Judicial Monarchs

Judicial Monarchs

Court Power and the Case for Restoring Popular Sovereignty in the United States

William J. Watkins, Jr.

Foreword by William J. Quirk

McFarland & Company, Inc., Publishers
Jefferson, North Carolina, and London

LIBRARY OF CONGRESS CATALOGUING-IN-PUBLICATION DATA

Watkins, William J., Jr.
    Judicial monarchs : court power and the case for restoring popular sovereignty in the United States / William J. Watkins, Jr. ; foreword by William J. Quirk.
        p.   cm.
    Includes bibliographical references and index.

    ISBN 978-0-7864-6866-9
    softcover : acid free paper ∞

    1. People (Constitutional law)— United States. 2. Political questions and judicial power — United States. 3. Constitutional history — United States. I. Title.
KF4880.5.W38 2012
342.7308'5 — dc23   2011051538

BRITISH LIBRARY CATALOGUING DATA ARE AVAILABLE

© 2012 William J. Watkins, Jr. All rights reserved

No part of this book may be reproduced or transmitted in any form or by any means, electronic or mechanical, including photocopying or recording, or by any information storage and retrieval system, without permission in writing from the publisher.

Cover art © 2012 Images.com
Front cover design by Bernadette Skok (bskok@ptd.net)

Manufactured in the United States of America

McFarland & Company, Inc., Publishers
  Box 611, Jefferson, North Carolina 28640
    www.mcfarlandpub.com

Table of Contents

Foreword by William J. Quirk 1

Preface 6

1. The Divinely Anointed Stuarts 9
2. Civil War, Restoration, and Revolution 31
3. Rethinking Sovereignty 55
4. Sovereignty and the Courts 74
5. Jefferson, Marshall, and Marbury 100
6. Curbing the Courts 119

Appendix A: The Agreement of the People, as Presented to the Council of the Army (October 28, 1647) 149

Appendix B: Kamper v. Hawkins *(November 16, 1793)* 152

Appendix C: Abbreviations Used in the Notes and Bibliography 186

Notes 188

Bibliography 208

Index 214

Foreword

by William J. Quirk

"Who is to decide?" is always the critical question. If you know *who* is deciding the question, you have a pretty good idea *how* it will be decided. America's law schools teach that the Supreme Court is the decider in constitutional questions. It interprets the Constitution for the other branches and the rest of us. It is the last word, it is the law of the land. If you don't like a Court ruling you have only two long-shot chances to reverse it: (1) convince the Court to reverse itself, or (2) get the Constitution amended. For all practical purposes, then, the Court's rulings are final.

Is this what the Founders intended? Bill Watkins, in his new book *Judicial Monarchs*, answers the question. He examines the evolution of sovereignty in the seventeenth and eighteenth centuries tracing the history from (1) Divine Right Sovereignty — the Stuart Kings, the Civil War, the beheading of Charles I, the Rule of Cromwell, and the dissenters; to (2) Parliamentary Sovereignty — coming to full form with the Glorious Revolution of William and Mary; to (3) Popular Sovereignty — from the seventeenth century English dissenters to the Declaration of Independence. Each of these stories is rich and fascinating in itself and together they enable Watkins to answer the question: Did the Founders intend our present system? Did they intend for the Court to have the last word? The big surprise is that the Founders intended exactly the opposite.

Watkins sets out to solve the biggest mystery surrounding the Founders' work in Philadelphia. There was no question the Constitution was to be written — England's unwritten constitution placed ultimate power in Parliament and the colonies were ill-served by it. But if everyone agreed the new Constitution was to be written that leaves open the big question:

Who is to interpret the words? The Founders were well aware of the power of interpretation, that the interpreter of a document—not the author—controls its meaning. So why were the Founders silent? Why did they fail to spell out who was supposed to interpret the Constitution?

What were the possibilities? They could have written down the system we now have. The Supreme Court interprets the Constitution and the other branches and the people follow. That would have been easy to draft and would have settled the issue without any further question. But there was something wrong with that approach. No one at the Convention believed it.

Another possibility, consistent with separation of powers theory, was that each branch interprets the Constitution for its own purposes. Thus, the Court, if necessary to decide a case, could rule on the constitutionality of a law. That finding, however, had no impact on the other branches unless they agreed with it. The point of the Revolution was not to replace a set of parliamentary rulers with judicial ones—it was to establish an experiment in self-rule. The Founders were not sure the experiment would succeed but as Jefferson said of Washington's view, "he would give his life to see it got a fair chance."

But the puzzle remains—if some form of judicial review was to be expected with a written constitution, why not specify what kind in the Constitution? The role of the judiciary on constitutional issues in England was simple—it was zero. What would it be here? Watkins' new scholarship is particularly helpful here. He has uncovered some state court decisions which answer the question. In several Virginia cases, the judges outlined their different approach of judicial review.

In *Caton* (1782), Edmond Pendleton noted that the separation of powers found in the Virginia Constitution required each branch of government to stay within its delegated powers. Could the judiciary exercise legislative power by overruling what the legislature passes? "[H]ow far this court ... shall have the power to declare the nullity of a law passed in its forms by the legislative power, without exercising the power of that branch contrary to the plain terms of that constitution, is indeed a deep, important, and, I will add, a tremendous question..." (*Commonwealth v. Caton*, 8 Va. [4 call] 5 [1782]). Judicial review, to Pendleton, appeared to violate separation of powers theory. Many Republicans believed exactly that.

Spencer Roane, in the 1793 *Kamper* decision, put judicial review in a different setting—since the Revolution the people were "the only sovereign power" and the legislature was subordinate to the people and constitution (*Kamper v. Hawkins*, 1793 WL 248, at *6 [1793]). The people had a right to alter the Constitution by a convention, but the legislature enjoyed no such power. The legislature has no power to change the fundamental law. St. George Tucker, in the same decision, wrote that since the Revolution the people possessed *"sovereign, unlimited* and *unlimitable* authority" (*Kamper*, 1 Va. Cas. at 21 [emphasis in original]). Governments possessed only that authority delegated by the people. It followed, he thought, that the legislature cannot alter the Constitution "without destroying the foundation of their authority" (*Id.* [quoting Vattel, *The Law of Nations: Book I*, ch. III, § 34]). The judiciary, he thought, was obligated to find such laws a nullity.

Alexander Hamilton in *Federalist* No. 78, described judicial review in simple terms. It was a matter of principal-agent. The legislature, as the people's agent, could not exceed the principal's instruction. The Court, according to Hamilton, assumed the role and stood for the people to assure their instructions were followed. Hamilton offered the example that supposed the legislature passed a law requiring only one citizen to prove treason while the Constitution requires two. How could such a law stand? Hamilton does not, however, respond to the separation of powers issues raised by Pendleton. Of course, judicial review, if limited to the simple Hamilton-type example, would not be controversial. But nothing on the Supreme Court docket is simple.

The Convention's silence on the question, in view of Watkins' discoveries, is understandable. It set out each branch — Article I, the Legislative; Article II, the Executive; and Article III, the Judiciary. Separation of powers theory requires each branch to stay within its delegated powers. The judiciary is not authorized to exercise a legislative function — such as altering or repealing a law. If the Convention intended a result inconsistent with separation of powers theory, it would need to expressly provide for that. The Hamilton view, for example, would need to be spelled out since allowing one branch to perform functions belonging to another contravenes separation of powers theory. No special provision was needed if the Constitution intended to incorporate normal separation of powers theory, meaning each branch exercises the powers granted and interprets the Constitution for its own purposes.

Under separation of powers theory, each branch receives its power from the people delegated by them through the Constitution. The holder of a delegated power, of course, before he acts must decide whether or not the proposed action is within his grant. He may be wrong, but if he is, he's accountable to the grantor and no one else. The branches are separate and coequal and the grantor is the people; the executive and legislature are directly accountable to the grantor.

An example of separation of powers theory is Thomas Jefferson and the Alien and Sedition laws. In 1798 the Adams administration enacted the Alien and Sedition laws. The laws made criticism of the administration a crime — a number of newspaper editors were imprisoned. Jefferson, upon his election, released every person in jail or being prosecuted under the Alien and Sedition Laws. He later wrote to Abigail Adams that the law was a "nullity, as absolute and as palpable as if Congress had ordered us to fall down and worship a golden image; and that it was as much my duty to arrest its execution in every stage, as it would have been to have rescued from the fiery furnace those who should have been cast into it for refusing to worship the image" (Letter from Thomas Jefferson to Abigail Adams [July 22, 1804], reprinted in 11 *The Writings of Thomas Jefferson* 42, 43–44 [Andrew A. Lipscomb & Albert Ellery Bergh, eds., 1904]). Nothing in the Constitution, Jefferson wrote to Abigail Adams, gave the judges power "to decide for the Executive, more than to the Executive to decide for them" (Letter from Thomas Jefferson to Abigail Adams [Sept. 11, 1804], reprinted in 8 *The Writings of Thomas Jefferson* (Paul L. Ford, ed., 1897]).

We know a good deal about the Founders. Is it plausible that they would want to create a judicial oligarchy? Madison's Notes of the Convention do not record Ben Franklin one day standing up and saying "I've got a good idea: Let's find nine really bright people and turn over most of our important decisions to them." Would the Convention authorize an institution that defines its own powers? Watkins' constitutional history makes this seem unlikely.

The Founders all referred to the Baron de Montesquieu as the "celebrated" Montesquieu. Montesquieu wrote *The Spirit of the Laws* which sets forth the theory of the separation of powers (1748). Montesquieu wrote, "Of the three powers..., the judiciary is in some measure next to nothing: there remain, therefore, only two..." (Baron de Montesquieu, *The Spirit of the Laws* bk. 11, ch. 6 [1748]).

The Divine Right of Kings, wrote the first Stuart King, James I, placed him just under God in the great chain of being. The people should realize that the King is "a Judge set by God over them, having the power to judge them but to be judged only by God..." (*King James VI & I: Selected Writings* 268 [Neil Rhodes et al. eds., 2003]). These beliefs led to the beheading of his son, Charles I, in 1649.

Following Cromwell, and the brief return of the Stuarts, the English brought in William and Mary for the Glorious Revolution in 1688. The Revolution established parliamentary sovereignty in its full form. Blackstone described it:

It hath sovereign and uncontrollable authority in the making, confirming, enlarging, restraining, abrogating, repealing, reviving, and expounding of laws, concerning matters of all possible denominations; ecclesiastical or temporal; civil, military, maritime, or criminal; this being the place where that absolute despotic power which must, in all governments, reside somewhere, is intrusted by the Constitution of these kingdoms....

The colonies' bitter experience with parliamentary sovereignty shaped our response. American theory denied the existence of any central ultimate sovereign power. Power could be separated and each branch so constructed that each branch would limit the other's power. Where there was conflict — the branches disagreed — it would have to be worked out. The Founders experiment involved two unique ideas: (1) can you limit power by words on a piece of paper?; and (2) the nature of power had always been indivisible — could it be divided into three parts that would not impinge on one another? Henry Adams, writing in the late nineteenth century, called the Founders' experiment the most fascinating in history even if it failed.

A major contribution of Watkins is his deconstruction of *Marbury v. Madison* (1803). Our law schools teach that this case establishes judicial supremacy. Watkins, however, explains that Marshall intended only to establish that the Court could rule on constitutionality to decide the case before it. He made no claim that the other branches needed to consider his ruling. Had he claimed any such thing, he would probably have been impeached. He answered the Pendleton question. Courts could declare laws unconstitutional if it was necessary to decide the case in front of them. Marshall, in short, simply followed separation of powers theory. Our law schools need to assign the Virginia cases Watkins has discovered when students read *Marbury*. It is only understandable when placed in its historical context.

Watkins' book should change the way constitutional law is taught in our law schools. The Founders would be astonished to learn that their Constitution is currently interpreted to establish judicial supremacy. Watkins believes, like Jefferson, that the people are "the only safeguard of the public liberty." His book gives the people a roadmap on how to go about exercising their power.

William J. Quirk joined the faculty of the University of South Carolina School of Law in 1970 after ten years in New York City in private practice and the Corporate Counsel's Office of the City of New York. Professor Quirk's most recent book is *Courts and Congress: America's Unwritten Constitution*. A former contributing editor to *The New Republic*, he has published many articles.

Preface

Who has the final say on what the Constitution means? Most citizens, lawyers, and judges will respond, "The Supreme Court of the United States." From high school civics to law school, Americans are taught that the Framers of the Constitution designed the Court to be the ultimate arbiter of constitutional issues and that Chief Justice John Marshall recognized this when deciding *Marbury v. Madison* in 1803. Lest anyone doubt these self-evident truths, the modern Supreme Court has expressly held that "the federal judiciary is supreme in the exposition of the law of the Constitution."[1]

Via judicial supremacy, the judiciary enjoys the final word on a host of "constitutional" issues. The courts make the ultimate decision on such diverse matters as affirmative action, abortion, and capital punishment. But is this role of the judiciary congruent with the first principles of America's creation?

To answer this question, we must travel back to our English roots and the constitutional framework that existed when the first English settlers began constructing the Jamestown colony in 1607. In the early seventeenth century, most English subjects recognized the king as the ultimate sovereign. James I and the Church of England emphasized that kings ruled by divine right and that subjects should dutifully submit to all of the king's decrees.

The Stuarts' abuses of power impelled many Englishmen to reexamine the locus of sovereignty. In the turbulent years of the English Civil War, heterodox opinions surfaced pointing to Parliament or the people as the source of power. After Oliver Cromwell's reign, these opinions were suppressed once the English monarchy was restored in 1660. Royal abuses, however, continued and England rejected divine-right theory in the Glorious Revolution of 1688. With the Glorious Revolution, Englishmen recognized Parliament as the ultimate sovereign. To paraphrase the eminent jurist William Blackstone, Parliament could make or undo any law as it saw fit.

Parliamentary sovereignty became the bedrock of British liberty. But when Parliament began to meddle in the internal affairs of the North American colonies in the 1760s, the colonists challenged conventional ideas about ultimate power. On the eve of the American Revolution, Thomas Jefferson and other leaders contended that the colonial legislatures possessed ultimate sovereignty and that the king was the glue that held the empire together. Because neither George III nor Parliament would accept this formula, the American War of Independence began.

With the advent of independence, and based on prior American arguments, most assumed that the legislatures of the newly independent states would act as mini-parliaments and exercise ultimate power. Instead, ideas about the people's sovereignty, which were first concretely expressed during the English Civil War, took root in America. Americans rejected the notion that an artificial body such as a legislature could wield ultimate sovereignty. Starting in Massachusetts, the people used popular conventions to ratify written constitutions. Under these constitutions, legislatures, governors, and judges were but servants of the people exercising delegated powers.

At first, state court judges were unsure how popular sovereignty affected judicial functions. Blackstone had taught that Parliament was the master of the British constitution. British judges did not review Parliament's acts to determine constitutionality. Parliament, in some sense, was the constitution.

Moving cautiously, state court judges accepted that popular sovereignty mandated a form of judicial review, that is, the power of the courts to review decisions of other departments of government. The judiciary realized that it was a coequal branch of government bound to take note of relevant constitutional provisions when adjudicating a particular case.

By the time *Marbury* was decided in 1803, judicial review was widely accepted in the American states. If we read Chief Justice Marshall's opinion in the context of popular sovereignty and published state cases adopting judicial review, we see that *Marbury* did not declare the Supreme Court to be the final arbiter on the meaning of the United States Constitution. Following in the footsteps of state court judges, Marshall simply held that, as a coequal branch, the Supreme Court must take note of constitutional provisions when deciding a case or controversy. He also suggested that the Court must show deference to the elected branches of government.

Marshall's modest holding in *Marbury* has been twisted to cloak the

Supreme Court with preeminent power in the federal system. Beginning in the late 1800s, the Court claimed the power to judge the reasonableness of laws passed by the national and state legislatures. If the laws were unpalatable to a majority of the Court, they were struck down as unconstitutional. Little has changed in the twenty-first century.

Modern judicial supremacy has turned the clock back regarding sovereignty. Rather than a coequal branch of government, the Supreme Court resembles a divinely anointed monarch of the 1600s or the omnipotent British Parliament of the 1700s. Popular sovereignty — the legacy of the American Revolution — has been forgotten.

To remedy this situation, Americans must remember that judicial independence, to the founding generation, never meant independence from the people. State and federal judges are not high priests of the constitutional order. Just like governors, senators, and representatives, judges are mere agents of the people. When judges begin to make public policy decisions, they rebel against their masters and usurp power.

What can Americans do to end this rule of the judges? The final chapter offers several suggestions, including a revival of judicial restraint, augmenting the power of juries, mechanisms for the removal of activist judges or the nullifying of their policy determinations, term limits, popular selection of the Supreme Court, and use of jurisdiction-stripping provisions already in the Constitution. Some combination of remedies is needed to return the people to their proper place in our constitutional order.

Chapter 1

The Divinely Anointed Stuarts

In *Federalist No. 2*, John Jay marveled that Providence had blessed the people of the former colonies with a common ancestry, similar customs, and attachment "to the same principles of government."[1] Jay did not define the origin of these commonalties; such was unnecessary for his late-eighteenth-century audience. The majority of Americans traced their lineage to England, Scotland, Wales, and Ireland.[2] In the beginning of the struggle against George III, the colonists staked claims to liberty on "the rights of Englishmen." They invoked the British constitution and precedents from English history.

Although Americans took pride in their connection with British political and constitutional ideals, they did not desire to, nor did they, simply adopt British institutions and theories when setting up state governments or the national government. The most patent example is the executive branch of government. No independent state established a hereditary executive modeled on the British monarchy. The terms of state governors were limited and the state legislatures took on tasks formerly performed by royal executive officials. America's first national constitution, the Articles of Confederation, had no president exercising executive power. Congress performed all legislative and executive functions. Even the Constitution of 1787, although it established an executive branch, limited the president's term to four years.

Perhaps the most glaring departure from British theory and practice was the locus of sovereignty, that is, ultimate power. At the time of the American Revolution, sovereignty rested in the British Parliament. Parliament could make or repeal laws as it saw fit. This principle applied not only to statutory law, but to what we recognize today as fundamental law or constitutional law. America, however, took a different course and accepted popular sovereignty. The people, not the legislatures or other artificial bodies, possessed ultimate power. Authority could be delegated to agents such as governors, representatives, or judges, but true sovereignty rested with the people.

The acceptance of popular sovereignty in the United States cannot be understood outside the context of English history and the conflict between Crown and Parliament. The English Civil War and Glorious Revolution set the stage for the American Revolution and radical ideas about the power of the people. Principles of popular sovereignty were first seriously debated during the 1640s in England. With the defeat of royalist forces and execution of the king, Englishmen examined the tenets of monarchical and republican theory. But for the instability of the Interregnum, theorists and soldiers arguing for popular sovereignty could have taken a tremendous leap forward in the realm of political science. Although unsuccessful in England, these heterodox theorists put forward ideas that would later take hold in America.

The 24th day of March in 1603 marked the end of an era. Elizabeth I had ruled England since her succession to the throne in 1558.[3] The daughter of Henry VIII, she was the last monarch of the Tudor dynasty. Her four decades of rule are associated with exemplary statecraft, exploration, imperial expansion, and myriad literary and cultural achievements. Under Elizabeth, Englishmen defeated the Spanish Armada, Shakespeare wrote masterpieces of the English language, Sir Francis Drake circumnavigated the globe, and the population enjoyed economic prosperity. Matching and maintaining the success of the Elizabethan Age would be a challenge for any successor.

Because Elizabeth had no children, her cousin James Stuart of Scotland was proclaimed James I of England shortly after her death.[4] At first glance, James appeared to be an excellent choice. Having ruled Scotland for 18 years before succession to the English throne, he did not begin his reign as a novice monarch. This long rule in Scotland made James at his ascension the most experienced English monarch since William the Conqueror. Subjects hoped that he could maintain the upward trajectory that the kingdom enjoyed under good Queen Bess.

James, however, brought much baggage along with him. He had been raised in a turbulent and dangerous period in Scottish history. When James was an infant, the Scottish nobility forced his mother, Mary, Queen of Scots, to abdicate.[5] The removal of Mary did not quell the dynastic rivalries. James lived under three regents before attaining the age of five, while the Scottish nobility fought for control over his person so they could govern in his name.[6] From a young age, he realized just how precarious his existence and rule were. His mother's execution in 1587 further imprinted the uncertainty of life on James' psyche and he took to wearing padded clothes to aid his chances of surviving an assassination attempt.

James underwent a classical humanist education with an emphasis on politics, Greek, and history. In his religious studies, he received heavy doses of Protestant theology and the heroes of the Reformation. Two of James' tutors were close confidants of Reformation icon Theodore Beza, who followed John Calvin as the leader of the church in Geneva, Switzerland. Unquestionably, James' caretakers were grooming him as a possible successor to the Protestant Elizabeth.

Approximately two weeks after Elizabeth's death, James set off for London. As he traveled, the people greeted him with cheers, gifts, and bonfires. The English nobility also warmly received him and had high hopes for his reign. First impressions at court were favorable. Elizabeth's circle of advisors described James as alert, intelligent, and educated. The Act of Succession, obsequiously and somewhat correctly, described him as "a Sovereign adorned with the rarest gifts of mind and body in such admirable peace and quietness."[7] While these impressions were accurate, it did not take long for other characteristics to surface.

James quickly proved to be improvident with money. In 1604, he spent £47,000 on jewels — an amount that equaled his annual revenue as King of Scotland. James' entourage dwarfed that of Elizabeth and caused many to take note of his extravagant living.[8] Always one to take care of his friends, he spent approximately £30,000 per year on pensions for his favorites. Jewels, pensions, and other forms of reckless spending soon caused the government to accumulate extraordinary annual deficits.[9] Englishmen were also unhappy that many of the beneficiaries of James' munificence were Scots who had followed him to London. These Scots were soon the only individuals with ready access to the king.[10] Even high-ranking government officials complained about the difficulty in gaining an audience with their monarch.

Officials accustomed to the hands-on rule of Elizabeth were further disappointed to find the able James detached from the day-to-day affairs of government. The king made clear that he preferred not to be bothered with details or paperwork. In fact, James spent many weeks away from court, in the country, hunting. Horses and hounds were far more interesting to him than the affairs of state. The new king described hunting as "the most honorable and noblest" activity "in making a man hardy and skillfully ridden in all grounds."[11] Frequent trips to the country, according to James, were necessary to maintain his health. He found London to be a dirty city and could not bear to spend long intervals there. He expected the Privy Council to keep the government running while he sojourned in his various hunting lodges.

The Stuarts and Divine Right

The government James inherited in England was based on the theory that the king exercised unlimited dominion over his subjects' lives and property.[12] This suited him inasmuch as he was a firm believer in the divine right of kings[13] and expected total obedience from his subjects.[14] James saw the realm as one great chain of being[15] in which he occupied a spot just under God. His brand of divine right consisted of four elements: indefeasibility of hereditary right, accountability of kings to God alone, non-resistance of subjects, and divine ordination of monarchy as a governing institution.[16]

In 1598, James wrote *The True Law of Free Monarchies*, in which he discussed at length the relationship between a king and his subjects. He began his treatise by describing monarchy as the form of government "resembling divinity" and "approach[ing] nearest to perfection."[17] James reasoned that the institution of monarchy was founded by "God himself" with "the erection of ... monarchy among the Jews" in the Old Testament.[18] Accordingly, only monarchy is suitable for a Christian people expressing allegiance to Yahweh and his Son.[19] A king was no mere man, but served as "God's lieutenant in earth."[20] Subjects should realize that the king is "a judge set by God over them, having the power to judge them but to be judged only by God."[21] In other words, the people had no power to call a monarch to account for misdeeds — this power was reserved to God alone.[22] "I grant, indeed," lectured James, "that a wicked king is sent by God for a curse to his people and a plague for their sins; but that it is lawful to them to shake off that curse at their own hand, which God hath laid on them, that I deny and may do so justly."[23]

James' view of sovereignty and kingship was not novel. Many of his points had earlier been made by Jean Bodin in *Les Six Livres de la République*, which was first published in 1576.[24] This book is the earliest known comprehensive discussion of the doctrine of sovereignty[25] and should serve as a starting point whenever the supreme power of governance is discussed.[26] In *République*, Bodin began with the proposition that a ruler "is absolutely sovereign who recognizes nothing, after God, that is greater than himself."[27] Sovereign princes were, in Bodin's words, God's "lieutenants for commanding other men"; therefore, "[c]ontempt for one's sovereign prince is contempt toward God, of whom he is the earthly image."[28] For Bodin, there were seven prerogatives of sovereignty: (1) declaring war and peace, (2) hearing appeals from inferior officials, (3) removing and appointing government functionaries, (4) imposing taxes, (5) granting pardons, (6) coining money, and (7) requiring subjects to swear loyalty oaths.[29] One who could exercise the prerogatives was a sovereign or lawgiver.[30]

Bodin recognized that a sovereign might delegate certain functions to others. Such delegation, however, could not make the possessor of the authority "sovereign." These officials "are but trustees and custodians of power until such time as it pleases" the true sovereign to reclaim the grant.[31] "For just as those who lend someone else their goods remain its owners and possessors, so also those who give power and authority to judge or to command, either for some limited and definite period of time or for as much and as long as it shall please them."[32] If it were otherwise, Bodin argued, then the subject could control his lord—an "absurd" result.[33]

Importantly, Bodin believed that the prerogatives of sovereign power were "indivisible."[34] Only one entity could possess the seven prerogatives and this sovereign authority could "not [be] limited in either power, or in function, or in length of time."[35] If sovereign prerogatives were divisible, the supposed co-sovereigns would clash until one prevailed as the ultimate sovereign. Bodin did recognize that the sovereign entity could be one man (monarchy), a few elite (aristocracy), or the entire people (democracy).[36] But the tenor of his work is geared to that of a monarchy—the system with which he and his contemporaries were most familiar.

Although Bodin spoke of absolute sovereignty, he believed that natural law placed certain limits on the sovereign's power.[37] Precise natural law principles are difficult to define, but Bodin claimed that at a minimum the natural law required a sovereign to respect the property of his people. According to Bodin, "If the prince, then, does not have the power to overstep the bounds of natural law, which has been established by God, of whom he is the image, he will also not be able to take another's property without just and reasonable cause—as by purchase, exchange, lawful confiscation."[38] If the king did violate the natural law by wrongfully depriving a subject of his property, the only remedy was a polite remonstrance. The real wrong, in Bodin's mind, was to God. Thus, the subject was forbidden to resist the sovereign prince in cases where natural law had been violated.[39]

The Bodin and Stuart view of royal authority and its association with the Creator of the universe was hammered home by the English clergy.

Considering that under the Act of Supremacy (1534)[40] the king was the head of the Church in England, such propaganda from the pulpit is not surprising.[41] Under this act, the monarch "shall be taken, accepted, and reputed the only Supreme Head in earth of the Church of England, called *Anglicana Ecclesia*."[42] Based on this statute, the king possessed the power to "repress, redress, reform, order, correct, restrain, and amend all such errors, heresies, abuses" that touched upon the Christian religion.[43]

The clergy's partnership with the monarchy in instilling obedience began long before James assumed the throne. For instance, the authorized sermons for use in the Church of England, known as the *Books of Homilies*, offered a stern message to the people. In "An Homily against Disobedience and Wylful Rebellion," parishioners were instructed that "obedience is the principal virtue of all virtues."[44] Lucifer, once a glorious angel, was the first author of rebellion and thus became "the blackest and most foulest fiend and devil."[45] Subjects who rebelled against the king were children of the devil and would be tossed "into the pit and bottom of hell" on Judgment Day.[46] Monarchs, both good and evil, "reign by God's ordinance"; therefore, a subject who contemplates the overthrow of a monarch challenges the authority of God.[47] "[W]hat a perilous thing were it to commit unto the subjects the judgment which prince is wise and godly, and his government good, and which is otherwise."[48]

This type of teaching continued into the reign of James. William Goodwin, vice chancellor of Oxford University, preached a sermon in 1614 on the dignity of kingship and duties of subjects. "Who can lay his hand upon God's annointed [sic]," asked Goodwin, "and be innocent? Who can? No man, Because God hath planted him above all men, and hath given no man authority to punish Him; God alone will take vengeance on his sinnes."[49] Goodwin recognized that a monarch could be cruel to his people, but he averred that this was but a curse sent by the Almighty "to chastise his children."[50] Because God preferred order to rebellion, He prohibited any kind of revolutionary act:

> God, which is the God of order, & not of confusion, foresaw in his wisdome, that it were better for the estates of Kingdomes, & lesse injurious to his Church, if the insolency of a wicked King, were sometimes tolerated without controll, than that the estate of his chiefe deputy, and Lieutenant upon the earth should be subjected to change and alteration, to deprivation, or deposing, at the pleasure and partialitie of either Priest, or of People.[51]

Roger Maynwaring, the king's chaplain, shared Goodwin's view of divine right. Monarchs were "inferior to none, to no *man*, to no *multitudes* of men, to no *Angell*, to no *order* of *Angels*."[52] No subject could even question the king's decision making "because, the heart of *a King is in the hand of God, and hee turneth it which way hee pleaseth.*"[53] Maynwaring further advised the people that suffering would make them "martyars," whereas civil disobedience would make them "traitors" in the eyes of God and thus deserving of eternal damnation.[54]

In light of this teaching about divine right and royal sovereignty, it is not surprising that James and his supporters had little regard for Parliament. James unabashedly informed Parliament that laws "were properly made by the king alone."[55] Parliament, the royalists believed, was not a necessary ingredient for the realm's governance. To James, Parliament's duty was to confirm a monarch's succession and to offer advice on momentous occasions such as in time of threatened invasion. Parliament was the king's servant, not his partner or his adversary.

At this time in English history, the king did exercise great control over Parliament. He decided when it should convene and disperse, and no statute could pass without his consent. Kings seldom used the veto power because bills that did not meet with royal approval were rarely passed. The king convened Parliament to conduct his business, not the business that its members thought prudent or necessary.[56] Subjects were repeatedly warned that the king could easily fall "out of love with parliaments" and "be enforced to use new counsels" in governing the country.[57]

While the king could claim that he "was beholden to no elective power,"[58] Parliament had much control over the purse strings and ordinary legislation. As early as the fourteenth century, English kings had agreed that no tallage or aid would be levied without the consent of the freemen of the realm.[59] The monarch certainly formulated foreign policy, but unless Parliament agreed to fund the monarch's foreign wars and adventures, the monarch's plans and strategies could not be carried out.[60] Hence, actual practice differed somewhat from royalist theory.

In contrast to the royalists' appeal to the king's sovereignty, parliamentarians emphasized the doctrine of king-in-Parliament.[61] "The sovereign power is agreed to be in the king," observed MP James Whitelocke in 1610, "but in the king is a twofold power — the one in parliament, as he is assisted with the consent of the whole state; the other out of parliament, as he is sole and singular, guided merely by his own will."[62] The power of the king in Parliament, argued Whitelocke, was far superior to that exercised by the king alone. "[F]or acts of parliament, be they laws, grounds, or whatsoever else," Whitelocke continued, "the act and power is the king's but with the assent of the Lords and Commons, which maketh it the most sovereign and supreme power above all and controllable by none."[63] Under parliamentarian theory, the king, Lords, and Commons together in one house were omni-competent. God had conferred the power of governance on the entire community, and this community, in turn, delegated powers to the king "subject to the conditions that he make laws and impose taxes only in Parliament."[64] In other words, the Lords and Commons were the king's partners in governance of the realm.

The Development of Parliament

Parliament's origins were quite humble; it certainly did not originate as the powerful institution described by Whitelocke. Parliament developed over time from the principle that the great magnates of the realm owed the king a duty of counsel and consent.[65] Of course, since time immemorial kings solicited the advice of the great barons.[66] For example, in 1086 William the Conqueror held a colloquy with his magnates before launching the Domesday survey of the wealth of his vassals.[67] Christmas, Easter, and Whitsunday conveniently provided three yearly opportunities for the king and his barons to feast and discuss the pressing issues of the day.[68] No great man of the realm would miss these feasts without risking his favor with the ruler. The travel to the king's court was often burdensome and inconvenient to the magnates. Many would have preferred to tend to business on their estates. They were not, at this early time, seeking to exert control over the king.[69]

In addition to providing advice on political and administrative issues, the assemblies of barons also performed judicial functions in that they advised the king's court on judgments to be rendered.[70] The great barons, not formally trained lawyers, were the judges holding court. It was not until the 1100s that England developed what moderns would recognize as a "judicial system." Henry II designed a royal court system that "would administer a law common to all England and all men."[71] Over time the various courts became specialized[72] and the king appointed numerous judges; however, the great barons advising the king retained judicial duties.

By the 1230s, the word "parliament" denoted a special meeting of the king's council.[73] But more formal organized parliaments did not begin until 1258.[74] In that year, Henry III was in an impecunious position. He had attempted to purchase the Sicilian crown for his son Edmund. In exchange for the crown, Henry agreed to provide the pope with an army and to serve as surety for papal debts.[75] Before coming to the financial aid of the king, the magnates demanded reform of the government — reforms placing much power in the barons' hands. Seeing no way out, the king agreed to institute changes known today as the Provisions of Oxford. The main reform crafted by the baronial and royal parties was the creation of a council of 15 chosen to advise and assist the king. This council would be elected by two persons from the royal camp and two from the barons' camp, which was described as "the community of the realm."[76] In addition, Parliament was scheduled to meet three times per year.[77] Hence, we see the "community of the realm" choosing the king's advisors and the community's representatives[78] meeting thrice each year in Parliament.

Although the power of the barons waxed and waned in the years after the Provisions of Oxford, Parliament would remain a key English institution from 1258 forward. By the middle of the next century, representatives of certain towns and counties began to participate in Parliament.[79] The increasing need for the "commons" can be traced to England's involvement in the Hundred Years' War beginning in 1337 and the army's constant need for supplies. With the tax burden growing, the king required the consent of not just the magnates, but also the burgesses and knights.[80] As Parliament became more representative, we see a commensurate decline in its judicial functions.[81] According to Jeffrey Goldsworthy, "After 1327, [Parliament's] judicial functions began to diminish in importance, and political business assumed greater prominence."[82] A relatively new feature of this political business was the origination of legislation from the petitions of the Commons.[83] While this practice was significant, these petitions were freely amended by the king and barons for years to come.[84]

The brief discussion above is not to imply that some sort of constitutional monarchy developed in the Middle Ages. Often kings eschewed calling a parliament and instead summoned great councils of barons to assist in governance.[85] For example, from 1485 to 1509 Henry VII called only seven parliaments — a far cry from the three times per year mandated by the Provisions of Oxford.[86] During Elizabeth's reign, Parliament was "rarely in session" and "met on average for a few weeks every three years."[87] In addition, via the royal prerogative the king had the "power to dispense with any legislative provision."[88] Real power remained with the Crown, but Parliament's influence continued to grow.

James Quarrels with Parliament

James' first dispute with Parliament occurred in the spring of 1604 — on the meeting of his very first Parliament. The election of Sir Thomas

Goodwin as a knight of the shire for Buckinghamshire had been voided by Lord Chancellor Egerton. The voters then elected the court's favored candidate, privy councilor Sir John Fortescue in a second election. The House of Commons protested this manipulation and declared Goodwin the legitimate representative for Buckinghamshire. In other words, the Commons claimed the right and privilege to judge the returns of its own members.

In an effort at compromise, James and the Commons agreed to void both Buckinghamshire elections. However, during the course of discussions, James asserted that he respected the privileges of the Commons inasmuch as they were grants from the monarch. The statement frightened some in the Commons because they interpreted it as a veiled threat to take away privileges. The Commons reasoned that the beginning of James' reign was the proper time to educate him on the English constitution.

A committee prepared a document that history knows as the Apology of the Commons. After expressing an expectation that "under your Majesty's reign, religion, peace, justice, and all virtue should renew again and flourish," the Commons quickly moved to the issue of privileges.[89] The Commons feared that "misinformation" had been delivered to the king.[90] Unnamed royal advisors had informed James that "we held not our privileges of right, but of grace only, renewed every parliament by way of donature upon petition, and so to be limited."[91] The Commons explained that this was not the case: "Our privileges and liberties are our right and due inheritance, no less than our very lands and goods."[92] If the king attempted to restrict these privileges, he did "wrong to the whole state of the realm."[93] Considering that "the prerogatives of princes may easily and do daily grow," the Commons was duty bound to lodge this protest to preserve what belonged to it.[94] Ominously, the Commons observed that privileges lost "are not recovered but with much disquiet."[95] While the Commons never officially presented the Apology to the king, James certainly was aware of it and probably had the Apology in mind when he addressed Parliament in July 1604 and urged the members to "use your liberty with more modesty in time to come."[96]

James and the Commons often clashed over what matters could be debated in Parliament. One example is impositions, customs duties levied by the king above rates authorized by Parliament. As previously discussed, James' extravagant spending kept him constantly in debt. Profligate spending caused skepticism in Parliament about granting the king additional funds. To bypass Parliament, James resorted to impositions. In so doing, he did have a precedent on his side. John Bate, a merchant who bought and sold seedless raisins grown in the Levant, refused to pay the duty because it had not been approved by Parliament. In *Bate's Case*, the Court of Exchequer held that "all commerce and affairs with foreigners" are governed "by the absolute power of the king."[97] The court reasoned that "[n]o exportation or importation can be but at the king's ports, they are the gates of the king, and he hath absolute power" over the goods and persons entering and exiting.[98]

In 1610, Parliament began a debate on the constitutionality of impositions. The members were afraid that extraparliamentary revenue would give the king too much independence. The purse strings provided Parliament with much power and it did not want this check on the monarch reduced. James vehemently scolded Parliament for this debate. He lectured that Parliament could address possible abuses in the collection of the imposts, but it could not delve into his authority to impose them. Parliament retorted that it possessed "the special privilege ... to debate freely of all things that shall concern any of the subjects in particular, or the commonwealth in general, without any restraint or inhibition."[99] James ultimately relented and permitted Parliament to continue the examination of the issue.

Outbreak of the Thirty Years' War caused further clashes between Parliament and king over the scope of parliamentary authority. In 1617, the Protestants of Bohemia rebelled against King Ferdinand II, a Roman Catholic ruler. Ferdinand's crown was offered to and accepted by Frederick V, a Calvinist and James' son-in-law. Austrian and Spanish troops quickly overran Bohemia and then the Rhenish Palatinate, Frederick's seat of power as the Prince-Elector. James, guided by advice from the Duke of Buckingham, sought to restore peace and his son-in-law by seeking an alliance with Roman Catholic Spain. The mechanism for this undertaking was a proposed marriage of the Prince of Wales to the Spanish Infanta, the youngest daughter of King Phillip III of Spain and Margaret of Austria.

English Protestants feared that the marriage would result in a Roman Catholic heir to the throne and an undoing of much of the English Reformation. Parliament deplored James' negotiations with Spain and lamented that more had not been done to relieve beleaguered Protestants in Europe. The Commons urged James to "speedily and effectually take the sword into your hand" and resolve to assist "those of our own religion in foreign parts."[100] The Commons also insisted that "our most noble prince may be timely and happily married to one of our own religion."[101] James took umbrage at what he considered an improper intrusion into matters of royal prerogative. He instructed Parliament to cease meddling in foreign affairs and the search for his son's bride.¹⁰² Undeterred, the Commons responded that "the arduous and urgent affairs concerning kings, state and defence of the realm ... are proper subjects and matters of counsel and debate in parliament."¹⁰³

Parliament, in James' eyes, had gone too far. The so-called "Spanish Match" was his panacea for a variety of ills and he would not tolerate criticism. James took the journal book from the Clerk of Parliament, found the Commons' protestation recorded therein, and ripped the offending entries from the official record. The king ordered Parliament adjourned before it could undertake any more debate.

The aged king, however, would soon have egg on his face. Prince Charles and Buckingham, impatient with the negotiations and impelled by the prospect of adventure, traveled to Madrid to woo the Infanta. The Infanta was personally appalled at the prospect of marrying a Protestant, but she was encouraged to act as a missionary for the Catholic faith. Through her, the priests in Madrid counseled, England could be led back to Rome or, at a minimum, the situation of English Catholics bettered.

The Spanish treated Charles and Buckingham to feasts, entertainment, and multiple receptions. Rome blessed the proposed union, but only if the Infanta could raise any children born to her and Charles in the Catholic faith. The pope also demanded toleration for Catholics in England, though he opposed toleration for Protestants residing in Catholic countries. Sensing that the love-struck Charles would agree to almost any condition, the Spanish further demanded that Parliament repeal all anti-Catholic laws and that the Infanta remain in Spain while Parliament completed the task. When Charles raised the issue of his brother-in-law Frederick and the loss of his central European territories, King Phillip showed no inclination to assist.

Buckingham realized that the conditions set by Rome and Madrid would never be agreed to in Parliament. Incensed at the Spanish manipulation of Charles, Buckingham knew that further negotiations were futile. He eventually persuaded Charles that the marriage would never happen and that they had both been duped by the Spanish. They returned to England with a hatred of all things reminding them of Spain.

Buckingham and Charles persuaded James to call another Parliament and to solicit funds and advice on foreign policy. James was feeble and approaching the end of his life. He had not the strength to argue with his son and favorite. The same king who had ripped the pages from the journal book now came crawling to Parliament. Gone were James' rebukes and reminders that parliamentary privileges were held at the pleasure of the king. Within a year, James would be dead. Charles I, despite having forced his father into an awkward situation with Parliament, would soon take an even stronger stand for royal power and prerogative rule.

Charles I and Parliament at Odds

Charles ascended to the throne in March 1625. Still stinging from the episode in Madrid, he planned to recover the Palatinate for Frederick and to attack Spanish ports. Parliament did not enthusiastically back Charles, regardless of lectures given to James on the need to wield the sword. James had been granted subsidies for war, but he never fought a battle. Consequently, Parliament was hesitant to grant more money unless the monarch could show concrete results.

Charles sent Buckingham and a band of ill-equipped sailors to raid Spanish treasure ships, but the expedition ended in failure. Most of the Spanish ships had arrived in port before Buckingham had even set sail. Buckingham also failed in an effort to relieve besieged Huguenots at La Rochelle. He gave an order to storm a key fortress, but in the middle of the attack his troops learned that their scaling ladders were too short to reach the tops of the walls. The attack was easily repulsed and Buckingham's men suffered losses as they scurried back to the boats.

Buckingham's enemies took this opportunity to bring impeachment proceedings. The duke had made many enemies over the years and now they sought revenge. Wild rumors spread that Buckingham, who attended James in his waning days, had given the king poison instead of medicine. Charles warned Parliament that he would not tolerate attacks on Buckingham and even sent one of his advisor's more vocal critics to the Tower of London.

In 1628, the military situation on the Continent worsened for Protestants, and English liberties were restricted at home. Many feared that the king was prepared to sweep aside constitutional safeguards. Charles had already compelled a "forced loan" from his subjects and jailed the men who refused to comply.[104] Five of these prisoners, known as the "five knights," objected to the loans and asserted that such "taxes" could not be levied absent the consent of Parliament. The knights challenged their confinement in the Court of King's Bench by requesting a writ of habeas corpus. This "Great Writ" requires that a prisoner be brought before a judge so the lawfulness of the confinement can be tested.[105] King's Bench denied relief on the ground that the king had the power to imprison citizens "for matters of state" and that the courts could not interfere with the king's prerogative powers.[106]

Englishmen were also concerned about the quartering of troops and use of martial law. The situation was especially bad on the Isle of Wight. Short on funds, Charles forced private citizens to accept soldiers in their homes while the soldiers awaited deployment to the Continent. The soldiers were ill clothed, undisciplined, and riotous. Multiple disputes arose between civilians and the soldiers. Rather than permitting civil courts to adjudicate these disputes, military courts were appointed to handle the unrest. This quick resort to martial law worried many inasmuch as there existed no compelling reason why the civil justice system could not function.

The Petition of Right

Under the leadership of Sir Edward Coke, Parliament began to debate the rights of Englishmen and the threats to those rights posed by the king's recent conduct. Referencing the *Five Knights Case*, Coke observed that "nothing is more precious to a man in this life than liberty."[107] To imprison a man without showing cause, Coke continued, is an act bereft of reason and reduces Englishmen to slavery. "If Freemen of England might be imprisoned at the will and pleasure of the king, or his commandment, then were they in worse case than bond-men or villains."[108] Even the most despotic lord of the manor "cannot command another to imprison his villain without cause."[109] Indefinite imprisonment, Coke continued, was "a kind of hell" and "very dangerous for the king and kingdom."[110] Coke, somewhat disingenuously, denied that he thought Charles was evil. He claimed that he only sought to protect "posterity" from a future tyrannical ruler.[111]

Coke also tackled the use of martial law. "If there be an uproar, if the King's courts be open you can do no martial law."[112] Coke also recognized that in cases of rebellion the Crown's forces could meet rebels on the battlefield and kill them in combat. But if the rebel is captured and the civil courts remain operational, "he cannot be put to death by martial law."[113] Coke recognized that the military needed much leeway to defend the realm, but he refused to permit military courts to usurp the authority of the common law courts unless there was no other option.

Charles' ears bristled as he heard reports of the debates in Parliament.

He did not terminate the parliamentary session because he knew some compromise was needed. Both king and Parliament were anxious to aid their coreligionists on the Continent. To do so, Charles agreed that he would not resort to extraconstitutional sources of revenue and he would confirm traditional rights of his subjects. Parliament would then grant subsidies and cease efforts to destroy Buckingham. This compact became the Petition of Right.[114]

The Petition began by tracing English precedent, dating back to Edward I, holding that no "tallage or aid shall be laid or levied without the good will and assent" of Parliament.[115] The Petition explained that in the reign of Edward III, Parliament "declared and enacted" that "no person shall be compelled to make any loans to the King against his will, because such loans were against reason and the franchise of the land."[116] The current generation had "inherited this freedom" and thus it "should not be compelled to contribute to any tax, tallage, aid, or other like charge, not set by common consent in Parliament."[117]

Despite the clear precedent against forced loans, the Petition complained that "of late" royal proclamations had been issued that "required [Englishmen] to lend certain sums of money unto your Majesty."[118] On top of this abomination, "many of them upon their refusal ... have been ... imprisoned, confined, and in sundry other ways molested and disquieted."[119] How could this treatment, the Petition asked, be consistent with the guarantees of the Magna Carta? In 1215, the Great Charter declared that "no freeman may be taken or imprisoned or be disseised of his freehold or liberties, or any of his free customs ... but by the lawful judgment of his peers, or by the law of the land."[120] Parliament had further enacted in the fourteenth century "that no man of what estate or condition that he be, should be put out of his lands or tenements, nor taken, imprisoned, nor disherited, nor put to death, without being brought to answer by due process of law."[121]

The Petition then turned to the quartering of troops: "Of late great companies of soldiers and mariners have been dispersed into divers counties of the realm, and the inhabitants against their wills have been compelled to receive them into their houses, and there to suffer them to sojourn, against the laws and customs of this realm, and to the great grievance and vexation of the people."[122] The Petition also complained of the use of martial law in military commissions, rather than common law in the civilian courts, to deal with the tension between the citizens and the soldiers. The result, according to the Petition, was that "[b]y pretext" some subjects had been unlawfully put to death and many soldiers had escaped punishment for acts of "murder, robbery, felony, mutiny" and other crimes against the population.[123]

The Petition concluded with a four-pronged prayer for relief. First, it stated "that no man hereafter be compelled to make or yield any gift, loan, benevolence, tax, or such like charge, without common consent by Act of Parliament."[124] Second, no subject should be imprisoned or harassed for a refusal to pay taxes that Parliament had not approved. Third, the soldiers and sailors quartered in civilian homes should be removed. Finally, military commissions proceeding under martial law should be "revoked and annulled."[125]

Charles believed that the Petition was an infringement upon his prerogative powers. The king consulted with his legal advisors and they opined that his approval of the Petition would not affect his divinely granted power to rule without Parliament. In further maneuvering to limit the punch of the Petition, Charles declined to treat it like a statute and instead merely said he would give it his "royal word." Realizing that mischief was afoot, the House of Commons protested and asked that the king give his official assent to the Petition as he would to a duly enacted statute. Charles acceded to this demand and remarked: "This I am sure is full, yet no more than I granted you on my first answer."[126] With the king seemingly pinned down, Parliament voted him subsidies for the prosecution of the war effort.

Disaster appeared to have been averted. Emotions and principles, however, would destabilize the situation. On August 23, 1628, Buckingham was assassinated. Charles lost his principal advisor and his best friend. The fact that the people and Parliament celebrated the duke's demise caused Charles' temper to flare. Although the murderer, a disgruntled army officer who had been passed over for promotion, acted alone, Charles blamed Buckingham's enemies in the House of Commons.[127] His distrust of Parliament grew.

Parliament continued to lose confidence in the king. The Petition of Right, by agreement of the Parliament and the Crown, had been included in the Parliament roll and printed for dissemination. On his own initiative, Charles gave orders to replace the final version with another that incorporated the king's original lukewarm response that simply gave his "royal word." The new version also incorporated a speech wherein Charles defended his prerogative power.[128] With money from the subsidies in his pocket, the king chose to play games with the Petition rather than treat it as a binding agreement.

Charles was also angry that Parliament had not granted him tonnage and poundage duties for life. Under the Tudors, Parliament customarily granted these duties for the life of the monarch.[129] Parliament did grant Charles tonnage and poundage duties for one year, but Charles continued to collect the duties as if it were a lifelong grant. Parliament reminded the king that "the receiving of Tonnage and Poundage, and other impositions not granted by Parliament, is a breach of the fundamental liberties of this kingdom, and contrary to your Majesty's royal answer to the said Petition of Right."[130]

Charles and the Commons further divided when the Commons began debating matters of religion. As head of the Church of England, Charles promoted a number of Arminian bishops and relied on their counsel. Arminianism, according to the Commons, was counter to the Reformed tradition of the Church of England.[131] At base, Reformed theology is closely associated with the scholarship of John Calvin and St. Augustine and emphasizes the sovereignty of God.[132] The Reformers believed that the sovereign Lord chooses the sinner rather than the sinner first choosing God; for those chosen by God His grace is irresistible and draws the person to Him. Dutch theologian James Arminius, on the other hand, argued that grace (or God's calling) is resistible — the person has the ability to make a choice.[133] For the Reformers, salvation is the monergistic work of God, whereas for the Arminians it is a synergistic work where man cooperates with God. Thus, the Commons feared that Charles was taking initial steps to alter the Reformed doctrine of the Church of England.

Angered that the Commons would debate issues solely within his powers, Charles demanded that Parliament adjourn. When the Speaker of the House informed the Commons that there could be no more speeches because of the king's command, pandemonium reigned. Members of the Commons forced the Speaker to keep his seat and then locked the doors so that no one could enter or leave. Agents of the king, attempting to free the Speaker and end the session, banged on the door but were denied admittance. The Commons passed resolutions condemning the levying of tonnage and poundage without consent of Parliament and dangerous "innovations of religion."[134] At last, the doors opened and the MPs returned to their respective boroughs. Eleven years would pass before Parliament could debate another matter.

Personal Rule

In a royal declaration, Charles decried what he saw as parliamentary infringement of his prerogative power and promised to "never permit again" such challenges to his divinely granted authority to rule.[135] He resolved to rule without Parliament, but he faced the question of funding. To survive financially, Charles implemented a policy of retrenchment and resorted to even more extraparliamentary revenues. For example, the Crown revived the medieval practice known as distraint of knighthood. Under this custom, owners of lands valued at £40 per year or more were required to become knights. By the 1630s, inflation had made many small landowners eligible for knighthood, but they eschewed this "honor" because corresponding obligations could consume much of their time and resources. Via distraint of knighthood, Charles fined men who had not been knighted and raised £175,000 in the process. While this medieval precedent brought in much-needed money, it also alienated approximately 9,000 small landholders from whom the fines were exacted.[136]

Charles also fined subjects for allegedly encroaching upon the royal forests. The forests had traditionally been hunting reserves for the king and his barons. Over the years, patterns of land use changed and areas that had once been teeming with game or capable of supporting game were under cultivation. In the 1630s, the Crown extended the limits of the royal forests to their medieval boundaries. Thus, many people who were never subject to forest law faced a bevy of fines. Once again, Charles succeeded in raising revenue and in raising the ire of his subjects.

Perhaps the most infamous source of extraparliamentary revenue resorted to was "ship money," a tax traditionally levied by the king on coastal towns for naval defense.[137] Ship money was not a yearly tax, but an extraordinary levy in times of danger. In 1634, Charles sent out writs of ship money to the coastal areas because "thieves, pirates, and robbers of the sea, as well as Turks, enemies of the Christian name" have "gathered together wickedly taking by force and spoiling the ships, and goods, and merchandises, not only of our subjects, but also the subjects of our friends in the sea."[138] Piracy was on the increase and the Spanish had based warships at Dunkirk. Accordingly, good reasons existed for a tax to add ships to the royal navy.

In 1635, Charles went a step further and broke with precedent. The Crown demanded ship money not only from coastal settlements, but also from inland communities. By expanding ship money, Charles could add £200,000 to the royal coffers each year.[139] With such sums, Charles could also live without the check of Parliament for the foreseeable future. Recognizing the danger, several prominent Englishmen refused to pay the levy and brought legal action against officials who seized their property. The case was styled as *Rex v. Hampden* and heard in the special Court of

Exchequer Chamber. The question presented was not whether the king could demand extraparliamentary aids in time of emergency, but whether the king was the sole judge of what constituted an emergency.[140] Hampden's counsel conceded that the king, without consent of Parliament, could demand assistance from his subjects when hostilities were imminent. Counsel argued that the law forbade the king, in times of peace, to extract money from his subjects without the consent of Parliament. Counsel's arguments for limitation of royal authority drew applause from the packed gallery — a very unusual display in the Westminster Great Hall and a sign that the people were very leery of Charles' personal rule.[141]

In response to Hampden's arguments, the court held that "[t]he law knows no such king-yoking policy." Rather, the law is "an old and trusty servant of the king's."[142] The court reasoned that the "king is bound to defend the realm" and the subjects are "bound to obey" and provide the provisions requisitioned.[143] Regarding who determines the existence of a danger, the court held squarely for the king: "And his averment of the danger is not traversable, it must be binding when he perceives and says there is a danger."[144]

The opinion in *Rex v. Hampden* sent shock waves through the country. Charles now had judicial cover for extraparliamentary revenues so long as he perceived a danger to the kingdom. "There is no Tyranny more abhorred," wrote parliamentarian Henry Parker, "than that which hath a controlling power over all Law, and knowes no bounds but its owne will."[145] Parker rightly believed that "danger" would be proclaimed anytime the king needed revenue.

But for a serious miscalculation in Scottish affairs, Charles might have sustained his government on extraparliamentary revenue and medieval precedents. Parliament might never have been summoned again in his reign. Instead, Charles and the Arminian archbishop William Laud chose to force the Scots to conform their religious practice to the Church of England. The Scots were primarily Presbyterian and Calvinist. Compared to the services preferred by Laud, the Scots worshipped in a plain and simple manner, preferring extempore prayers and sermons to high church liturgy. Laud, however, believed that the Scottish service was devoid of order and beauty.

On Laud's advice, Charles used his prerogative power to forbid extempore prayers and to prohibit ministers from preaching outside their parishes without a license from a bishop. Episcopal church government and the accompanying use of bishops was never popular with the Scots. They especially disliked Laud's assertion that the bishops ruled by "divine right."[146]

Hence, this additional power given to an office they already distrusted caused much vexation.

Charles and Laud also forced a new prayer book on the Scots. The new liturgy was decidedly Anglican and not well received. The prayer book was first used at St. Giles' Cathedral in Edinburgh. The congregation, unhappy with the high church liturgy, rebelled. A stool heaved toward the pulpit narrowly missed the bishop's head. Fearful for their safety, the clergy fled. To the chagrin of Charles and Laud, the Scottish bishops suspended use of the new prayer book. This concession to the people was seen as cowardice by the Crown. A few Calvinist milkmaids, according to Laud, had brought the bishops of Scotland to their knees. Charles scoffed when informed that it would take an army of 40,000 men to force the new prayer book on the people.

Charles and Laud soon learned that the opposition to religious innovation was composed of more than just milkmaids and laborers. Beginning in February 1638, clergy, nobility, and commoners signed the National Covenant, a document objecting to religious innovation forced on the people absent consultation with either the Scottish Parliament or General Assembly of the Scottish Kirk (church). The Covenant began by expressing the Scots' loyalty to the king: "We ... promise with all our hearts under the same oath, hand-writ, and pains, that we shall defend [the king's] person and authority with our goods, bodies, and lives."[147] It also expressed their love for "God's true religion, Christ's true religion, the true and Christian religion" as it had been established by the Scottish Reformation.[148] The Covenanters, confident that the true religion reigned in Scotland, promised to "defend the same, and resist all these contrary errors and corruptions."[149] Thus, they were bound to oppose the new prayer book and other religious novelties favored by Charles and his Arminian bishops.

Charles was not impressed with the claims of loyalty to him and the lecture on true religion. Fearing that rebellion would spread to England, he resolved to bring the Scots in line. The king began preparations to raise an army, but he soon realized that such an expense was well beyond the budget permitted by personal rule. Charles called for his loyal subjects to make voluntary contributions for the support of the army, but he received a lukewarm response. A ragtag army was raised and skirmished with the Scots near Kelso. Realizing that a full-blown war would not go well for his forces, Charles negotiated with the Scots while pondering how to raise the necessary money for a real army. Under the Pacification of Berwick, Charles promised to submit the disputed matters to the Scottish Parliament and General Assembly. He certainly never planned to keep this promise, but he needed to buy time.

Forgetting the reaction to his requests for voluntary support, Charles reasoned that national pride would trump his English subjects' disillusionment with personal rule. Accordingly, in April 1640, he summoned Parliament to grant subsidies to suppress the Scots.[150] Once convened, Parliament demanded redress of grievances before any subsidies were considered. John Pym took the floor and divided the issues into three topics: (1) actions taken in the past 11 years against the liberties of parliament, (2) innovations in religion, and (3) "grievances against the property of our goods."[151]

Pym blistered the king for ordering dissolution of the previous Parliament before matters of great import to the people could be debated and brought to the king's attention. He dredged up the Buckingham affair and how the king unjustly imprisoned several of the duke's enemies for no just cause. Such a treatment or "breaking of the parliament," Pym continued, "is death to a good subject."[152] Turning to religion,[153] Pym expressed satisfaction with the "reformed religion" of England and protested against the Arminian innovations of Archbishop Laud. He accused Laud of "introducing popish ceremonies, as altars, bowing towards the east, pictures, crosses, crucifixes and the like, which of themselves considered, are so many dry bones, but being put together make the man."[154]

Lastly, Pym turned to the king's years of personal rule. Pym began with a discussion of tonnage and poundage and reminded Charles that these duties had not been granted for life. No precedent existed, lectured Pym, for collecting these taxes without the consent of Parliament. Pym then discussed distraint of knighthood, enlargement of the forest, and ship money. As for the latter grievance, Pym recognized that the king received a favorable ruling from his judges, but opined that the king's levying of ship money on inland communities was "against all former precedents and laws."[155]

This extraconstitutional government sprang, explained Pym, from the king's refusal to call a parliament. Had the king done so, he would have had sufficient money and his subjects would have had a forum to "make known their petitions."[156] Instead, the monarch and the people were left without a means of communication: "Where the intercourse of the spirits betwixt the head and the members is hindered the body prospers not."[157] The cure to this disease, postulated Pym, was the calling of yearly parliaments. This would strengthen the monarchy as well as protect the liberties of the people.

Pym's speech angered Charles and persuaded him to dissolve what is known as the "Short Parliament." Still determined to restore his authority in Scotland, the king assembled another ill-equipped army and marched northward. The troops rioted along the way and many deserted. Upon seeing this pathetic band of men, the Scots took the initiative. Their forces crossed the River Tweed and routed the English units. The Scots occupied the English town of Newcastle and dared the king to remove them.

In the face of this disaster, Charles still thought he could prevail without Parliament. The king called a great council of peers to meet him in York. Charles perhaps expected a revival of the Middle Ages when the great lords would appear with armed knights in tow. This did not happen and Charles knew he had to call Parliament to save him. Charles made another temporary peace with the Scots and agreed to pay the occupying forces £850 per day for their expenses. A humiliated Charles issued writs for a new Parliament.

The first four decades of the 1600s were a period of conflict between Crown and Parliament. James I and Charles I, claiming to be God's lieutenants on earth, treated Parliament as an advisory body. Parliament was not, in the Stuarts' opinion, a partner in government. Parliament existed to affirm succession to the throne and grant money when called on by the monarch. It existed to serve the Crown, and was not necessary to the English system of government.

In reality, Parliament was essential to the English constitution — especially when the monarch became embroiled in wars and other foreign ventures. But for Charles and Laud picking a fight with the Scots, Charles might have enjoyed many decades of personal rule. Instead, God's anointed learned that, without the backing of Parliament, his prepotency was circumscribed. The people and their representatives also appreciated that Parliament was an indispensable check on royal power. They grasped just how precarious liberty could be when a monarch takes divine right theory to its ultimate conclusion.

CHAPTER 2

Civil War, Restoration, and Revolution

When the Long Parliament assembled on November 3, 1640, its members were emboldened. They knew that they could not be summarily dismissed as Charles had done with the Short Parliament. The Scots had the king cornered and he could not bully his subjects into providing funding. Unlike ever before in his reign, Charles needed Parliament. But the members had not forgotten the abuses suffered throughout the first 15 years of Charles' rule. They remembered forced loans, imprisonments with no just cause, royal gamesmanship with the Petition of Right, expansion of the forest, ship money, and a host of other issues arising from the years of personal rule.

Working within the fiction that the king can do no wrong, the members launched an attack on Charles' chief advisors. Through impeachment and other procedures, Parliament showed the king what it thought of him and his policies. The judges who had upheld Charles' forced loans were called to account for their actions. Charles watched uncomfortably as Parliament attacked his favorites. Queen Consort Henrietta Maria, whom Charles had married in 1625, suggested that he arrest Pym and other leaders in the House of Commons. Decisive action, she urged, must be taken to preserve the gleam of the Crown. The divinely appointed monarch, however, held his tongue and hoped the unpleasantness would pass.

Parliament rightly asserted that the king's failure to call regular parliaments "produced sundry and great mischiefs."[1] Via the Triennial Act, the members declared that subsequent parliaments would meet at least for one 50-day session every three years. They designed an independent mechanism for the summoning of Parliament should the king fail to honor the statute. The Long Parliament also passed legislation prohibiting Charles from dissolving it without the consent of both houses.[2] Though he believed the measures infringed upon his prerogative powers, Charles acquiesced.

Parliament also passed legislation dealing with ship money, the king's expansion of the forest, prerogative courts, and extraparliamentary taxation. Charles did not fight these measures and actually gained some support as Parliament became divided over religious issues. Events in Ireland led to greater distress when native Irish Catholics rebelled against English and Scottish settlers. England needed to raise an army to restore order in Ireland, but Parliament did not trust the king to lead a large military force. Many feared that Charles would use the army to destroy Parliament and establish autocratic rule. Hence, Pym and his supporters demanded parliamentary control over any Irish expedition and a say in the appointment of the king's advisors.[3]

The English Civil War

At the urging of the queen, Charles took action to restore his authority. The king ordered the arrest of his most vocal parliamentary opponents. When Parliament refused to surrender the men, the queen demanded that Charles himself "pull those rogues out by the ears, or never see my face again."[4] Accompanied by 400 armed men, Charles entered Westminster Hall and commanded that the men named in the warrants come forward. As he scanned the assembly, Charles realized that Pym and the others had escaped. Charles returned to his palace and Londoners rioted upon hearing the news that the king had gone to personally arrest his opponents. Rumors circulated that Charles would soon assail the city with royal forces, locate Pym, and hang him in front of the Royal Exchange.

People poured into the streets and prepared to battle Charles' dragoons. The city's residents brandished weapons and promised to defend Parliament from royal attack. Charles wisely fled the city with his family and closest advisors. He put the queen and Princess Mary on a boat bound for Holland and then began to gather military supplies. Parliament also organized bands of soldiers and rations but offered the king one last chance at peace. In the Nineteen Propositions, Parliament entreated Charles to agree to a limited monarchy in which the legislature exercised most important powers.[5] Parliament even demanded control over the education of the king's children and consultation before the king arranged for a foreign marriage. Not surprisingly, Charles saw the terms offered as his unconditional surrender and refused to part with so much power. Within a few months, the English Civil War would begin.

The first few years of the war went poorly for Parliament. The majority of the English population was not excited about the war, but instead simply wanted to grow their crops, feed their families, and sell the surplus at market. They wanted the king and Parliament to settle their differences so daily life could continue uninterrupted. Moreover, after hearing years of sermons about the monarch being God's lieutenant on earth, many were hesitant to take up arms even though they resented the period of personal rule. A number of parliamentarians also kept up the fiction that they were not fighting the king, but fighting for the king and against his evil advisors who were leading him astray.[6] Thus, parliamentary leaders and soldiers mounted a conservative campaign that lacked zeal when confronting Charles and his men on the battlefields.

Of course, not all the parliamentarians adhered to such a conventional mindset. A prime example is Henry Parker, an Oxford-educated barrister, an original thinker, and a close parliamentary ally of Pym. Parker is rightly regarded as the father of parliamentary sovereignty. In a pamphlet published in 1642, he denied that God ordained monarchial government and he postulated that "power is originally inherent in the people." In a just system of government, Parker continued, the consent of the people is "the proper foundation of all power." The people needed good laws and just magistrates because the Fall of Adam left man in a sinful condition and prone to transgress upon the liberty and property of his neighbor. Thus, the people could rightly institute a form of government to check the evil inclinations resulting from the Fall.

Parker recognized that the people could appoint a king as their agent. But Parliament did not occupy the same footing as a minister or agent of the people. To Parker, the people and Parliament "were the same thing in a different mode."[7] If Parliament was the people and the people possessed all power, then Parker reasoned that the king could not complain about parliamentary efforts to curb monarchial power. Charles should be happy that Parliament planned to retain the office of king. Parker's theory was far from the theory of king-in-Parliament put forward by members sparring with James I, but it also was not an argument for popular sovereignty.

Others picked up on Parker's radical assertions. In discussing the king's veto and power over the military, an anonymous pamphleteer argued in 1643 that laws are transmitted from the people (i.e., Parliament) to the king.[8] If the people's good judgment causes a measure to pass both houses of Parliament, then the king must assent or confirm the decision. Otherwise, the writer contended, the people are left to the king's whim.⁹ As for the struggle between Charles and Parliament for control over the troops, the pamphleteer began with the first principle that "God and nature hath ordained Government for the preservation of the governed."¹⁰ Even if the people through Parliament had delegated to the monarch control of the militia, this was solely to better preserve the liberty and property of Englishmen. When the king threatens the welfare of the people, it is proper for Parliament to "reassume" control over the militia so the people can protect and preserve themselves.¹¹

Parker's and Anonymous' arguments for parliamentary sovereignty were heterodox, but mild compared to other offerings. William Ball, for example, pushed the envelope in 1646 and argued for popular sovereignty. Ball viewed all power as coming from the people, with the king and Parliament serving as guardians of the people's laws and liberties.¹² The people possessed, according to Ball, a primary, primitive, and intensive power that trumped the king and Parliament's secondary power. "So that the English Nation, or People," averred Ball, "never gave, or voluntarily assented, that their Kings, or Parliaments, or Both, should have an absolute Domineering, or Arbitrary Power over them...."¹³ If king-in-Parliament ceases to protect the people and abuses the trust powers granted, then the people may exercise their primary powers to correct the situation. Ball did not argue for the people to step in for a mere slight or doubtful exercise of royal or parliamentary power, but only when "their Liberties, and Propertie are destroyed or violated *ad placitum.*"¹⁴

The turning point in the war came not when Parker's or Ball's ideas gained ascendency, but when innovators began to purge the military of certain aristocratic elements. Under the leadership of Thomas Fairfax and Oliver Cromwell, a New Model Army (NMA) arose.¹⁵ Unlike past armies, a soldier's success in the NMA was based more on merit than bloodlines. In previous English military establishments, competent soldiers with genuine combat experience were passed over in favor of the sons of the great barons. While the NMA was not a perfect meritocracy, it did reward merit to a greater extent than its predecessors.

The initial step in creating the NMA was the Self-Denying Ordinance. Under this measure, all members of parliament — except the military genius Oliver Cromwell — were discharged "from all and every office or command military or civil, granted or conferred by both or either of the said Houses of this present Parliament."¹⁶ The Lords, associating their high birth with military service, were deeply offended by their exclusion. However, the military situation was such that the Lords accepted the need for experimentation and approved the ordinance. Indeed, many lords knew that military advantage had been lost because aristocrats commanding Parliament's forces were unsure whether they truly wanted to defeat Charles.[17]

Prior English armies had also been limited geographically. Units were raised by counties and other local bodies. Consequently, the part-time soldiers were tied to particular areas and did not want to fight in other parts of the country. They were a militia and not a professional army. The NMA, on the other hand, was a professional army that could and would fight anywhere in the country. It was controlled and paid by Parliament and viewed itself as a national organization.

So effective was the NMA that by 1646 Charles surrendered to Scottish authorities. Military success, however, was but a small part of the NMA's legacy. In the months and years after Charles' surrender, the NMA became an active political participant. With military victory, Parliament ceased to pay the NMA on a regular basis and did nothing for war widows and disabled soldiers.[18] Soldiers also feared legal proceedings related to the NMA's "requisitions" of horses and other materials during the war. They wanted an indemnity ordinance passed to protect them from these lawsuits. Parliament made matters worse when it planned to ship some NMA regiments to Ireland to quell rebellion and to demobilize others — all without first dealing with the issue of back pay.

The actions of Parliament caused the NMA to elect representatives and to engage the political process. These elected representatives were charged "to act in the name and on behalf of the whole soldiery ... in the prosecution of their rights and desires."[19] NMA leaders created a General Council consisting of these representatives plus officers and commanders. The NMA made it clear to Parliament that the soldiers would not disband or be sent to Ireland until grievances were addressed.[20] The situation escalated when Parliament denied that the soldiers had a right to petition for grievances.

The soldiers refused to occupy a second-class status. The NMA reminded Parliament that it was not a "mercenary army" but had been brought into being "for the defence of our own and the people's just rights and liberties."[21] Because elections had not been held since 1640 and the "temptation ... of unlimited power" had overtaken some in Parliament, the NMA called for a new round of voting.[22] The NMA also suggested that electoral reform take place so that Parliament would be a "more equal representative of the whole ... kingdom."[23] A close reading of the NMA's declarations reveals a belief that the Army was more representative of the people than Parliament was. Indeed, the NMA assumed the position of a "third estate" of the kingdom.[24]

With the end of hostilities, the soldiers had an opportunity to contemplate the future of England. The collapse of the old order permitted soldiers as well as civilians to put forward heterodox opinions representing viewpoints from across the political spectrum. For example, on the extreme left were the "Diggers," a group advocating the abolishment of private property and the creation of a communistic state.[25] More conservative elements favored establishment of some sort of limited monarchy. Others argued that a new government should be grounded in republican principles.

One of the groups that had the most influence upon the NMA was the "Levellers."[26] Led by John Lilburne,[27] the Levellers advocated religious toleration, translation of laws from Latin or French into English, social legislation to "keep men, women, and children from begging and wickedness," improvement of the harsh conditions found in English prisons, frequent elections, an end to imprisonment for debt, and many other forward-thinking proposals.[28] Just as Parliament met NMA petitions with hostility, so too did Parliament treat the Levellers. Soldiers and civilian Leveller leaders saw much common ground and the NMA became vital to the Leveller movement.[29] The Levellers argued that military defeat of the king had not brought much relief because Parliament had become intoxicated with power and oppressed the people. Civilian Levellers began to see the NMA, rather than Parliament, as "the natural head of the body natural of the people at present."[30] Parliament, in Leveller eyes, was no better than Charles.[31] Its members, rather than using the NMA victory as an opportunity to reform the country, were continuing with business as usual.

To the dismay of many in Parliament, the Levellers rejected theories of divine right, king-in-Parliament, and parliamentary sovereignty. The Levellers forcefully argued that ultimate authority resided in the people themselves. Institutions of government, under the Leveller theory, were but agents of the people and could only exercise delegated powers with the consent of the people. In the words of John Lilburne, it was "tyrannical" for any person to "assume unto himself a power, authority and jurisdiction, to rule, govern or reign over any sort of men in the world without their free consent."[32] And if ever the people's agents exceeded the delegated powers, all power "returneth from whence it came, even to the hands of the [people]."[33]

To put theory into practice, the Levellers created the Agreement of the People, which would have required the signature of all citizens before it became effective. In essence, this was a written constitution whereby the people, as ultimate sovereigns, delegated certain powers to their representatives.

> That the power of this, and all future Representatives of this nation is inferior only to theirs who choose them, and doth extend, without the consent or concurrence of any other person or persons, to the enacting, altering, and repealing of laws; to the erecting and abolishing of offices and courts; to the appointing, removing, and calling to account magistrates and officers of all degrees; to the making of war and peace; to the treating with foreign states; and generally to whatsoever is not expressly or impliedly reserved by the represented themselves.[34]

There then followed a reservation of rights that prohibited the representatives from doing such things as interfering with religion or conscripting citizens.[35]

In the midst of these radical ideas, agents of Parliament and the Army continued to negotiate with Charles for terms of his restoration. Acting as if he had won the war, Charles refused to compromise. With multitudes complaining about parliamentary tyranny, he speculated that the nation would beg him to reassume the throne with few, if any, restrictions on his power. To hurry the process along, Charles entered into an agreement with the Scots whereby he promised to restore Presbyterianism to England for three years and to suppress religious opinions contrary to Presbyterianism. It is unlikely Charles planned to keep his end of the bargain, but a Scottish army invaded England to do his bidding.

The invading army, however, was no match for the NMA. With the destruction of the Scottish regiments, Charles' fortunes took a turn for the worse. This use of "foreign" troops against England increased the hatred of the king. Many parliamentary and NMA leaders who favored negotiations with Charles now believed that the king could never be trusted with any authority. Charles was a "man of blood" who deserved punishment for his treachery.

Charles on Trial

On December 6, 1648, Colonel Thomas Pride and a detachment of soldiers forcibly excluded members of the Commons who opposed bringing Charles to trial. Pride excluded 143 members, leaving only 78. Of these, 20 refused to take their seats. The "Rump" left after Pride's purge inferred that it was expected to do the bidding of the NMA or face purgation itself.

Approximately one month after Pride's purge, the Rump passed three resolutions. First, the Rump declared that "the people are, under God, the original of all just power."[36] It followed that the Commons (or what was left of it), having been elected by the people, has "the supreme power in this nation."[37] Based on this supreme power, any measure that passed the Commons, with or without assent of the Lords or king, "hath the force of law."[38] This resolution was prompted not by a desire to state first principles, but by the Lords' refusal to collaborate in the trial of Charles for treason.

Prior to the trial of Charles, the law punished treason if one "compasses or imagines the death of our Lord the King," makes war against the king, or adheres to the enemies of the king.[39] Even the most inventive lawyer would have had difficulty charging Charles within the established definition of treason. Accordingly, the Commons modified the definition to also include the levying of war by the king "against the Parliament and Kingdom of England."[40] At first blush, this addition to the standard definition of treason seemed to make the outcome of any trial obvious: the conviction and execution of the king. This is not so. Many leaders still sought some sort of settlement with Charles, but the stubborn king refused to bend. Moreover, regicide was not required if Charles was found guilty; many simply wanted a formal finding that the king was to blame for the war and the deprivations that accompanied the fighting.[41] Such a finding, they believed, might form the basis for persuading Charles to accept a limited monarchy.

With the new treason law on the books, the Commons passed an Act Erecting a High Court of Justice to try Charles. The court consisted of 135 commissioners, few of whom were trained in the legal profession. Fearful of having their names associated with the trial of the king, the most influential judges and lawyers wanted no part in the proceedings. These legal giants also saw their refusal to serve as a mechanism to thwart the Rump and to preserve the ancient constitution.

The act averred that the king, "not content with the many encroachments which his predecessors had made upon the people in their rights and freedom, hath had a wicked design totally to subvert the ancient and fundamental laws and liberties of this nation, and in their place to introduce an arbitrary and tyrannical government."[42] In furtherance of this scheme for arbitrary government, the king "hath prosecuted it with fire and sword, levied and maintained a civil war in the land, against the Parliament and kingdom; whereby this country hath been miserably wasted, the public treasure exhausted, trade decayed, thousands of people murdered, and infinite other mischiefs committed."[43] With this background concerning the king's behavior, the court was instructed "to take order for the charging of him, the said Charles Stuart, with the crimes and treasons above mentioned, and for receiving his personal answer thereunto, and for examination of witnesses upon oath."[44]

With so many lawyers wanting no part of the trial, the Commons turned to John Cooke to serve as solicitor general in the case. Although the son of a poor tenant farmer, thanks to hard work and family sacrifice, Cooke was educated at Oxford. The legal community knew him for his devotion to social and legal reforms much akin to those advanced by the Levellers.[45] Rather than flee London with his colleagues, Cooke believed that Charles had committed great crimes against the people and embraced the opportunity to prosecute the case.

The actual trial began on January 20, 1649, with Cooke reading the indictment against Charles. Cooke charged the king with seeking to establish "an unlimited tyrannical power to rule according to his will."[46] In securing this objective, Cooke alleged that the king levied war "against the present Parliament, and the people therein represented."[47] Charles sought to disrupt the reading of the charge by hitting Cooke with a walking stick and crying "hold." Keeping his cool, Cooke ignored the king and continued with his work. With his last attempt to strike Cooke, a silver tip dislodged from the stick and rolled to the floor. Charles motioned for Cooke to pick up the tip, but Cooke refused to move. In front of the packed gallery, Charles stooped and picked up the tip himself. This event had more potency than the reading of the charge. Here was the king of England stooping while a commoner stood erect and proud in his work.

After the reading of the charge, the court called upon the king to answer. Charles refused to enter a plea and instead demanded to know whence the court derived its authority. Charles viewed himself as the font of all justice and knew he did not authorize this new court; therefore, he believed that the court was illegitimate and lacked jurisdiction. When Lord President John Bradshawe informed Charles that the court existed "in the name of the people of England, of which you are elected King," Charles scoffed.[48] The king lectured Bradshawe that he was not an elected king, but had received his office by divine appointment. Of course, Bradshawe did not mean an election as we moderns view the term, but rather that Charles was invited by Parliament to assume the throne and confirmed as king by a vote of the Lords and Commons.[49] Charles lectured the court that God would judge them harshly for participating in the legal proceedings and continued to inquire into the court's authority. Seeing that Charles was not going to enter a plea, Bradshawe adjourned court and gave the king one day to reconsider.

Under the common law, Charles could plead guilty or not guilty. A refusal to enter a plea amounted to an admission of every allegation made in the charging document. When he returned to court, Charles attempted to give a speech on why the judges had no authority over him. He lectured that "a King cannot be tried by any superior jurisdiction on earth."[50] In other words, he averred that no court on the planet Earth had authority to put God's anointed on trial. Bradshawe permitted Charles to ramble for a short while and then reminded the king that he was "a prisoner ... charged as a high delinquent."[51] Bradshawe made clear that the pleading stage of a trial was not the time for speeches. He again asked Charles to enter a plea to the charges. Charles refused to plead and was promptly removed from the court.

Charles gave the court no choice but to consider his refusal to plead as admission of the crimes charged. Because of Charles' recalcitrance, Cooke would not be permitted to present witnesses in Westminster Hall to testify about the king's misdeeds and wartime conduct. There was, however, a private sentencing hearing at which witness statements were taken to satisfy the court of the king's de facto admission of guilt. Many of the witnesses called testified that the king led troops in battle, starved English towns into surrender, and encouraged his soldiers to mistreat prisoners of war.[52] Cooke also showed the court captured correspondence in which Charles sought military aid from Continental powers. Based on this evidentiary hearing, the court had no misgivings about condemning Charles as a tyrant, traitor, and murderer.

When the court reconvened to sentence Charles, the king asked that he be permitted to meet with the Commons and the Lords. When asked what he would propose to Parliament, the king refused to answer. The court adjourned to consider Charles' request, but decided that no further delay was warranted. The king's refusal to outline what he would propose to Parliament caused many to decide that Charles was not acting in good faith. The court returned to Westminster Hall, declared Charles guilty, and sentenced him to death by beheading. Charles requested that Parliament permit him to see his children and to be attended by clergy. Parliament granted this last request; three days after sentencing, an axe severed Charles' head from his body.

The Commonwealth

With the restoration of Charles I now out of the question, England needed an executive power. The Rump held the reins of power, but such a body was too unwieldy to implement and enforce the laws of England. To remedy this problem, the Commons created a Council of State with broad executive powers.[53] The Commons authorized the Council to conduct foreign affairs, govern the military, regulate trade, imprison offenders, suppress royalist rebellions, etcetera. The Council brought some stability, but leaders of the new commonwealth recognized the need for major reform. The last parliamentary elections occurred in 1640 and the current members were but a "rump" of that duly elected body. New elections should have been a given, but many in the Commons fretted that royalists and Presbyterians would win at the polls. Some MPs toyed with the idea of "recruiter" elections whereby members of the Rump would recruit new members to take their places. These so-called elections would have been farcical and the resulting body would have had less support than the Rump.

Word of these proposed shenanigans caused the Rump to lose respect. Failure to pass the baton of power to another duly elected body, coupled with the Rump's inability to pass reform legislation, persuaded Cromwell that the Rump had to be dissolved by force. On April 20, 1653, he and a detachment of soldiers paid a visit to the Rump. In an angry speech, Cromwell informed the MPs that "[i]t is not fit that you should sit as a Parliament any longer. You have sat long enough unless you had done more good."[54] Cromwell ordered the soldiers to remove the Speaker of the House and ordered Parliament dissolved.

In June of 1653, Cromwell sent out writs of summons for a new body that he expected to function as a constituent assembly.[55] The members were nominated by Cromwell and a council of NMA officers assisting him. History knows this body as the Barebones Parliament, so named after Praisegod Barebones, an Anabaptist preacher who was otherwise a nondescript member. Cromwell stressed to the assembly that the Council of State was an ephemeral body and that the assembly possessed the real power.[56] In time, the Barebones Parliament rather than Cromwell's council proved short-lived. Parliament, badly split over religious issues, dissolved itself in December 1653. Full authority returned to Cromwell and the NMA.

At this point, many believed Cromwell would take the crown. Although there was much support for a monarchy, Cromwell understood the dangers. The ranks of the NMA contained numerous republicans for whom kingship was anathema. The country was tired of war and Cromwell did not want to see the NMA divided and battling brothers in arms. Cromwell also disliked the permanent connotation of kingship.[57] He could stomach being a lord protector, but not king. The English associated protectors with a regent and the handling of affairs during the minority of the monarch. The very term "protector" implied a temporary period.

With the end of the Barebones Parliament, Cromwell and his officers adopted the Instrument of Government.[58] This written constitution omitted any statements about the locus of sovereignty. Instead, it began with the assertion that "the supreme legislative authority of the Commonwealth ... shall be and reside in one person, and the people assembled in Parliament; the style of which person shall be the Lord Protector of the Commonwealth of England, Scotland, and Ireland."[59] The administration of the government was charged to "the Lord Protector, assisted with a council, the number whereof shall not exceed twenty-one, nor be less than thirteen."[60] To avoid temptations of personal rule, the Instrument provided that Parliament should be summoned every third year. The office of lord protector was made elective, not hereditary. Upon the death of the protector, the Instrument empowered the Council to choose a successor. The Instrument extended freedom of religion to all Christians except to Catholics, Episcopalians, and those who "hold forth and practice licentiousness."[61]

The commonwealth was built upon the military establishment and this created a financial strain. This challenge of keeping a standing army paid and provisioned ultimately led to the demise of the commonwealth. To support the NMA, Englishmen were taxed at high levels — rates bordering on those paid by Frenchmen living under the absolutism of Louis XIV. Even with enormous revenues flowing into the government, deficits ran high. Cromwell further displeased the populace when he resorted to the rule of the major generals. In essence, Cromwell and the Council divided England into 11 districts and placed a major general in charge of each area.[62] The major generals, backed by professional soldiers, exercised despotic power and caused many civilians to lose faith in the protectorate. Government's hand seemed heavy on the people with the major generals imposing fines for cursing, gambling, and excessive use of alcohol.[63] During this time Cromwell agreed that the office of lord protector should be hereditary and thus inched further toward the restoration of monarchy to England.

When Cromwell died on September 3, 1658, his son Richard became lord protector. Richard lacked the vigor and decisiveness of Oliver. A country gentleman rather than a soldier, he did not command the respect of the NMA. Without support of the military, his reign was doomed and lasted a mere eight months. The generals recalled the Rump, dissolved the Rump, and then ruled via a Committee of Safety. England was in chaos; people great and small wanted order and stability.

The Stuarts Restored

General George Monck, commander of the army in Scotland, became the spokesman of all Englishmen who demanded a return to a stable, constitutional government. He led his forces south and was joined by likeminded persons. Monck had been in communication with Prince Charles and explained to him that the army could restore the Stuart line if Charles offered certain concessions.[64] Acting on Monck's advice, Charles issued the Declaration of Breda.[65] He promised a full pardon to all (except for those whom Parliament would later enumerate), payment of amounts owed by the army, and confirmation of land sales concluded since the war began in 1642.[66] Based on the promises made at Breda, the new Parliament (or convention, as it was called) invited the son of the murdered king to return to England.

The Stuart restoration unfortunately settled very little. Although king and Parliament had struggled throughout the 1600s — culminating in a civil war — there was no Restoration agreement concerning Charles' powers. The Declaration of Breda avoided the issue altogether. Despite the nationwide debates and governmental experiments in the 1640s and 1650s, no one understood just what, if any, restrictions limited Charles II. Englishmen hoped that Charles and Parliament would work together in the best interests of the realm, but there were no guarantees.

Charles II returned to England as a somber man, determined never again to experience the hardships and embarrassments of exile. Thirty years old when he assumed the throne, Charles appeared distant, cynical, and guarded. Extensive time abroad had made him more French than English in personal and political tastes. He appreciated the cheering crowds that lined the route from Dover to London, but he did not trust them. He speculated that many in the crowds had also cheered the regicide, or at least declined to lift a finger to protect his father. In a word, Charles was a melancholy king.[67]

Charles combated dolefulness by indulging himself in drink, revelry, and sundry mistresses. Initially such activity was a welcomed signal that the strict codes of the major generals were no more. Englishmen, however, soon grew weary of Charles' expenses, extravagant court, and bastard children on which the king spent enormous sums.[68] Parliament had voted Charles custom duties for life and budgeted £1.2 million for royal expenditures. While such a budget would have seemed infinite to his predecessors, Charles was constantly in debt. Difficult economic times certainly added to the financial problems inasmuch as tax revenues often fell short of the mark, but Charles greatly contributed to the situation by mismanagement.

Charles' financial problems, in part, led him to sign the Treaty of Dover in 1670. He agreed to support Louis XIV's efforts to conquer and dismember the Netherlands. If the combined English and French forces were successful, Charles would receive a stretch of Dutch territory. This much of the treaty was made public. The treaty also contained secret clauses that only a few of Charles' closest advisors knew about. Louis agreed to pay Charles an annual subsidy of £160,000 to free his cousin from reliance upon the English Parliament. In exchange for the money, Charles promised to publicly announce his allegiance to the Roman Catholic Church at an opportune time. He further agreed to suspend penal laws against English Catholics.[69]

Now on the Sun King's payroll, Charles issued the Declaration of Indulgence.[70] Citing "unhappy differences in matters of religion which we found among our subjects upon our return," Charles suspended penal laws affecting "noncomformists or recusants."[71] The Declaration permitted Protestant dissenters to worship in public places so long as "the teacher of that congregation be approved by us."[72] Charles declared that Roman Catholics could "worship in their private houses," but declined to permit them to gather for public worship services. To justify his authority to set aside parliamentary enactments concerning religion, Charles cited his position as head of the Church of England.

While most Englishmen conceded that the king could occasionally excuse individual compliance with certain statutes, his unilateral nullification of an entire statutory scheme was another matter. Charles and Louis sensed the hostility of the English people to both the Dutch war and the voiding of English laws. Thus, Louis persuaded Charles to adjourn Parliament for two years. The cousins hoped their combined forces would overwhelm the Dutch and that the English people would be placated by martial success. Despite the combined English and French onslaught, the Dutch fought valiantly under the leadership of William of Orange (Charles' nephew). While the armies and navies clashed, Dutch propagandists flooded England with pamphlets decrying Charles' succor given to Catholic France against the Protestant Dutch. The pamphlets accused Charles of being a puppet of the Sun King and raised the ire of the English people. Englishmen had no qualms about fighting the Dutch for commercial advantage, but they could not stomach aiding and abetting the absolutist French regime.[73]

When Parliament reconvened, it refused to vote Charles additional monies for the Dutch war. If Charles wanted money, he would have to accept the Test Act, which required all civilian and military officers to take Anglican communion and to swear an oath denying transubstantiation. His back to the wall, Charles accepted the Test Act, withdrew the Declaration of Indulgence, and watched as several of his loyal advisors stepped down because their closet Catholicism prevented them from denying the Roman Church's sacramental teaching. Charles' brother and the heir to the throne, James, Duke of York, resigned his naval post. James' resignation made clear that if Charles fathered no legitimate heir, England would once again be ruled by a Catholic monarch.[74] This revelation led to panic and wild rumors of popish conspiracies and plots.[75]

By the end of the 1670s, Parliament attempted to force Charles to accept legislation excluding James from the throne. Parliament would accept James' Protestant daughter Mary, who was married to William of Orange, as Charles' successor, but it would not consider a Catholic on the throne. With the seemingly inseparable union of church and state, Parliament could not countenance a Catholic monarch. It feared a return to the days of Bloody Mary and the persecution of Protestants.[76]

At this point, Charles realized that far more was at stake than his brother. As discussed in the first chapter, indefeasibility of hereditary right was central tenet of the Stuarts' brand of divine right. Charles was very much the grandson of James I and an adherent to his grandfather's teachings. Parliament, Charles believed, was an instrument of the monarchy and thus prohibited from meddling in matters of succession.[77] Numerous royalist writers took up their pens to support Charles' claims.[78] Such a debate on the nature of kingship and Parliament had not been held since the 1640s.

John Brydall, for instance, asserted that "the King is our only Soveraign" and denied that the Lords and Commons were "Co-partners in the Soveraignty."[79] The king was "the sole Legislator" who alone "gives Life, and Being, and Title of Laws" with or without the consent of Parliament.[80] Parliament, in Brydall's words, was "only Consultative or Preparative" in the making of law.[81] An anonymous writer was even more direct:

"In the presence of His Majesty, both, or either Houses of Parliament have no power to command."[82] In case anyone missed his argument, the anonymous writer emphasized that "the *King* is the only *Supreme Governor of this Realm.*"

In 1680, royalists published Robert Filmer's *Patriarcha*. Most likely written in the 1630s or 1640s, this book was a classic statement of divine right theory. Filmer argued that just as a father rules over his household, so too does the king rule over England.[83] He traced the divine ordination of monarchy from Adam and averred that Jehovah "hath taught us by Natural Instinct, signified to us by the Creation, and confirmed by his own Example ... the Excellency of Monarchy."[84] Filmer recognized that kings could be tyrants, but he rejected tyranny as an objection to monarchy inasmuch as, in his view, popular governments were more dangerous to order and liberty.[85] "[E]very Tyrant desires to preserve the Lives, and protect the Goods of his Subjects," whereas popular assemblies have no such motive.[86]

Filmer denied that any law or custom could limit a king's power. He described the king as possessing an "Unlimited Jurisdiction."[87] The only reason laws were recorded, Filmer continued, was so that a subject "might find his *Prince's Pleasure* deciphered to him in the Tables of his Laws, that so there might be no need to resort unto the King."[88] Common law and custom were not limits because they were "Originally the Laws and Commands of Kings at first unwritten."[89] Parliament had become an advisory body in the law-making process, but even in Parliament "all Statutes or Laws are made properly by the King alone."[90] If a law did not please the people or Parliament they had no choice but to obey; resistance to the king was tantamount to resisting the will of God.

Perhaps the greatest answer to Filmer's work is Algernon Sydney's *Discourses Concerning Government*. Written in the early 1680s, the book was first published in 1698—fifteen years after Sydney's death. Sydney was a republican and fought against Charles I during the Civil War. Upon the restoration of Charles II, Sydney could not bring himself to apologize for his service to Cromwell's regime; therefore, he lived in exile until he was given permission to return to England in 1677. The government put Sydney to death in 1683 for his part in a conspiracy to assassinate Charles II. Sydney was a coconspirator, but his trial will always be remembered for irregularities and little respect for due process of law.

In his *Discourses*, Sydney mocked the notion that any person could trace his family history back to some original grant of power from God. To do so, Sydney asserted, would require "the genealogies of everyone from

Noah" or special revelation from heaven.[91] Sydney's reason and study of the Scriptures led him to conclude that there had never been such a grant of power and that "[w]e may enter into, form, and continue in greater or lesser societies, as best pleases ourselves."[92] The only inheritance man has "is that exemption from the domination of another." This inheritance Sydney called "liberty," and described it as "the gift of God and nature."[93]

A monarch, in Sydney's view, was not God's special lieutenant on earth. Instead, "all magistrates are equally the ministers of God, who perform the work for which they were instituted."[94] And the work of just rulers was simply "the doing of justice, and procuring the welfare of those that create them."[95] If the people become unhappy with a magistrate or form of government, they "may proportion, regulate and terminate their power, as to time, measure, and number of persons, as seems convenient to themselves."[96]

Gilbert Burnet's pamphlet on supreme authority is another example of opposition to divine right theory. Burnet, however, was no republican, having served as one of Charles' chaplains and later advising William and Mary and Queen Anne. In exploring the locus of supreme power, Burnet looked to the legislative branch.[97] He went on to define the legislative power as king-in-Parliament.[98] The king's executive power was not supreme, but merely a delegated trust power.[99] Burnet agreed with Sydney that monarchy was not ordained by God as the only authorized form of government.[100] Hence, if a king subverted the English constitution, he fell from power and could be stopped from exercising authority.[101]

Charles reacted to the constitutional debate much as his father had. He saw Parliament as an evil to be avoided and allowed over three years to pass without calling another after dissolving Parliament in 1681. This was in blatant defiance of the Triennial Act of 1664. Charles was emboldened to live without Parliament when Louis XIV promised him a large subsidy if he would dispense with summoning the legislature.[102] An increase in foreign trade and correspondingly the custom duties also helped the king enjoy a period of personal rule.

Desiring to shore up royal power, Charles did not sit idly as his income increased. In a bold move, he tried to pack local governing bodies with his supporters. The mechanism he used was *quo warranto* proceedings whereby the king could revoke the charter of a municipal corporation for petty infractions.[103] Charles would reissue the charter and in the process pack the local governing body with supporters of royal power. Typically, the revised charter gave the king a veto on the selection of local officers. Because well over 75 percent of MPs were city or borough members,[104] this move meant that if a king ever called another Parliament, the MPs would be royal allies.[105]

Charles also began forming a complaint judiciary. During the beginning of his reign, he appointed judges to serve "during good behavior." This meant, in theory, that they could not be dismissed for a ruling that displeased the king. Towards the end of his reign, Charles appointed judges to serve "during pleasure." This meant that the king could dismiss them for any reason or no reason. The judiciary in England was not a separate branch of government; it was part of the executive/royal branch. Hence, the judiciary was never a real check on royal power. Instead, it often served to suppress activity viewed by the Crown as seditious. Charles' decision to appoint judges "during pleasure" rendered the judiciary an even greater tool for the suppression of subjects who favored limits on royal authority.

When Charles died on February 6, 1685, his brother James[106] received a kingdom with waxing royal power. Aware of concerns about his religion and Charles' efforts to prostrate Parliament, James II issued a declaration promising to preserve the church and state under established law. Although he made clear that he would not accept restrictions on prerogative power, James also promised to safeguard the property of his subjects. The people happily received the new king's declaration. Because James was more upright in his personal conduct than Charles and also possessed a reputation as a hard worker, some believed that his reign might be more successful than his brother's. Such hopes soon proved foolhardy.

At the same time that James was assuring his subjects of his love for the British constitution, he candidly informed the French ambassador that he distrusted parliaments and desired to make himself financially independent of them.[107] In violation of his promise to protect the people's property, James contemplated using troops to forcibly collect taxes that had not been voted by Parliament. Using an insignificant uprising in western England as an excuse, James doubled the size of the standing army and, in violation of law, appointed Catholic officers to lead the men. James did not build housing for his soldiers and instead required his subjects to billet them. While he assured Englishmen that these houseguests were for protection of the realm, he ordered the army to march on London. James' forces encamped at Hounslow Heath and began maneuvers meant to intimidate the city dwellers.

James was very open about his Catholicism and soon reestablished diplomatic relations with the Vatican. As head of the Church of England, he forbade the clergy from preaching anti–Catholic sermons. These measures, coupled with James' appointment of Catholics to civil and military posts, frightened many Englishmen. In October 1685, Louis XIV revoked the Edict of Nantes, which had granted French Protestants a measure of toleration.[108] As Protestant Frenchmen fled to England and other countries, they brought with them stories of oppression and mistreatment. English Protestants, aware of James' close relationship with Louis, were confident that they would face similar ordeals.[109]

James continued his brother's purge of the judiciary. When complaints were voiced that he had violated the Test Act in appointing Catholics to military posts, he arranged a collusive lawsuit to affirm his prerogative power. Prior to the initiation of the suit, he dismissed six judges whom he did not trust to rule for the Crown. With a packed judiciary, James got the desired result. In *Godden v. Hales*, the Court of King's Bench held that because the king is sovereign and all laws are his laws, the king has the power to "dispense with penal laws in particular cases."[110]

As previously discussed, while the majority of Englishmen agreed that the king could suspend the application of a law in a particular case not anticipated by Parliament, they did not believe that the king could void an entire statutory scheme. With the favorable decision in *Godden v. Hales*, James decided to push the envelope a bit further. In the spring of 1687, he set aside the Test Acts that barred Catholics and Protestant dissenters from holding office. James expected the dissenters to join with England's tiny Catholic population in supporting the Crown. To his chagrin, the dissenters—fearing an alliance between James and Louis XIV—did not embrace the king's Declaration of Indulgence.[111]

The dissenters' reaction left James in a pickle. In an ill-advised gambit, he cast aside conservative Anglicans, who typically supported divine right theory, for a Catholic-dissenter alliance that never materialized. In modern political parlance, James alienated his base and failed to garner support from outside the English mainstream.[112] Unable to recognize his isolated position, James further blundered when he ordered the conservative Anglican fellows of Magdalen College, Oxford, to elect a pro–Vatican president. When the fellows refused to bow to his wishes, James had 25 of them ejected and declared them ineligible to hold any office in the Church of England. With the events at Oxford, Anglicans became convinced that James intended to destroy their church and force Englishmen to accept papal authority.

Despite concern about James' religious policies and moves to consolidate power in the monarchy, a number of Englishmen believed that better days were on the horizon. James' two daughters were firm in the Protestant faith and could be counted on to reverse their father's most incendiary measures. Many were surprised that James had outlived the robust Charles II and, considering that James was 51 years old when he ascended to the throne, his reign was expected to be brief. Such optimism ceased when James' second wife, Mary of Modena, gave birth to a son on June 10, 1688. James' enemies spread rumors that the child had been smuggled into Mary's bedchamber in a warming pan, but this was rank speculation. Rather than getting a Protestant queen upon James' death, England would now be ruled by James Francis Edward Stuart. Undoubtedly James and Mary would raise the child as a Roman Catholic and a defender of his father's policies.

To celebrate the birth of a son, James stepped up efforts to silence his critics. On the day of the birth, James' cabinet council charged seven prominent bishops with seditious libel. The bishops had refused to read James' Declaration of Indulgence from their pulpits on the grounds that the king could not unilaterally suspend acts of Parliament by royal prerogative. Angered by the bishops' dedication to the rule of law, James interned them in the Tower of London. Londoners cheered the bishops as they traveled by barge down the Thames to prison. In June 1688, the bishops were tried and acquitted by a jury. Both Anglicans and dissenters knelt together and gave thanks for the bishops' deliverance. Londoners lit bonfires to celebrate the king's defeat. A bellicose James ordered the prosecution of the revelers, but grand juries refused to return "true bills" that would have permitted the cases to go forward.

Unrest was growing, but Englishmen could not coerce James without foreign assistance. James' expansion of the army meant that only a professional force from across the Channel could threaten his personal rule. On the same night that Londoners lit bonfires in celebration of the bishops' acquittal, leading English magnates met and signed a letter asking William of Orange for military assistance.[113] They assured William that "the people are so generally dissatisfied with the present conduct of the government in relation to their religion, liberties, and properties" that William could expect many to welcome an invasion.[114] Concerned that James and Louis XIV would soon combine to destroy the Dutch Republic,[115] William agreed to make a preemptive strike. He assembled an invasion fleet and, thanks to a favorable wind, landed in England on November 5, 1688.

In a declaration issued prior to the landing, William denied that he coveted the English throne. Instead, he stated his ultimate goal as the meeting of "a free and lawful Parliament." This was a brilliant move because the desire for a legitimate Parliament — not one packed with the king's myrmidons — united all of James' enemies, whether they were Anglicans or dissenters, republicans or archconservatives. William castigated James' wicked advisors for overturning the religion, laws, and liberties of the realm. He doubted that the queen actually birthed a son and described her pregnancy as "pretended bigness." Affirming that he was an invited guest by certain lords spiritual and temporal, William averred that his soldiers were meant to protect him from the king's counselors and that they would not be used to the detriment of the English people.[116]

William was saying the right things, but his army was still half the size of James'. Had James acted decisively and immediately engaged the foe, he might have prevailed. Instead, he contemplated remaining in London and concentrating his forces there. James feared that if he left the city, the same people who celebrated the bishops' acquittal would rule the streets and threaten his Catholic friends and advisors. Once James decided that he had to engage William, he was the victim of poor intelligence. Many of the scouts sent out to track William defected to the Dutch forces; therefore, James was left guessing at William's movements. William's army slowly grew as the great landholders declared for him and English army units left James' service. When James took the field to rally the troops, he became afflicted with severe nosebleeds and retreated to his bed. Failing to inspire the soldiers and hearing of the growth of William's army, he returned to London.

James summoned a number of peers residing in London to advise him. They suggested that James negotiate with William and summon a free Parliament. They further advised James that if he wished to retain power he needed to make concessions; he needed to stop his emulation of his father's personal rule of the 1630s. William offered James very fair terms: James would remain king, a free Parliament would be held, William's forces would be provisioned, and key areas in London would be turned over to the City of London. James was unwilling to make concessions. He believed that Charles I's downfall resulted from conceding too much to the leaders of the Long Parliament. He sent his wife and son to France and made plans to follow them. Prior to leaving, James tossed the Great Seal into the Thames (hoping this would frustrate the conducting of government business) and rode for the coast. Fishermen captured him and, to William's vexation, returned him to London. William arranged for the guards around James to be somewhat neglectful of their duties so James could successfully escape. This time no fisherman intervened and James fled to the court of the Sun King.

Seeking advice, William summoned members of Charles II's final Parliament and the Lord Mayor and aldermen of the City of London.[117]

This assembly thanked William for rescuing them from the tyranny of James II and asked him to assume the administration of the government until Englishmen could craft a permanent solution to filling the empty throne.[118] Consistent with his earlier declaration and upon the recommendation of the MPs, William issued letters calling for election of a Convention Parliament. This was not a regular Parliament because the king had not issued writs of election; however, elections went smoothly and the Convention met January 22, 1689. MPs and their constituents predominantly agreed that William should head the executive branch of government. There were, of course, a few who supported the recall of James on certain conditions. Ever petulant, James torpedoed this idea by declaring unambiguously that he would return on his terms and his alone.

The conservative faction, known as Tories, recognized that James would no longer steer the course for England. Even so, they did not want to part with the hereditary element of divine right theory. They most certainly did not want an elective kingship. Thus, leading Tories considered declaring William regent, as if James were a minor, and permitting him to rule in James' name. The more reformed-minded faction, the Whigs, opposed a regency because it ignored problems that could arise if James outlived William, such as the claim of young James Francis Edward Stuart to the throne. Under the cherished principle of hereditary right, this infant, who would be raised in the French court, would be king upon James II's death.

Acknowledging the problem created by the recent birth, some Tories suggested making William's wife Mary queen and declaring that James' baby boy was not his natural child. While this took care of the infant's claim, it did not sit well with William. He did not want to be his wife's consort, but rather wanted the English throne for himself. At a minimum, he demanded that he and Mary be cosovereigns.

After much debate, the Convention agreed that James had "abdicated the government" and that the throne was "thereby vacant."[119] In a carefully crafted ceremony, the Convention offered the crown to William and Mary — but only *after* reading them the Declaration of Rights.[120] In this Declaration, the Convention proclaimed that many of the acts and practices of James II were contrary to the ancient constitution and thus illegal. The Convention condemned James' suspension of laws without the consent of Parliament, extraparliamentary methods of raising revenue, raising and keeping of standing armies, and James' tampering with parliamentary elections. The Declaration affirmed essential individual rights such as bearing arms and the petitioning of the king for redress of grievances. The Declaration was later passed as a statute and became known as the Bill of Rights.

The Bill of Rights did not put forth the doctrine of parliamentary supremacy nor did it disclaim the divine right of kings.[121] But in reality the Glorious Revolution marked the beginning of parliamentary sovereignty in the Bodin mold.[122] With the monarch unable to raise significant revenues without parliamentary consent, Parliament effectively assumed control of the ship of state. What began as an advisory council of great magnates was fast becoming the ultimate sovereign in the English political system.

By the 1760s, when the great William Blackstone wrote his *Commentaries on the Laws of England*, the power of Parliament was a given. Parliament, according to Blackstone, consisted of "the king's majesty, sitting there in his royal political capacity, and the three estates of the realm; the lords spiritual, the lords temporal, (who sit, together with the king, in one house) and the commons, whom sit by themselves in another."[123] The *Commentaries* thus recognized that the principle of king-in-Parliament was settled. The Stuart proposition that the Lords and Commons were dispensable was but a part of history. Blackstone was clear that the "crown cannot begin of itself any alteration in the present established law."[124]

Regarding the power of Parliament, Blackstone described it as follows:

> It hath sovereign and uncontrollable authority in making, confirming, enlarging, restraining, abrogating, repealing, reviving, and expounding of laws, concerning matters of all profitable denominations, ecclesiastical, or temporal, civil, military, maritime, or criminal: this being the place where *absolute despotic power*, which must in all governments reside somewhere, is entrusted by the constitution of these kingdoms.[125]

Nor was fundamental law beyond the reach of Parliament in Blackstone's estimation: "It can change and create afresh even the Constitution of the kingdom...."[126] Once Parliament takes an action regarding the constitution or a lesser matter, "no authority upon earth can undo" it.[127]

The phrase "no authority" also included the people of Great Britain. Under the accepted doctrine, if Parliament enacted pernicious laws that threatened the liberty of the people, "the subjects of this kingdom are left without all manner of remedy."[128] Parliament was not an agent or trustee of the people and thus subject to their sanction — it was sovereign.[129] Blackstone specifically took aim at John Locke's assertion that Parliament was "only a fiduciary power to act for certain ends" and that the people possessed "supreme power to remove or alter the legislative ... when they find the legislative act contrary to the trust reposed in them."[130] Blackstone derided Locke's logic as "theory" and alien to the British Constitution as it had actually developed.[131] Without elaboration, he refused to adopt or argue from Locke's reasoning and instead affirmed "that the power of parliament is absolute and without control."[132]

In sum, the 1600s were a century of great change and debate. The century began with a monarch devoted to the divine right of kings and ended with the ignominious flight of his grandson. The efforts of the Stuarts to rule without Parliament resulted in the demise of their beloved divine right theory and the weakening of the monarchy. God's supposed "Lieutenant on Earth" lost much of his luster. Although it would be some time before Parliament reduced the monarch to a mere figurehead, the course steered by the Stuarts accelerated this process.

The instability caused by clashes between the Crown and Parliament in the 1640s permitted Englishmen to debate the first principles of society and some voices argued for popular sovereignty to replace divine right theory. Under Leveller theory, departments of government were but the servants of the omnipotent people. To put theory into practice, the Levellers created a written constitution called the Agreement of the People. The Agreement was ahead of its time and offered an alternative to divine right and parliamentary supremacy. Although England was not ready to embrace popular sovereignty, it would not be long until thirteen English colonies would do so.

The latter days of Charles II and the rule of James II brought an end to claims that the king was England's ultimate sovereign. With the offer of the throne to William and Mary and the Bill of Rights, Parliament would never again be eclipsed by the monarchy. By the mid–1700s, it was settled law that Parliament possessed all power under the constitution. Indeed, parliamentary sovereignty was closely associated with England's — and later Britain's — liberties. Certain colonies across the pond, however, would eventually challenge the validity of this association.

Chapter 3

Rethinking Sovereignty

The absolute power of Parliament, as described by Blackstone in his *Commentaries*, followed colonists to North America.[1] Parliament was the ultimate sovereign whether a subject lived in London or Boston. It could make or repeal laws as it saw fit. No court, collection of individuals, or divinely appointed prince could claim legal power to restrain Great Britain's Parliament. Indeed, just prior to the American Revolution, Martin Howard, Jr., a prominent figure in the colony of Rhode Island and Providence Plantations, observed that "[e]very Englishman … is subject to [Parliament's] jurisdiction, and it follows him wherever he goes. It is the essence of government, that there should be a supreme head, and it would be a solecism in politicks to talk of members independent of it."[2] Such a description of Parliament's power and jurisdiction was generally accepted on both sides of the Atlantic.

Settled principles, however, are often reexamined in times of strife. This was the case in the 1760s when Parliament sought to exercise greater control over its North American dominions. The American colonists bristled at the influx of tax collectors, soldiers, and other government agents. Parliamentary sovereignty, the bedrock of British liberty, did not seem so sacrosanct. Rather than the foundation of liberty, Parliament appeared to be inimical to colonial rights — especially the right of self-government. Consequently, the colonists began to rethink sovereignty just as the Levellers and others did during the turbulent years of the English Civil War.

In 1607, just over 100 intrepid settlers, who had been recruited by the Virginia Company, established the first permanent English-speaking settlement in North America. Named in honor of James I, Jamestown struggled in the face of Indian attacks, disease, and hunger. By the end of 1608, only 53 sickly settlers remained. Despite reports of hardship reaching home, Englishmen continued to brave the Atlantic and colonize in North America. Twenty-seven years after Jamestown's inauspicious beginnings, 5,000 settlers called North America home. Just seven decades later the number had topped 250,000.

Although settlers traveled to North America for a variety of reasons — such as freedom of religious practice, financial gain, and the desire to be left alone — England had but one purpose in encouraging colonization: enrichment of the mother country. England, like many of the European powers, adhered to mercantilism. In essence, mercantilism is a system of economic nationalism in which government strives to maintain a positive balance of trade by promoting domestic manufacturing and enacting tariffs to handicap foreign competition.[3] In a mercantilist colonial system, colonies were intended to provide England with raw materials and agricultural commodities and to purchase manufactured goods from the British Isles.

Mercantilist theory was put into practice with the Navigation Acts. Under these statutes, only British ships with predominantly British crews could carry goods to or from a colony. If, for example, a French manufacturer wanted to ship items to Virginia, his vessel was supposed to dock in London, pay duties, and load the items on a British ship for transportation to the New World. There were some commodities produced in America that could not be carried to foreign ports — even if loaded onto British vessels. Britain did not want its colonies feeding or clothing enemy nations. Hence, the American colonists could not export such items as rice, cotton, wool, or naval stores to foreign countries. The colonies were also forbidden to export certain items to Great Britain. For instance, the Hat Act of 1732 forbade the shipping of beaver hats out of the colonies. This act, to the chagrin of the colonists, protected hat makers in Britain from American competition. These regulations of colonial trade meant that British manufacturers and merchants, unhampered by foreign competitors, dictated the prices of goods bought and sold by the Americans.[4]

The results of the mercantilist system pleased the mother country. Historian Gordon S. Wood estimates that "[f]rom the late 1740s on, Americans were importing from Britain about £500,000 worth of goods more than they were exporting to the mother country."[5] The colonies purchased approximately one quarter of all British exports. British ship owners enjoyed great prosperity; almost half of British shipping was involved in trade with America.[6] Although mercantilism was meant for the benefit of the mother country, the colonies nonetheless prospered. By the mid–1750s, the American colonists enjoyed a higher standard of living than most Europeans.[7] The colonists had diets high in protein and produced better vegetables than their relatives back home.[8] Grinding poverty, as found in many European nations, simply did not exist in America.

The success of the American colonies was not the result of careful planning or oversight. The colonies developed naturally on the backs of enterprising individuals. Britain's imperial structure was dilapidated and inefficient — certainly incapable of hindering the growing colonies.[9] This neglect of colonial matters left Americans with a strong sense of self-sufficiency and self-government.[10] British officials were seldom in a position to interfere with colonists' economic and social pursuits, and the colonists took advantage of their independence — often to the benefit of the empire. Sir Robert Walpole, who served as prime minister from 1721 to 1742, took the position that "salutary neglect" of the colonies was best for all parties involved.[11] He rightly believed that so long as the colonies were at peace and governed by local laws ensuring domestic tranquility, the colonials and British merchants would enjoy economic prosperity.

This policy of colonial independence was the case not just in North America, but throughout the peripheries of the empire. Local bodies in Wales, Scotland, and Ireland enjoyed a freedom that would have been unthinkable under a more centralized, European monarchy.[12] Such a localization of power was a direct result of Parliament's triumph in the Glorious Revolution and the Crown's inability to raise revenue without resort to the British Parliament or the representative assemblies of the various colonies.[13]

Indeed, it was British policy to encourage creation of representative assemblies.[14] Assemblies were an integral part in colonial governance. Every American colony was governed by a governor, a council, and a house of representatives.[15] By the eve of the Revolution, the office of governor was controlled by the Crown in all colonies except Rhode Island and Connecticut. In these two colonies the office was elective.[16] The governor exercised broad powers, such as commanding the militia, appointing local officials (e.g., justices of the peace, sheriffs, judges) and vetoing of legislation.[17] The council assisted the governor with executive and administrative matters and often performed judicial duties.[18] Historians have described the council as a "combination of the House of Lords and the king's cabinet in the British government."[19] The lower houses represented the voices of the people. These bodies viewed themselves as mini-parliaments and were schooled in the battles between the Stuarts and the House of Commons.[20] Exercising the power of the purse, these assemblies proved to be an effective check on the governors' powers.

Imperial Restructuring

The hands-off approach to the colonies changed with the conclusion of the Seven Years' War in 1763. The victorious British forces won vast new territories from France and Spain in North America: Canada, East and West Florida, and a fertile swath of land situated between the Appalachian Mountains and the Mississippi River. Not only did Britain acquire additional land in North America, but it also secured a paramount position in controlling trade with Africa and Asia.[21]

While the spoils of war held the promise of new wealth, the cost of territorial acquisition was high. Britain's war debt rose to £137 million with £5 million in annual interest.[22] Considering that the empire's peacetime budget was about £8 million, the debt was staggering.[23] In addition to this preexisting debt, Britain faced the prospect of additional expenditures in organizing the new territories and appointing royal officials. Britain also faced the prospect of keeping the peace with hostile Indian tribes that unhappily found themselves under British jurisdiction. The ever-present colonial hunger for land made conflict inevitable; therefore, Britain estimated that it would need 10,000 regular troops stationed in North America to handle the peacekeeping duties.[24]

The raising of additional revenue was not an easy task. Britons suffered under a heavy tax burden and many felt that the colonists gained the most benefit from the victory over France.[25] Taxation in Britain had reached upwards of 30 percent of landowners' incomes before the Seven Years' War.[26] The British Treasury estimated that the average colonist paid one-fiftieth of the taxes paid by the average British subject living in the mother country.[27] Britons also resented that the colonists did not fully participate in fighting the French in North America until after they were promised reimbursement by the Crown.[28] As a result, at the end of hostilities the public debt was £18 per person in Great Britain versus 18 shillings per person in America.[29] Hence, Britons of all classes and parties believed it was time for the colonists to pay something towards their own defense.

The primary architect of George III's imperial restructuring was George Grenville, the king's third prime minister. The debts accumulated during the Seven Years' War caused Grenville loss of sleep. He even harbored doubts whether the territorial gains of the conflict could ever outweigh the financial implications. A countinghouse clerk at heart, Grenville looked for ways to balance the budget and retire debt. In examining the North American situation, he was shocked that the salaries of colonial customs officers exceeded the amounts they collected. Moreover, the Board of Trade estimated that smugglers brought £700,000 of goods into the colonies without paying one pence in duties.[30] Grenville believed that something should be done to extract more revenue from the colonies.

Grenville formulated his plans at a time when Americans felt betrayed by the mother country. Just eight months after the war ended, George III issued a proclamation prohibiting white settlement in the recently acquired interior lands.[31] The king hoped this would maintain peace with the Indians; he also heeded concerns of British creditors who worried that if the colonists moved from the seaboard to the interior, it would be almost impossible to track down debtors in the vast wilderness. The colonists viewed the proclamation as treachery. In American eyes, the primary purpose of fighting the French was to conquer territory that would be opened for westward expansion. The king's apparent preference for Indian hunting grounds did not sit well at all.

The first revenue-generating measure passed by Parliament was the Sugar Act of 1764.[32] The stated purpose of the act, in its preamble, was "defraying the expences of defending, protecting, and securing" the North American colonies.[33] The Sugar Act revised the Molasses Act of 1733, which imposed a sixpence tax per gallon on foreign molasses.[34] Molasses, a key component in manufacturing rum, was critical to the New England economy. Americans distilled rum and sold it to their neighbors, Indians, and fishermen operating near Newfoundland. Some rum was also shipped to Africa along with agricultural products as part of the triangular trade. Once the rum and other goods were offloaded in Africa, slaves were crammed into the ships and taken to the West Indies to work on the sugar cane plantations. The ships then delivered more molasses to New England.

The Molasses Act of 1733 was never enforced. Smugglers bribed customs officials and the supply of molasses continued unabated. With the Sugar Act, Parliament reduced the duty to three pence per gallon and employed the Royal Navy in enforcing the tax. Grenville believed that reducing the duty would squelch any complaint about actually paying it.[35] The newly imposed duties were ill timed because the North American colonies were experiencing a postwar economic downturn.[36] Grenville also did not realize that the profit margin on rum was so slim that the three-pence duty hurt many New England distillers. A flurry of protests followed as the colonists comprehended that the Sugar Act would be but the first of many parliamentary intrusions on their independent existence.

The next intervention was the infamous Stamp Act of 1765.[37] It was the first direct, internal tax to be levied on the North American colonies by Parliament.[38] The act required that almost every form of paper used in the colonies be affixed with an official stamp. Hence, the tax increased the price of legal documents, bills of sale, mortgages, almanacs, playing cards, newspapers, pamphlets, calendars, and numerous other items used by all classes of colonial society.[39] The stamps had to be purchased with British sterling; the colonists could not use foreign currency or paper money when buying them. The legislation also provided that the act would be enforced in vice-admiralty courts where judges determined the law and the facts of the case.[40] Colonists would be unable to depend on juries of their vicinage to relieve them from the burdens of the act.

Colonials regarded the Stamp Act with almost universal odium and believed that, if accepted, it would create a precedent harmful to American liberties. The importance of precedent or custom was central to the British constitution.[41] Although Parliament was the ultimate sovereign, custom provided certain "limits" on its authority. For example, most members of Parliament would have agreed that Parliament could not rightly prohibit the people from petitioning the government for redress of grievances. Custom and precedent dictated that the ability to petition was a right of freeborn Englishmen. Of course, no branch or component of government existed to nullify such a statute other than Parliament itself, pressured by the people using the ballot box or other means.

Because it was unwritten, the British constitution necessarily relied more on custom or precedent than does the current United States Constitution. Precedent certainly carries much weight in the modern American system, but those unhappy with precedent may also turn to the Constitution's text and history when arguing for the overturn of precedent. With no text and therefore no discussion or debate prior to adopting the text, British subjects necessarily were limited to the custom of the realm as evidenced by prior course of conduct. Accordingly, when subjects feared that Parliament or the king was inserting a dangerous innovation into the constitutional order, they were duty bound to create a "record" with protests and often refusals to abide by the act in question.[42] If they failed to do so, a subsequent king or Parliament could build further on the precedent.[43]

Colonial Protests

This understanding of precedent motivated the colonists to communicate their displeasure to the mother country via civil unrest and legislative resolutions.[44] In Boston, an underground group known as the Loyal Nine (later called Sons of Liberty) formed to combat the Stamp Act. The Loyal

Nine sagaciously recruited the leaders of the north and south end gangs so they would have foot soldiers for the campaign. The gangs were notorious in Boston and rioted every fifth of November, the anniversary of the Gunpowder Plot. The gangs started at opposite ends of the city and moved forward with wagons on which effigies of the pope sat. Then each gang fought to destroy their rival's pope. These brawls were brutal and had resulted in serious injuries and loss of life.[45] By channeling the power of the gangs to "patriotic ends," the Loyal Nine possessed the resources to overawe the Crown's forces present in the city.

On August 14, 1765, the Loyal Nine's allies sprang into action against Andrew Oliver. Oliver was a wealthy merchant and had been appointed the Stamp Act agent for the colony. Leaders of the gangs created an effigy of Oliver and hung it in a tree in Boston's south end. Attached to the arm of the effigy was a placard that read: "What greater joy did New England see / Than a stampman hanging on a tree."[46] Lieutenant Governor Thomas Hutchinson attempted to call out the militia to disperse the mob and remove the effigy, but quickly learned that many of the militia members were part of the mob and refused to break with their colleagues. As evening approached, the mob cut down the effigy and paraded it through the town on a plank. When the mob came to a newly constructed building on Oliver's dock, the rioters assumed this was the new stamp office and promptly destroyed the structure. The effigy was burned amid cheers and a contingent of the mob headed for Oliver's home. Fortunately for Oliver and his family, they escaped prior to the arrival of their uninvited guests. The mob helped itself to Oliver's wine cellar, destroyed the home's furnishings, and then retired for the evening. The next day Oliver resigned his commission.[47] Other colonies experienced similar riots and tumults as stamp men, having become pariahs, joined Oliver in resigning their posts.[48]

The colonies also registered their protests by passing resolutions. The most influential resolves were passed in Virginia, where young Patrick Henry and a group of representatives from the backcountry wanted to strike a decisive blow for American liberty.[49] Knowing that his resolves would offend the more conservative members of the legislature, Henry waited until the end of the session when many legislators had left Williamsburg for home. With only 39 of 166 assembly members present, Henry and his western allies struck. Henry criticized the Stamp Act and observed that "in former times tarquin and Julus [sic] had their Brutus, Charles had his Cromwell, and he Did not Doubt but some good american would stand up, in favor of his Country."[50] The Speaker immediately accused

Henry of treason, at which point Henry apologized, professed loyalty to the Crown, and continued his speech.

Henry and his allies had prepared seven resolutions, but only five of them were passed by the House of Burgesses. The largest majority for any resolve was 22 to 17. These resolutions were reprinted in newspapers throughout the colonies and stirred Americans to protest Grenville's latest revenue measure. The Virginia Resolutions and those from the various colonial assemblies shared a number of characteristics. First, they pointed to the lack of precedent for Parliament levying direct, internal taxes on the colonies. In the words of the Maryland assembly,

> his Majestys liege People of this Ancient Province have always enjoyed the Right of being Governed by Laws to which they themselves have consented in the Articles of Taxes and internal Polity and that the same hath never been forfeited or any other way Yielded up but hath been Constantly recognized by the King and People of Great Britain.[51]

Often connected to the precedent argument was a "knowledge" argument based on divergent local circumstances.[52] Patrick Henry's resolutions lectured Parliament that only representatives chosen by the people "can ... know what Taxes the People are able to bear, or the easiest Method of raising them."[53] Considering the challenges of travel and communications in the eighteenth century, this was a strong argument. Parliament was attempting to enact a comprehensive, one-size-fits-all tax on colonies as different as South Carolina and Massachusetts when no member of Parliament was from either colony and very few, if any, had personal knowledge of the colonial circumstances.

The knowledge problem aside, the colonials also protested that the members levying the tax on the colonies would not feel the pinch of the tax. According to Patrick Henry's resolutions, this shared burden by elected representatives "is the only Security against a burthensome Taxation, and the distinguishing Characteristic of British Freedom, without which the ancient Constitution cannot exist."[54] When legislating for Britain, the members would feel the bite of a tax or ill-conceived law in the same manner as electors and those nonelectors who were "virtually represented." This was not true for American colonists virtually represented in Parliament. Members of Parliament could not feel the effects of laws on colonials nor were they present to witness the results. Thus, the doctrine of shared burdens proved to be a compelling argument against virtual representation.[55]

Keying in on representation, the colonial assemblies also made the famous taxation-without-representation argument known by every schoolchild. The phrase "no taxation without representation," however, is a bit more complicated than most Americans have been led to believe. Under the customs of the British Constitution, taxation was a gift from the people to the king and was distinguished from ordinary legislation.[56] Because one cannot gift something if one does not have a claim to it, taxation was closely tied to representation.[57] The Connecticut assembly expressed the ideas as follows:

> That in the Opinion of this House, An Act for raising Money by Duties or Taxes differs from other Acts of Legislation, in that it is always considered as a free Gift of the People made by their legal, and elected Representatives, And that we cannot conceive, that the People of great Britain, or their Representatives, have Right, to dispose of our Property.[58]

Because the colonists, via the franchise, had authorized no one in Parliament to consent to taxation, the Stamp Act was void. It followed that colonial "gifts" to the king could only come from the colonial assemblies. In fact, the colonists, through Benjamin Franklin, suggested that the king should approach them directly if he desired revenue: "When aids to the Crown are wanted, they are to be asked of the several assemblies, according to the old established usage, who will, as they have always done, grant them freely."[59] The colonists' reasoning on this point was sound, and many Britons, including William Pitt and Edmund Burke, agreed that Parliament could not tax the colonies.[60]

Organized extralegal groups — all called "Sons of Liberty"— sprang up across the colonies.[61] These organizations carried out a successful campaign to boycott certain British goods. By this time Grenville's ministry had fallen and he was succeeded by the Marquis of Rockingham. Rockingham worked with British merchants and helped them form a lobby to urge repeal of the Stamp Act. Petitions from manufacturing towns poured into Parliament. Rumors spread that armies of unemployed workers would march on London and demand redress. Grenville, still an MP, advised Parliament to stand firm and to teach the rebellious colonies a lesson. Rockingham, aided by William Pitt, prevailed and secured repeal of the Stamp Act.

However, even those members of Parliament who joined with the Americans in seeking a repeal of the Act desired to reaffirm the power and ultimate sovereignty of Parliament. Pitt, in his speech urging repeal, counseled as follows:

> At the same time, let the sovereign authority of this country over the colonies be asserted in as strong terms as can be devised, and be made to extend to every point of legislation whatsoever. That we may bind their trade, confine their manufactures, and exercise every power whatsoever, except that of taking money out of their pockets without their consent.[62]

This sentiment would give rise to the Declaratory Act of 1766 in which Parliament claimed the power "to make all laws and statutes of sufficient force to bind the colonies and people of *America*, subjects of the crown of *Great Britain*, in all cases whatsoever."[63] This assertion of authority was not radical. With the Declaratory Act, Parliament was simply acknowledging its place in the constitutional order as established in the Glorious Revolution. This language could also be interpreted in multiple ways. Grenville could read the Declaratory Act to include the power to tax the colonies, whereas Pitt and Rockingham could read the act to refer only to legislation. The Declaratory Act settled very little.

Parliament continued the controversy with the colonies when it passed the Townshend Acts in 1767. Charles Townshend, a captivating speaker and eighteenth-century playboy, was chancellor of the exchequer and the de facto head of William Pitt's ministry. Pitt had succeeded Rockingham, but poor health prevented him, now Lord Chatham, from effectively steering the ship of state. Townshend gleaned from the Stamp Act crisis that although the Americans would not suffer internal taxes to be levied by Parliament, they would not oppose external taxes. He thus proposed levying customs duties on glass, lead, paint, tea, and paper. The revenue collected from the duties would be used to pay the salaries of royal officials serving in the colonies. No longer would these servants depend on the colonial assemblies for their pay. Townshend recognized that the new levies would only bring in about £40,000 per year, but he viewed the new duties as essential inasmuch as they would establish a precedent that could be used to expand the revenue.

The colonists balked at Townshend's efforts to use customs duties to raise revenue. The Americans claimed that Britain could regulate trade, but Britain could not use trade regulations to raise revenue that ought to come from internal taxes.[64] Americans also inveighed against Townshend's plans to free royal officials from the modest control the legislatures exercised via salary payments. The colonial assemblies protested the Townshend Acts and were dismissed by their respective royal governors.

Similar to the Stamp Act protests, the people agreed to stop purchasing British manufactured goods and also took to the streets. Not surprisingly, the Boston mob led the way and forced royal officials to request soldiers to restore order. By the end of 1768, 4,000 redcoats were stationed in Boston — a town of 15,000 residents. The townspeople resented the presence of a standing army which they viewed as inimical to liberty. The working class detested the soldiers because the redcoats often took second jobs and competed with Bostonians in the unskilled labor market. Friction between the soldiers and people led to the Boston Massacre in which five civilians were killed after threatening a young private on duty at the custom house. This was but a prelude to the bloodshed at places such as Bunker Hill, Saratoga, and Camden.

Limiting Parliament

The imperial restructuring caused American thinkers to study the power of Parliament and how it might be limited. At base, the colonists wanted to enshrine principles of home rule in the British constitution.[65] The colonists were proud of their British heritage and often appealed to their rights under the ancient constitution. That this constitution recognized the ultimate sovereignty of Parliament did not prove insurmountable to the flexible colonial writers. Throughout the 1760s, theories changed dramatically as the colonists responded to Britain's attempts to raise revenue and accompanying arguments supporting the new legislation.

Early efforts to limit parliamentary power proved clumsy and problematic. For example, in 1764, James Otis published his *Rights of the British Colonies Asserted and Proved* in which he argued for continued home rule and some form of colonial representation in the British Parliament.[66] Otis began by praising the Glorious Revolution and the defeat of the Stuarts. He described the British constitution as "the best national civil constitution in the world."[67] Otis identified Parliament as "the supreme legislative of the kingdom and in dominions" and argued that the colonists should submit to all parliamentary enactments.[68]

Though he accepted Blackstone's formulation of Parliament's sovereignty,[69] Otis nonetheless contended that parliamentary taxes levied on the colonies were "absolutely irreconcilable with the rights" of Americans as British subjects and violated natural law principles.[70] He made clear that the colonists could not nullify unconstitutional legislation but instead had to patiently wait for Parliament to discover the constitutional error. Otis believed that the remedy could either be repeal of the tax or acceptance of colonial representation in Parliament. But considering Otis was initially arguing for colonial home rule, the cure seemed incongruent with his stated purpose. Otis' tract was confusing and contradictory; it won him few accolades. If anything, it highlighted the fact that an institution exercising sovereignty on the Bodin model cannot be limited.[71] This was not a message the colonists were eager to hear.

Learning from Otis' mistakes, other thinkers chose to distinguish between the power of Parliament and the power of colonial assemblies.[72] They divided the powers of the colonial assemblies and those of Parliament into two distinct spheres. The powers of Parliament were described as external, general, or imperial, while the powers of the assemblies were described as internal or local.[73] For example, John Dickinson, writing in 1768, observed that in an empire composed of distinct provinces "there must exist a power somewhere to preside, and preserve the connection in due order."[74] If the issue concerned the empire as a whole, such as the regulation of trade among the members, Dickinson opined that the power must rest with Parliament.[75] Direct taxation, however, was an internal matter and therefore outside of Parliament's power.[76] Stephen Hopkins of Rhode Island agreed with Dickinson on this point and urged his fellow colonists to "patiently submit" to all laws passed by Parliament "for directing and governing all these general matters."[77] But for matters affecting only one part of the empire, Hopkins pointed to the "peculiar privileges" of the different provinces as the ultimate authority.[78]

The mother country understood that it was but a small step from the concept of divided sovereignty to an argument that Parliament had no sovereign power over the colonies. During questioning of Benjamin Franklin by Parliament, he was specifically asked whether the colonies might not soon voice objections to Parliament's regulation of external matters. Choosing his words carefully, Franklin responded that while some men had presented that position, the colonists were yet to be persuaded. However, he ominously warned that "in time they may possibly be convinced by these arguments."[79]

As Franklin predicted, it was not long until the colonists rejected the supremacy of Parliament. By the late 1760s, the colonists had already become suspicious of parliamentary sovereignty. In 1768, pamphleteer William Hicks observed that "while the power of the British parliament is acknowledged sovereign and supreme in every respect whatsoever, the liberty of America is no more than a flattering dream, and her privileges delusive shadows."[80]

Perhaps the best statement of the colonists' rejection of parliamentary supremacy is Thomas Jefferson's *A Summary View of the Rights of British America*.[81] According to Jefferson's version of history, the colonists left the mother country and only continued the union with Great Britain "by submitting themselves to the same common sovereign, who was thereby made the central link connecting the several parts of the empire thus newly multiplied."[82] Hence, the sole connection between the people of Britain and the colonists was George III. To Jefferson, Parliament was a foreign jurisdiction having no say in the affairs of the colonies. He declared a number of parliamentary enactments "void" on the "true ground ... that the British parliament has no right to exercise authority over us."[83] Past parliamentary measures regulating colonial affairs were usurpations of the American legislatures' authority.

Jefferson also offered George III a road map on how to preserve the union between the people of Britain and the North American colonists. Describing the king as "the only mediatory power between the several states of the British Empire," Jefferson asked George III to approach Parliament to recommend the repeal of unconstitutional acts which were the cause of "discontents and jealousies among us."[84] Without intercession of the king, "fraternal love and harmony through the whole empire" would be impossible.[85]

In reality, Jefferson's solution to the dispute between the colonies and mother country was impossible for the British to accept. At the time Jefferson penned his *Summary View*, the balance created by the Glorious Revolution was less than 100 years old. Although in 1774 the balance of power tilted decidedly toward Parliament, the royal prerogative was not yet dead and the king still exercised substantial power under the British constitution. Were the king to accept Jefferson's view of royal power, the constitutional balance would shift away from Parliament and back toward the monarchy. To a nation wedded to the principles of parliamentary sovereignty and suspicious of attempts to augment royal power, Jefferson's proposal was a constitutional heresy.

During this time, formal plans of union were drafted in an effort to avoid independence. For example, the loyalist Joseph Galloway proposed a plan that would have united the thirteen colonies within the British Empire. Galloway called for the creation of a continental assembly that he described as "a British and American legislature" that would "regulat[e] the administration of the general affairs of America."[86] In theory, this legislature would be "an inferior and distinct branch of the British legislature," although it would handle all continental matters.[87] Each colony would "retain its present constitution, and all powers of regulating and governing its own internal police, in all cases what[so]ever.[88] In recognition of the king's authority, he was to appoint a president general to execute the laws passed by the new legislature.[89]

With George III unwilling to intercede on behalf of the colonies or to accept proposals for union, the colonies declared independence. Consistent with the colonists' evolving theory of sovereignty, the Declaration of Independence primarily addressed the "history of the present King of Great Britain."[90] The Declaration only indirectly addressed Parliament by accusing the king of "combin[ing] with others to subject us to a jurisdiction foreign to our constitution."[91] By 1776, the colonists had jettisoned Parliament from the constitutional scheme. With the king serving as the only link between the colonists and the British Empire, there was no need to formally address Parliament or declare independence from parliamentary rule. Because of the king's multiple abuses, the colonies were "absolved from all allegiance ... to the British crown."[92]

The rejection of parliamentary sovereignty and connection with the king left ultimate sovereignty in each legislature. Since the mid–1760s, the Americans had been arguing that the state assemblies were the equivalent of the parliamentary body sitting at Westminster. John Adams, writing as "Novanglus," asserted in 1775 "that our provincial legislatures are the only supreme authorities in our colonies."[93] James Madison, some years after the Revolution, summed up this idea as follows: "The legislative power [at the time of the Revolution] was maintained to be as complete in each American Parliament, as in the British Parliament."[94] Parliamentary sovereignty, the heart of the British constitution, appeared likely to continue in the various state constitutions.[95] After all, the American Revolution was begun by invoking the colonists' rights as Englishmen.

Acceptance of Popular Sovereignty

Parliamentary or legislative sovereignty, however, was short-lived once redcoats and colonists clashed on the battlefield. The Revolutionary War years were much akin to the 1640s and 1650s in England. Just as the Levellers, Diggers, and a host of others reexamined fundamental principles, so too did the Americans. Akin to Lilburne and his followers, the Americans questioned whether ultimate sovereignty could rest in an artificial body such as a state assembly.[96]

In a proclamation issued prior to the Declaration of Independence, the General Court of Massachusetts averred:

> It is a maxim, that, in every government, there must exist, somewhere, a supreme, sovereign, absolute, and uncontroulable power; But this power resides always in the body of the people, and it never was, or can be delegated, to one man, or a few; the great Creator, having never given to men a right to vest others with authority over them, unlimited, either in duration or degree.[97]

Similarly, in June 1776, the Virginia Declaration of Rights stated that "all power is vested in, and consequently derived from, the People; that magistrates are their trustees and servants, and at all times amenable to them."[98] In the early months of the Revolution, we see a revival of the spirit of 1649 and the Levellers' Agreement of the People.[99] Massachusetts and Virginia, in no uncertain terms, declared that the people possess what Bodin or Blackstone would recognize as ultimate sovereignty, while the people's agents (e.g., representatives, governors, and judges) possess what we today call governmental or legislative sovereignty, which is derived from the people and is inferior to the people's ultimate sovereignty.[100]

Of course, eloquent declarations are one thing and action is another. The Levellers succeeded with the former but had no success with the latter. Having resurrected popular sovereignty from the graves of the English Civil War, Americans were tasked with implementing this principle.

The first state to use a special convention to draft a constitution and then to submit this product to the people was Massachusetts. In so doing, Massachusetts became the model of popular sovereignty in the making of constitutions.[101] This innovation in the theory of government did not come from the state's leading politicians, but rather from town meetings of farmers and tradesmen.[102] The elite envisioned government continuing as it had before, only without interference from royal officials or Parliament. The people wanted a new framework of government that guaranteed certain rights and, most importantly, received the consent of the governed.[103] Citizens from certain parts of the state contended that until they consented to a new form of government they were in a state of nature and no part of Massachusetts.[104]

Bending to the demands of the people, on June 15, 1779, the state house of representatives passed two resolutions. In the first resolution it "recommended to the several Inhabitants of the several towns in this State to form a Convention for the sole purpose of framing a new Constitution."[105] The delegates chosen were to meet in Cambridge to debate and draft a new plan of government. The second resolution provided that once the delegates finished their work, the document would be circulated among the people and for "the Selectmen of each town, and the Committee of each plantation at a regular meeting of the Male inhabitants thereof, being free and twenty one years of age, to be called for that purpose, in order to its being duly considered and approved or disapproved by said towns and plantations."[106]

The towns, in choosing delegates to the convention, often drafted instructions emphasizing popular sovereignty. For example, the town of Pittsfield reminded its delegates that "all power originates from the people, so, in a state of civil society, all power is founded in compact."[107] As a consequence of this ultimate power, "civil rulers derive their authority from the people, so they are accountable to them for the use of it."[108] The town of Sandisfield directed its delegates that once a draft constitution was completed, the document should be submitted to local bodies where the people could suggest amendments and express their approval or disapproval of the work of the convention. By this method, the convention could be "possessed of the minds of the People at Large" and thus better complete the work at hand.[109]

The convention followed the recommendation of Sandisfield and on March 2, 1780, it sent the proposed constitution, which was the handiwork of John Adams, to the towns for discussion and suggestions. The towns were given until June 7, 1780, to report back. At that point, the convention would make alterations favored by two-thirds of the people.[110] When the convention reconvened, it reviewed the returns from the towns and declared that the constitution had been ratified. Historians question the tabulation method used by the convention and observe that it is difficult if not impossible to determine whether the full constitution was properly ratified.[111] Nevertheless, the process used in Massachusetts broke new ground.

In the preamble, the constitution defined the body politic as "a voluntary association of individuals: It is a social compact, by which the whole people covenants with each citizen, and each citizen with the whole people."[112] In other words, this was Massachusetts' Agreement of the People. The people, according to the constitution's bill of rights, possessed "[a]ll power" such that government officers "are their substitutes and agents, and are at all times accountable to them."[113] As a derivative of this power in the people, they "alone have an incontestable, unalienable, and indefeasible right to institute government; and to reform, alter, or totally change the same, when their protection, safety, prosperity and happiness require it."[114] The people's agents (governor, legislators, and judges) were thus reminded that the ultimate sovereigns, if displeased with the new constitution, could abolish the framework and start anew.

Massachusetts taught its neighbors the proper way to adopt a constitution in light of principles of popular sovereignty: "Constitutions were formed or changed by specifically elected conventions and then placed before the people for ratification."[115] Between declaring independence and ratification of the Massachusetts Constitution in 1780, most of the former colonies adopted constitutions in the legislative branch.[116] This should not be surprising inasmuch as a parliament, under British constitutional theory, could make or unmake fundamental law. Massachusetts instructed Americans on the difference between legislative power and constituent power.

Only the people can exercise the latter, while their agents exercise the former *after* the people make a delegation of authority in a constitution. In his *Notes on the State of Virginia*, Thomas Jefferson praised Massachusetts for its chosen method of adopting a constitution and urged his state to follow this example: "To render a form of government unalterable by ordinary acts of assembly, the people must delegate persons with special powers. They have accordingly chosen special conventions to form and fix their government."[117] The failure of Virginia in 1776 to use a popular convention to ratify its constitution was, to Jefferson, a critical defect.

On the continental level, the issue of sovereignty did not arise under the Articles of Confederation. The thirteen states were united under the Articles from 1781 until implementation of the Constitution in 1789. The Articles did not extend Congress' power to individuals. For example, Congress could not tax citizens; it could only make requisitions of the state governments. Moreover, Article II made clear that the member states retained "sovereignty, freedom, and independence, and every power, jurisdiction and right which is not by this Confederation expressly delegated to the United States in Congress assembled."[118] Thus, for a majority of the 1780s, discussions of sovereignty took place at the state level.

Issues of sovereignty did arise with the Constitution of 1787. Many Americans believed that a more energetic general government was needed. In 1786, delegates from five states met in Annapolis, Maryland, to consider commercial matters. Disappointed at the poor attendance, Virginia invited the other states to assemble the next year in Philadelphia to consider "the Exigencies of the Union." The Confederation Congress concurred and endorsed the idea of a convention meeting for the "purpose of revising the Articles of Confederation."[119] Delegates from 12 states met in the summer of 1787 and proceeded to draft a new framework of government.

After compromise, study, and debate, the Framers created a system in which the people of each state delegated power to two governmental sovereigns: the state and national governments. "The Federal and State Governments are in fact but different agents and trustees of the people," Madison wrote in *Federalist No. 46*, "instituted with different powers, and designated for different purposes."[120] To accomplish such an act, the Constitution had to be ratified in separate state conventions so the people of each state could take a portion of the powers originally delegated to their state government (or retained themselves) and transfer this power to the national government.

From the beginning of the Philadelphia convention, the leading delegates urged that the new constitution should be submitted to the people in state conventions. At the start of proceedings, Edmund Randolph of Virginia presented 15 resolutions for the delegates to consider. These resolutions, known as the "Virginia Plan," formed the basis of the debate. The 15th resolution proposed that the new constitution be submitted to "assemblies ... expressly chosen by the people, to consider & decide thereon."[121] Speaking in favor of this method, Madison ",thought it indispensible that the new Constitution should be ratified in the most unexceptionable form, and by the supreme authority of the people themselves."[122] George Mason was more explicit: "The Legislatures have no power to ratify it. They are mere creatures of the State Constitutions, and cannot be greater than their creators."[123] Oliver Ellsworth of Connecticut objected to the convention requirement, but did concede that "a new sett of ideas seemed to have crept in since the articles of Confederation were established. Conventions of the people, or with power derived expressly from the people, were not thought of then."[124] The delegates, following this "new sett of ideas," opted for submission to the state conventions and Article VII eventually read: "The Ratification of the Conventions of nine States, shall be sufficient for the Establishment of this Constitution between the States so ratifying the Same."[125]

Postratification, the great legal minds of the United States taught their students about the people's power to adopt or abolish government. The American understanding of popular sovereignty was eventually enshrined in Blackstone's *Commentaries*—albeit in St. George Tucker's 1803 annotated version. Tucker was the preeminent legal theorist of the early 1800s.[126] His annotated edition of the *Commentaries* was the definitive American legal text used in the first half of the nineteenth century. In his Appendix A to the first volume, Tucker made clear that the British concept of sovereignty did not survive the American Revolution. He described the people as possessing "indefinite and unlimited power."[127] If a mere legislature exceeded a grant of power found in a constitution, Tucker stated that the resulting statute offended "against a greater power from whom all authority, among us, is derived" and that the offending act should be opposed.[128] With such annotations, Tucker attempted to render Blackstone usable for American lawyers brought up in the republican tradition.

Similarly, James Wilson lectured on the people's authority while teaching at the College of Philadelphia, which is now the University of Pennsylvania. Wilson explained to his students that "[t]he supreme power of the people is a doctrine unknown and unacknowledged in the British system of government. The omnipotent authority of parliament is the dernier resort...."[129] In the United States, on the other hand, "no prerogative or government can be set up as coequal with the authority of the people. The supreme power is in them; and in them, even when a constitution is formed, and government is in operation, the supreme power still remains."[130] Government operates based on a delegation of power from the people. The people choose how much authority to delegate, to whom, and for what period of time. The people are the ultimate sovereigns.

At the end of the Seven Years' War, parliamentary sovereignty was "black letter law" to the American colonists. Even in the early protests against Grenville's Stamp Act, the colonists still recognized the ultimate power of Parliament. Faced with the end of "salutary neglect" and aggressive imperial restructuring, the colonists struggled to confine Parliament to a certain sphere. They attempted to distinguish between external and internal matters, arguing that Parliament was sovereign over the former but not the latter. When the Townshend duties mocked this distinction, the colonists decided that Parliament could exercise no authority over them. George III, according to Jefferson's *Summary View*, was the sole link between the Americans and the empire. When George III refused to embrace this role and challenge Parliament on behalf of the colonies, the Americans accelerated towards independence.

With the Declaration of Independence, most colonists viewed their legislatures as the source of ultimate power. The assemblies were considered mini-parliaments on the British model. However, Americans continued to meditate on issues of power and quickly realized that no artificial body could possess ultimate power. Such power resided in the people themselves. Putting this principle into practice, the states — starting with Massachusetts — used popular conventions to adopt written constitutions. The act of a legislature was viewed as insufficient to create fundamental law. This view held sway at the Philadelphia convention where the Framers of the United States Constitution provided that the document had to be submitted to the people of each state. Popular sovereignty became the cardinal principle of the American constitutions.

CHAPTER 4

Sovereignty and the Courts

With the establishment of popular sovereignty, the judiciary moved into uncharted waters. American judges were unsure whether the courts would function as they had under the British constitution, or whether their role had changed. And if the function of the courts had changed, was their power augmented or reduced? Did it matter that the state and federal constitutions, unlike the British constitution, were written documents?

Until the 1780s, the courts played little or no role in the development of popular sovereignty. As outlined in the previous chapters, the evolution of sovereignty was primarily a struggle between the king and Parliament in England and between king-in-Parliament and the colonial assemblies in America (with the "sovereign" people of each state/colony claiming ultimate power early in the American Revolution). Noticeably absent from the front lines were courts of law. While the courts did make occasional appearances during the conflicts, for example, in the *Five Knights Case* and *Rex v. Hampden*, constitutional change originated elsewhere. There were no landmark decisions restraining the royal prerogative or exploring whether taxation was a gift that could be bestowed only by duly elected representatives. Over time in America, the role of the courts would be transformed.

In understanding the absence of judicial action against the excesses of the Stuarts, we must remember that English judges were appointed by the king and served at his pleasure.[1] If the king disagreed with a decision of a judge, the judge could be dismissed immediately. The king was the font of all justice and the judges were his agents. In the words of James I, "As kings borrow their power from God, so judges from kings; and as kings are to account to God, so judges unto God and kings."[2] If the judges were presented with a question concerning the king's prerogative, James instructed them to "deal not with it till you consult with the king or his Council."[3] Lacking independence, the judges were not in a position to interject themselves into disputes between the king and Parliament concerning the locus of ultimate sovereignty.

After the Glorious Revolution, the power of the judiciary did not increase. The courts of Common Pleas and King's Bench were subordinate to Parliament because Parliament was the highest court in the land and possessed ultimate sovereignty. While the court of King's Bench might review, say, the decisions of assize courts, review of parliamentary enactments was different. It would have been unthinkable for a judge to nullify a measure assented to by the king, Lords, and Commons.

The Early American Judicial System

On the eve of the Revolution, it appeared unlikely that the judiciary would ever occupy a prominent place in the American systems of government. The 1701 Act of Settlement had granted English judges tenure during "good behavior"—judges were no longer removable at the whim of the king. The Act of Settlement, however, did not extend to the colonies. Thus, the colonists complained in the Declaration of Independence that the king "has made judges dependent on his will alone, for the tenure of their offices, and the amount and payment of their salaries."[4] Inasmuch as the people viewed the judges as agents of oppressive royal authority, the courts were not highly esteemed.[5]

Of course, complaints about abuses by the executive branch extended much further than the judiciary. For example, colonial governors attempted to influence the colonial assemblies by appointing legislators to judicial and other offices and by offering legislators government contracts and other opportunities for personal profit.[6] If the legislators were not compliant with the governor's wishes, the governor could always remove the benefit conferred. During the Stamp Act crisis, the governor of Massachusetts took away commissions from legislators serving in the state militia as punishment for their opposition to British policy.[7]

To remedy these abuses, early American constitutions reduced the power of the executive branch and increased that of the legislature, the branch of government most closely connected with the people.[8] The governors' terms were limited and many state legislatures began to exercise what had been, and are recognized today as, executive functions (e.g., declaring war or pardoning persons convicted of crimes).[9] In ten of the newly independent states the executive was appointed by the legislature and in only two states could the executive serve more than one year.[10] In only four states did the executive enjoy the power of appointment — the remaining nine lodged that power in the legislature.[11] Although today we associate some sort of veto power with the executive branch, in the early constitutions only three states granted the executive this power.[12] Hence, via term limits, legislative control, and reduction in executive functions, the people sought to prevent the abuse they had suffered under royal governors.

The grievances against the king and royal governors did not translate immediately into establishment of the state judiciaries as independent, coequal branches of government. For instance, in South Carolina and New Jersey the judiciary was not considered as a separate and autonomous branch of government.[13] At first blush, such arrangements seem to violate basic separation of powers principles. Today, we recognize three general governmental functions: the making of laws, the execution of laws, and the application/interpretation of the laws as they relate to cases and controversies.[14] As stated above, for many years in England the judicial power was considered a branch of the executive department, and this view was accepted by some American thinkers.[15] However, the trend was to view governmental power as divided into three separate branches so that, in Jefferson's words, "no person should exercise the powers of more than one of them at the same time."[16] The Massachusetts Constitution of 1780 stated the predominant view as follows:

> In the government of this Commonwealth, the legislative department shall never exercise the executive and judicial powers, or either of them: The executive shall never exercise the legislative and judicial powers, or either of them: The judicial shall never exercise the legislative and executive powers, or either of them: to the end it may be a government of laws and not of men.[17]

While to modern Americans such sentiments seem to compel the creation of a separate and distinct judicial branch with the power of judicial review, this was not the understanding at the time of independence. When they were rushing to weaken the executive branch (which to some colonists would include the judicial[18]), Americans were not oblivious that the legislature could violate its delegated powers.[19] The people did not look to the courts to protect them from unconstitutional enactments. Instead, the people believed that the best security would be internal safeguards such as bicameralism, delaying veto, term limits, frequent elections, and juries.[20] And while not all of these safeguards appeared in each state constitution, some combination of them did.

Moreover, as pointed out by historian Gordon Wood, "The early constitution-makers had little sense that judicial independence meant independence from the people."[21] Juries were especially sacrosanct bodies and could not be overridden by a judge even if the judge believed the jury's decision was against the greater weight of the evidence.[22] It is difficult to date the origin of jury nullification. The first explicit argument for such a power in the jury, however, is traced to the Leveller movement and John Lilburne.[23] Records show that Lilburne, when on trial for treason in the late 1640s, addressed his jury and argued that it presided over both the law and facts of his case.[24] The packed gallery cheered Lilburne's assertion, but the Crown's judges protested and called for soldiers to restrain the spectators. This show of force did not influence the jury. After deliberating one hour, they found that Lilburne was not guilty of all charged crimes. To celebrate this victory, the Levellers had a medal struck. One side was the likeness of Lilburne. The other side had the following inscription: "John Lilburne saved by the power of the Lord and the integrity of his jury who are juge of law as wel as fact."[25]

True to Leveller principles, juries in prerevolutionary America possessed virtually unlimited power to determine both law and fact.[26] Judges were often relegated to deciding pretrial motions and other ministerial matters.[27] In the words of Thomas Jefferson, written shortly after he penned the Declaration of Independence, a judge should be "a mere machine" when performing his duties.[28] If judges took actions tending to undermine customary rights or republican government, citizens expected that the jurors would check them by ignoring or overturning the judges' opinions and determinations.[29]

In Georgia, for example, the juries of the county superior courts decided issues of law and fact, turning to judges only when they desired advice.[30] Decisions of the superior courts could be appealed to special juries, not a supreme court.[31] By placing such power in juries, the community could control the content of substantive law. A legislature could pass a statute and a judge could instruct on the common law, but juries possessed the power to veto both.

The power of early American juries is evident in examination of a case known as "the Parsons' Cause."[32] In 1758, Virginia experienced a drought that devastated the tobacco crop. Tobacco warehouse notes circulated as currency and the drought caused the value of tobacco to skyrocket. Recognizing the dire economic consequences for debtors, the colony's legislature passed the "Two Penny Act," which gave debtors the option of paying in tobacco notes or money at the rate of two pence per pound of tobacco. The Two Penny Act affected numerous Virginians, including the clergy. Anglican clergyman were supported by tax revenue and by statute their pay was 16,000 pounds of tobacco per year. If not paid in tobacco but rather two pence per pound, the clergy would suffer a significant financial loss. The clergy lobbied allies back in England to disallow the statute. Ultimately, its efforts were successful and the Privy Council declared the Two Penny Act void.

Some clergymen, who had been paid in money instead of tobacco, brought suit against their local vestrymen and tax collectors for back wages. One such plaintiff was the Reverend James Maury, rector of a parish in Fredericksville. Because the Privy Council had nullified the Two Penny Act, the court summoned a jury to consider the issue of damages. Maury's attorney introduced evidence of a £288 arrearage and rested his case. Patrick Henry represented the defendant and argued that, by disallowing the statute, George III and his advisors were tyrants and undeserving of the obedience of Virginians. Henry's arguments resonated with the jury and they awarded Reverend Maury one penny in damages. In essence, the jury decided that the Two Penny Act was valid and overruled the Privy Council.

The people simply did not trust judges to rule on the constitutionality of legislation as the Parson's Cause jury and others had done.[33] Juries implicitly possessed this power in America and some states also employed councils of revision to determine whether the legislature had deviated from its delegated powers.[34] In Pennsylvania, the Council of Censors, which served as a council of revision, was chosen every seven years by the people.[35] Based on a vote of two-thirds of the censors, a state constitutional convention could be summoned to correct constitutional abuses or mistakes.[36] In New York, the Council of Revision (although not popularly elected) examined all state legislation and reported its objections back to the legislature. The legislature could alter a bill as per the objections, abandon the bill, or override the objections by a two-thirds vote in both houses.[37] Popular control of the judiciary was also evident in states requiring judges to stand for re-election,[38] and states that permitted judges to serve for good behavior often gave their legislatures control over judicial salaries and provided for simple procedures to remove judges.[39]

The Judiciary and the Philadelphia Convention

There was no great national judiciary created under the Articles of Confederation. Article IX gave Congress the power of "appointing courts for the trial of piracies and felonies committed on the high seas and establishing courts for receiving and determining finally appeals in all cases of captures." The Articles also provided that the Confederation Congress was "the last resort on appeal" of disputes between states if Congress was requested to intervene. The Confederation Congress could determine the validity of competing state land grants to individuals if a party to the controversy petitioned Congress for redress. Thus, the Confederation's judicial functions were very limited and the courts that did exist — for admiralty and maritime matters — were not an independent branch of government.

In 1787, when the Philadelphia Convention began to debate revisions to the Articles and/or a new form of government, most of the delegates agreed that the judiciary's power should be expanded.[40] By the late 1780s, most Americans agreed that the judiciary should be a separate and independent branch of government; therefore, the delegates to the Philadelphia Convention insisted on a truly independent judiciary. Blackstone had taught that the "distinct and separate existence of the judicial power, in a particular body of men, nominated indeed, but not removable at pleasure, by the crown, consists one main preservative of the public liberty."[41] Accordingly, the ninth resolution of the Virginia Plan called for creation of a national judiciary consisting of "one or more supreme tribunals, and of inferior tribunals to be chosen by the National Legislature."[42] The resolution proposed that the judges would hold office "during good behavior" and prohibited increases or diminutions in salary "made so as to affect the persons actually in office at the time of such increase or diminution."[43] On the motion of Gouverneur Morris, the delegates struck the language prohibiting the increase in salaries.[44] Benjamin Franklin observed that the possibility of inflation or increased judicial duties counseled in favor of the authority to increase the pay of judges.[45] The motion passed with only Virginia and North Carolina voting against it.[46]

While the majority of delegates agreed on the creation of a national judiciary, there was much debate on the size of the judiciary. Many delegates opposed the creation of lower federal courts. They urged that the state courts should serve as the trial courts for the union. John Rutledge of South Carolina averred "that the State Tribunals might and ought to be left in all cases to decide in the first instance the right of appeal to the supreme national tribunal being sufficient to secure the national rights & uniformity of Judgmts."[47] In other words, Rutledge envisioned state courts adjudicating federal questions with the aggrieved parties having a right to appeal to a national supreme court.

Those agreeing with Rutledge argued that the creation of federal courts would be an unnecessary expense. Luther Martin of Maryland also feared that the lower federal courts would "create jealousies & oppositions in the State tribunals."[48] South Carolina delegate Pierce Butler saw federal trial courts as an innovation and encroachment that would cause revolt in the states.[49] Delegates insisting on the establishment of lower courts countered that the cost of creating lower federal courts would be well worth the money. Madison believed that state courts would be subject to local prejudices and thus there would be a bevy of appeals from state courts deciding federal matters. He prognosticated that the supreme court would be overwhelmed by the number of appeals and that federal trial courts, being independent from local politics, would more likely reach just results satisfactory to all parties and lessen the number of appeals.[50]

As with so many other issues, the delegates reached a compromise. They agreed to leave the creation of lower courts to the discretion of the national legislature. If the legislators so desired, they could experiment with the state courts serving as federal trial courts. If this experiment ended as predicted by Madison, legislation could be passed creating inferior courts. The Philadelphia Convention agreed to vest judicial power "in one Supreme Court, and in such inferior courts as the Congress may from time to time ordain and establish."[51] The first Congress, of course, thought that lower federal courts were necessary and passed the Judiciary Act of 1789.[52] The statute was adopted within just a few months of the new government beginning operations.

Judicial review, a subject of much debate today, was barely mentioned at the Convention. Most of the debate regarding the judiciary centered on who would choose the judges: Congress, the Senate, the president, or some combination thereof. The few references we do have to judicial review are in connection with a proposed council of revision. The eighth resolution of the Virginia Plan recommended that the executive and "a convenient number of the National Judiciary, ought to compose a Council of revision with authority to examine every act of the National Legislature before it shall operate."[53] If the council found a particular legislative act objectionable, it could veto the measure. The national legislature could override the veto if two-thirds of both houses again passed the act.

After the delegates agreed to a single executive, they turned to the proposed council of revision. Elbridge Gerry objected to the inclusion of the judiciary in the council because "they will have a sufficient check against encroachments on their own department by their exposition of the laws, which involved a power of deciding on their Constitutionality." Gerry continued by observing that "[i]n some States the Judges had actually set aside laws as being against the Constitution. This was done too with general approbation."[54]

Gerry feared that the proposed council of revision would establish judges "as the guardians of the Rights of the people"—a dangerous proposition in his view.[55] To protect the rights of the people, he preferred to rely "on the Representatives of the people as the guardians of their Rights & interests."[56] Gerry's rejection of a guardianship role for courts, coupled with his earlier comments about checking encroachments "on their own department," indicates a narrow notion of judicial review. For example, laws limiting rights to jury trial would come within the scope of the judicial department and the judges could presumably rule on the laws' constitutionality. But it is unclear whether this power of review would be permissible for statutes dealing with other matters such as laws establishing qualifications for electors. While Gerry's words point to a narrow understanding of judicial review, there is not enough evidence to draw a conclusion one way or the other.

Luther Martin echoed Gerry's broad sentiments that judges—separate and distinct from the council—had the power to rule on the constitutionality of laws, but Martin made no distinction about their own department. "In this character" (i.e., as judicial officials), Martin noted, "they will have a negative [impact] on the laws."[57] Rufus King agreed with Gerry's misgivings about composition of the council and cited separation of powers concerns. "Judges ought to be able to expound the law as it should come to them," King averred, "free from the bias of having participated in its formation."[58] Madison countered that participation in the council would "enable the Judiciary Department the better to defend itself against Legislative encroachments" while at the same time shoring up the executive.[59] Reference to judicial self-defense, like Gerry's statements about the judicial department, also hints at a narrower understanding of judicial review, with judges exercising this power to defend their constitutional functions.

Madison believed that the additional check in the council was needed because of the "tendency in the Legislature to absorb all power into its vortex."[60] He also argued that a veto in any branch other than the legislative violated pure separation of powers principles, and thus the separation of powers was not a valid objection to the judges' participation in the council. George Mason agreed with Madison, noting that "[t]he Executive power ought to be well secured against Legislative usurpations on it."[61] He also observed that when ruling from the bench judges "could impede in one case only, the operation of law."[62] Sitting on the council, judges could have a say on every unjust law and affect more than just a single case.

James Wilson supported Madison and Mason on judicial inclusion in the council. Articulating a sweeping understanding of judicial review, he noted that "[t]he judiciary ought to have an opportunity of remonstrating against projected encroachments on the people as well as themselves."[63] He recognized that in interpreting laws, the judges "would have an opportunity of defending their constitutional rights." But, in his opinion, this was not enough. "Laws may be unjust, may be unwise, may be dangerous, may be destructive," Wilson observed, "and yet may not be so unconstitutional as to justify the Judges in refusing to give them effect."[64] Oliver Ellsworth of Connecticut also spoke in favor of judicial inclusion, noting that it would give more "firmness to the Executive" and it would give an additional opportunity for the judiciary to defend itself.[65]

Despite forceful arguments for creating a council of revision composed of judges and the executive, the eighth resolution of the Virginia Plan was defeated. The debate is instructive on the delegates' views on the judiciary. Without question, the delegates offering opinions on the matter seemed to have contemplated a form of judicial review.[66] When deciding an actual case or controversy, they expected the judges to strike unconstitutional laws. The purpose of this power was twofold: (1) for the judges to defend their constitutional sphere and (2) for the judges to defend the rights of the people. But defense of the people should not be overstated. For instance, although Gerry applauded judicial review, he made clear that representatives were better defenders of the people's liberties, and in his comments contemplated the judiciary defending its constitutional prerogatives rather than striking all sorts of legislative enactments. Most likely, the idea of frequent elections played into Gerry's thinking here.

In setting boundaries of judicial review, James Wilson articulated what we know as the doubtful-case rule.[67] A court should not negative an act of the legislature unless the act is a blatant violation of the Constitution. If there is any doubt about the legitimacy of a statute, it should be resolved in favor of the people's representatives by permitting the law to stand. Close calls are not the business of the judiciary. Wilson's remarks indicate that the Framers had some understanding of the threat of "judicial activism" and expected the judiciary to exercise power in modest fashion.

Discussion of judicial review is also found in debates regarding state veto. The sixth resolve of the Virginia Plan gave Congress a veto on "all laws passed by the several States contravening in the opinion of the National Legislature the articles of Union."[68] On the motion of Benjamin Franklin, the delegates added to the end of the clause "or any treaties subsisting under the authority of the Union."[69] Charles Pinckney of South Carolina wanted to broaden the veto power to all state laws that Congress believed to "be improper."[70] Madison seconded the motion, noting that such a veto was "absolutely necessary to a perfect system."[71] Madison feared that without a legislative veto "the only remedy will lie in an appeal to coercion."[72] Gerry and others opposed this measure, observing that a national government with such a power "may enslave the States."[73] Gouverneur Morris feared that the proposed negative "would disgust all the States."[74] Morris believed that the proposal was also unnecessary because an unconstitutional law would "be set aside in the Judiciary department."[75] Pinckney's motion ultimately failed by the vote of seven states to three.

Upon the rejection of the proposed negative, Luther Martin of Maryland suggested a supremacy clause:

> That the Legislative acts of the U.S. made by virtue & in pursuance of the articles of Union, and all Treaties made & ratified under the authority of the U.S. shall be the supreme law of the respective States, as far as those acts or treaties shall relate to the said States, or their Citizens and inhabitants — & that the Judiciaries of the several States shall be bound thereby in their decisions, any thing in the respective laws of the individual States to the contrary notwithstanding.[76]

This was clearly meant as an alternative to the negative and there was very little debate on the clause. The committee of detail changed Martin's phraseology from "the Judiciaries of the several States" to "the judges in the several States."[77] This excluded juries from the supremacy clause and made clear that the clause applied to national as well as state judges.[78] The committee made other revisions including changing "supreme law of the respective states" to "supreme law of the land."[79] Without question, the supremacy clause contemplated federal and state judges reviewing the constitutionality of legislative enactments because they were bound by "the supreme law of the land." The Constitution required them to exercise judgment on just what constituted supreme law and thus contemplated judicial review.

After the Philadelphia Convention, Alexander Hamilton in *Federalist No. 78* offered a defense of the power of judicial review under the proposed Constitution. Hamilton began with the proposition that an act contrary to Congress' enumerated powers is void.[80] Hamilton viewed the people as the ultimate sovereigns who would be expressing their will by adopting the Constitution.[81] The people's Constitution would thus be superior to statutory law.[82] If Congress could pass a law outside of its delegated powers, Hamilton reasoned, this would "affirm that the deputy is greater than his principal."[83]

Hamilton focused on the fact that the proposed Constitution placed written limits on government power, something unknown under the British constitution.[84] These limitations, he argued, could be preserved only in "the courts of justice; whose duty it must be to declare all acts contrary to the manifest tenor of the constitution void."[85] To Hamilton, courts served as an "intermediate body between the people and the legislature ... to keep the latter within in the limits assigned to their authority."[86] This judicial power did not place the judiciary above the legislature, Hamilton averred, but rather put the people above both.[87]

Even with this power of judicial review, Hamilton contended that the judiciary was the "least dangerous branch to the political rights of the constitution."[88] Unlike the executive, the judiciary has no power to dispense honors or call out troops to enforce its decisions. The judiciary is less powerful than the legislature because it cannot appropriate funds nor regulate the conduct of the people via the enumerated powers. Possessing "neither Force nor Will," Hamilton asserted, the judiciary was "the weakest of the three departments of power."[89]

Hamilton echoed James Wilson's stress on the doubtful-case rule. The judges should only strike a law when an "irreconcilable variance" exists between a statute and the Constitution.[90] This suggests that the courts act only if a duly passed law is implacably opposed to the clear import of the Constitution. If reasonable persons, acting in good faith, can harmonize the statute and the Constitution, there is no "irreconcilable variance." If it is possible to square the statute and Constitution, but the judges nonetheless overturn the law, they have "substitute[d] their own pleasure to the constitutional intentions of the legislature" and thus have "exercised WILL instead of JUDGEMENT."[91]

Evidence from the state conventions for the ratification of the Constitution also supports judicial review. For example, in the Virginia convention John Marshall, speaking in favor of ratification, observed that a federal statute contrary to the enumerated powers would be struck by the judiciary. "If they were to make a law not warranted by any of the powers enumerated, it would be considered by the judges as an infringement of the Constitution which they are to guard. They would not consider such a law as coming under their jurisdiction. They would declare it void."[92] Patrick Henry, urging against ratification, boasted that Virginia courts had "opposed acts of the legislature" on constitutional grounds.[93] Henry wondered whether the federal judiciary—if created by the first Congress— would have the fortitude to act in similar fashion.[94] Edmund Pendleton assured Henry and the other delegates that the people would be secure from tyrannical laws because "honest, independent judges will never admit an oppressive construction."[95]

In lamenting the lack of a bill of rights in the Constitution of 1787, some Anti-Federalists argued for judicial review. "An Old Whig" feared that under the proposed Constitution Congress would assume powers not delegated. A bill of rights would provide some protection because it could be used by the judiciary to combat congressional usurpations. Without "a bill of rights to which we might appeal, and under which we might contend against any assumption of undue power and appeal to the judicial branch of the government to protect us by their judgments," Congress would be at liberty to increase its powers.[96]

Oliver Elsworth in the Connecticut convention explained to his colleagues that the judiciary would be a check on the powers of Congress and the state legislatures:

> This Constitution defines the extent of the powers of the general government. If the general legislature should at any time overleap their limits, the judicial department is a constitutional check. If the United States go beyond their powers, if they make a law which the Constitution does not authorize, it is void; and the judicial power, the national judges, who, to secure their impartiality, are to be made independent, will declare it to be void. On the other hand, if the states go beyond their limits, if they make a law which is a usurpation upon the general government, the law is void; and upright, independent judges will declare it so.[97]

In North Carolina, William R. Davie averred that "the judiciary ought to be competent to the decision of any question arising out of the Constitution."[98] The judiciary, as a coequal branch of government, would prevent Congress from disregarding "the injunctions of the Constitution."[99] Davie further observed that an independent federal judiciary would benefit North Carolina because federal judges would enforce the Constitution's prohibition against state taxes on imports and exports.[100] Virginia had allegedly extracted large sums from North Carolinians and now would be checked by the federal courts.[101] In the Pennsylvania ratifying convention, James Wilson, similar to Connecticut's Elsworth, touted the proposed Constitution as checking Congress via the judicial authority. "I say, under this Constitution, the legislature may be restrained, and kept within its prescribed bounds, by the interposition of the judicial department."[102] If the judges find that a statute is inconsistent with the Constitution's fundamental law, "it is their duty to pronounce it void."[103] Holding office during good behavior and without fear of Congress reducing their salaries, the judges would be defenders of the Constitution.

In sum, the approval of judicial review as expressed by many delegates to the Philadelphia Convention and the state conventions is consistent with the evolution of sovereignty in American thinking. Under the British constitution, Parliament could make or unmake any law as it saw fit. Although courts interpreted parliamentary enactments, a court could not declare an act of Parliament void. By 1787 in America, most agreed that the people possessed ultimate sovereignty. Hence, the delegates in Philadelphia and the various states understood that the courts would play a role unknown to the British system. No longer did a particular branch of government hold ultimate power. Certainly the legislative branch predominated, but with a written constitution all three branches were charged with interpreting the document. Hence, a form of judicial review was a natural outcome of the Revolution and was expected by the Constitution's drafters and ratifiers.

Judicial Review in State Courts

As discussed above, the American theory of sovereignty and the arguments of the Constitution's drafters and ratifiers support the idea of judicial review. Debates and theory, however, are no substitute for an examination of actual practice in American courts during these formative years. The decision whether to exercise judicial review ultimately rested with the courts. Early state court decisions are especially instructive on the evolution of the idea of judicial review. These decisions demonstrate how judges struggled with the exercise of judicial review in light of their education and experience with parliamentary sovereignty. What follows is a discussion of three cases that are merely illustrative of the judges' intellectual labors.[104]

Commonwealth v. Caton (1782)

Approximately one year before the Treaty of Paris officially ended the War of Independence, judges in the Commonwealth of Virginia encountered a weighty constitutional question. The case, *Commonwealth v. Caton*, 8 Va. (4 Call) 5 (1782),[105] dealt with a pardon granted to three loyalists by the Virginia House of Delegates.[106] The loyalists had been convicted and sentenced to death in the summer of 1782 for providing assistance to British troops occupying portions of the state. Under Virginia's Treason Act of 1776, the power of pardon in treason cases was transferred from the executive to both houses of the legislature.[107] Offering mercy to the three condemned loyalists, the lower house granted the pardon and referred the matter to the Senate for concurrence. The Senate, however, thought the prisoners unworthy of clemency and voted to deny a pardon.[108] The prisoners demanded that the sheriff release them based on the action of the lower house. The sheriff demurred and kept them imprisoned until the next meeting of the general court.[109]

The prisoners filed a petition arguing that although the Treason Act referred to "the general assembly," the Virginia Constitution in certain cases vested the power to pardon in the House of Burgesses and that this was in fact such a case.[110] Because the state constitution must control the issuance of a pardon, the prisoners argued that the Treason Act was void.[111] The attorney general countered that the provisions of the state constitution did not run counter to the Treason Act; as a validly enacted statute, the Treason Act controlled and the putative pardon was invalid because the upper house had failed to concur.[112]

Caton was of interest to the entire Virginia bar. In fact, the general court asked "the Gentlemen of the Bar, tho' not engaged as Counsel" to "generally deliver their Sentiments upon the Question" of "[w]hether a Court of Law could declare an Act of the Legislature void because it was repugnant to the Act for the Constitution of Government."[113]

At the sitting of the general court, Edmund Randolph, the attorney general for the Commonwealth, appeared on behalf of the government. Andrew Arnold represented the prisoners and addressed the court after Randolph. In addition to these counsel of record, John Francis Mercer, William Mercer, and St. George Tucker addressed the court as amicus counsel.

Randolph argued that the alleged pardon carried no legal weight because the Senate had not concurred. He offered the court two possible interpretations of the constitution. The first would limit the pardoning power of the House of Burgesses to impeachments. The second was to regard the "obvious" meaning of the constitution that "although the house of delegates must originate the resolution [for a pardon], the senate must in all cases concur."[114] Regarding the question of judicial review, Randolph expressed his personal opinion that a court could declare a legislative enactment void. Randolph based his position on the Revolution: "The Revolution has given me a coat of mail for my defense, while I adhere to its principles. That bench too is reared on the revolution, and will arrogate no undue power."[115] Randolph's reference to the Revolution and his notes from the argument reveal that he rejected legislative supremacy and realized the impact of popular sovereignty on the judicial department.

Counsel for the prisoners argued that the "power of pardoning belonged to the house of delegates" and that, because the Treason Act was inconsistent with the state constitution, the general court was obliged to declare the statute void.[116] Amicus counsel concurred that the general court could exercise judicial review. The most notable of the arguments presented came from St. George Tucker. Tucker explained to the court that the state constitution is "not lyable to any alteration whatsoever by the Legislative."[117] If the legislature did attempt to alter the constitution by a mere statute, this would destroy the foundations of constitutional government. Accordingly, the judiciary must act as "a counterpoise to the legislature."[118]

The judges of the general court issued their opinions seriatim on November 2, 1782.[119] The report of the case contains written opinions of Judges George Wythe and Edmund Pendleton. Wythe, who would later be a delegate to the Philadelphia Convention, began by noting that it was his duty to protect the senate and the community against usurpations from the House of Burgesses.[120] When traitors are properly convicted and sentenced to death, Wythe lectured, a single house of the legislature cannot rescue them. A chamber that tries such a thing is a "usurping branch" and the judiciary must take action.[121]

In dealing with the constitutional authority of the legislative or executive, Wythe promised to inform them that "here is the limit of your authority; and, hither, shall you go, but no further."[122] Wythe ruled that "the pretensions of the house of delegates cannot be sustained."[123] The state constitution, according to Wythe, permitted the House to issue pardons without consent of the Senate only in cases of impeachment prosecuted by the House.[124] Because this was not an impeachment case, the House's pardon of the loyalists was insufficient.

Writing separately, Edmund Pendleton remarked that Virginia was different from the countries of Europe because it had a written constitution adopted by its citizens as "their social compact."[125] Pendleton believed that the separation of powers found in the Virginia Constitution required each branch of government to stay within its delegated powers.[126] For him, this separation of powers brought into question judicial review, and he was less cavalier than Judge Wythe in touting the power of the judiciary:

> But how far this court, in whom the judiciary powers may be in some sort said to be concentrated, shall have power to declare the nullity of a law passed in its forms by the legislative power, without exercising the power of that branch, contrary to the plain terms of that constitution, is indeed a deep, important, and I will add, tremendous question.... I am happy in being of opinion there is no occasion to consider it upon this occasion; and still more happy in the hope that the wisdom and prudence of the legislature will prevent the disagreeable necessity of ever deciding it, by suggesting the

propriety of making the principles of the constitution the great rule to direct the spirit of the laws.[127]

Pendleton contended that the legislature, in passing the Treason Act, "pursued, and [has] not violated the constitution."[128] He believed that the House understood and knew that the concurrence of the Senate was necessary inasmuch as it asked for the upper house to join it in the pardon. Hence, like Wythe, he found that the pardon was invalid.[129]

This view that the prisoners did not receive a valid pardon carried the day by a vote of six judges to two.[130] Although we only have the written opinions of Wythe and Pendleton, at least one of the other judges expressed a view that he "would sooner quit the bench" than ever declare an act of the legislature void.[131]

Caton provides a basic but not an in-depth analysis of judicial review. We must also remember that any statement on the power of courts to strike an act of the legislature is dicta. The Treason Act was not struck down—the ultimate holding was that a pardon in the case of treason required the action of both houses. The Pendleton and Wythe opinions are valuable because of their pioneering nature. Wythe believed that the judiciary had the power to instruct the other two branches on the scope of their powers—something unheard of under the British constitution. He also thought it his duty as a judge to protect both the people and the other branches of government from encroachments. While Wythe obviously rejected the British doctrine that only the legislature can interpret the constitution, he did not discuss the scope of judicial review.

In contrast to Wythe's opinion, Pendleton approached judicial review much more cautiously. He recognized that the court was entering new territory and understood that when declaring a statute unconstitutional a court was arguably taking on a legislative function in violation of the Virginia Constitution. Although not ruling judicial review out of bounds, he preferred to save the issue for the proper case or controversy.

Rutgers v. Waddington (1784)

On the eve of peace with Great Britain, a court in New York City faced a question about the validity of a popular state statute: the Trespass Act. The act became law in March 1783 and was passed to assist property owners who had fled New York during the British occupation of the city. In 1776, when British troops marched in, thousands of New Yorkers abandoned businesses and property, and left with only as much as they could carry. The Trespass Act authorized the returning patriots, whose property had been confiscated and used by the British and their loyalist allies, to file trespass actions for compensation. The act specifically prohibited the pleading of military orders as a defense to suit.[132]

In 1776, Elizabeth Rutgers fled New York and her brew house located on Maiden Lane.[133] Her abandoned property was confiscated for the use of the army by the British commissary and given to Benjamin Waddington and Evelyn Pierrepont.[134] According to court documents, the property was in great disrepair, having been "stripped of everything of any value, except an old Copper, two old Pumps, & a Cistern full of Holes."[135] Waddington and Pierrepont expended £700 to restore the premises.[136]

They enjoyed the rent-free use of the property until May 1, 1780, when the British commander decreed that they pay £150 per year to the Vestry for the Poor.[137] On June 20, 1783, with the evacuation of the redcoats imminent, the British commander ordered Waddington and Pierrepont to pay rent to Rutgers' agent retroactive to May 1, 1783.[138] In the winter of 1783 a fire broke out and destroyed the brewery.[139] Pursuant to the Trespass Act, Rutgers brought suit for £8,000 back rent. She hired the attorney general of New York, Egbert Benson, to represent her. Waddington retained Alexander Hamilton and two other legal heavyweights to defend the suit.[140] Hamilton was an opponent of anti–Tory legislation and postulated that such punitive measures would hurt the reputation and economy of New York.[141] *Rutgers v. Waddington* (1784),[142] as the case was styled, caused much chatter in the state's legal circles.

Hamilton argued that the Trespass Act was inconsistent with settled principles of the law of nations (i.e., a conqueror has the right to use property under the conqueror's control) which had been incorporated into the New York Constitution. He also contended that the act was violative of provisions of the Treaty of Paris waiving private damages "in consequence of or in any wise relating to the war."[143] In briefing the issues, Hamilton urged that the court declare the Trespass Act unconstitutional because "[a] statute against Law and reason especially if a private statute is void"[144] even if "the legislature intended the results of the Act."[145]

Hamilton based his judicial review argument on Sir Edward Coke's opinion in *Dr. Bonham's Case*[146] in which Coke stated that "when an act of parliament is against common right and reason, or repugnant, or impossible to be performed, the common law will controul it, and adjudge such act to be void."[147] Taken out of context, this statement sounds much akin to the modern concept of judicial review with which American lawyers are familiar.

Dr. Bonham's Case arose out of a dispute between Dr. Thomas Bonham and the Royal College of Physicians. Pursuant to a charter granted by Henry VII that was later confirmed by an act of Parliament,[148] the college was authorized to (1) fine persons practicing medicine in London without a license from the college, (2) govern London's medical community, and (3) fine and imprison those guilty of malpractice.[149] The president and censors of the college were permitted to retain half of the money they received for fines imposed.[150] In 1605, Dr. Bonham attempted to join the college, but the membership rejected him and ultimately had him fined and imprisoned for continuing to practice in London.

Coke detested anticompetitive monopolies such as that possessed by the college.[151] Construing the college's royal charter narrowly, Coke ruled that the college could fine a person for illicit practice, but it could only imprison for malpractice.[152] Further, to the extent that the college could be a judge and party to a case via its judicial powers, Coke construed the clause as an absurdity. Right before his famous statement about common right and reason, Coke noted that "censors cannot be judges, ministers, and parties; judges to give sentence or judgment; ministers to make summons; and parties to have the moiety of the forfeiture."[153] In other words, he was merely exercising a canon of statutory interpretation whereby a statute contradicting established legal principles is narrowly construed so the result is not absurd (because Parliament, in its wisdom, could not have intended an absurd result).[154] This is exactly how Blackstone read the holding in *Dr. Bonham's Case*. Blackstone also emphasized that had Parliament clearly intended an absurd result, "there is no court that has power to defeat the intent of the legislature, when couched in such evident and express words, as leaves no doubt whether it was the intent of the legislature to do so."[155]

In advocating for his client, Hamilton rejected Blackstone's explanation of *Dr. Bonham's Case* as a mere exercise of the canons of statutory interpretation whereby a statute contradicting established legal principles is narrowly construed so the result is not absurd. Hamilton surely understood the preeminence of Parliament in the British system and it is unlikely that he seriously believed that English courts possessed a power of judicial review. Hamilton was certainly familiar with Coke's famed *Institutes*, a comprehensive study of English law, in which Coke described the power of Parliament to pass statutes as "so transcendent and absolute" that "it cannot be confined either for causes or persons within any bounds."[156]

Hamilton's arguments were heard by a panel of seven judges in the mayor's court. On August 27, 1784, Judge James Duane issued a carefully crafted opinion in which he began by observing that the issues presented "affect the *national character*," illuminate "the spirit of our Courts to posterity," and "embrace the whole law of nations."[157] Duane complimented the attorneys for their efforts in presenting argument that "spared [the court] much labour."[158] He noted that the Trespass Act was a remedial law and thus had to be construed to have full force in advancement of the remedy as intended by the state legislature.[159] He further observed that under principles of statutory construction the legislature certainly intended the law to apply to the defendants because a reasonable legislator would have considered British merchants, "who merely for the purpose of commerce" relocated to New York upon the city's conquest, to be proper subjects of the act.[160]

Turning to the law of nations, Judge Duane recognized that it had been incorporated into the state's common law and was applicable in the instant case.[161] He rejected Rutgers' argument that Britain's war against the colonies was unjust and thus loyalists could claim no right or protection derived from the law of nations. The "happiness of mankind" dictated that neither party to the conflict be bound to acknowledge the solemnity or injustice of their part in the conflict.[162] Accordingly, the court held that the law of nations applied to the case.

In holding that the law of nations applied — and thus that military orders were a defense to a trespass action — Judge Duane emphasized that he was not overturning the Trespass Act. The court, he explained, was simply applying the canons of statutory interpretation. The legislature must not have foreseen a repeal of the law of nations with the general expressions of the statute. "The repeal of the law of nations, or any interference with it, could not have been in contemplation, in our opinion, when the Legislature passed this statute; and we think ourselves bound to exempt that law from its operation."[163] Had the legislature used specific language suspending operation of the law of nations in the Trespass Act, the court would have been bound to respect this decision.

Judge Duane declined to adopt Hamilton's broad arguments about the power of courts to strike a legislative enactment as against law and reason. Relying on Blackstone, Judge Duane did not challenge legislative supremacy:

> The supremacy of the Legislative need not be called into question; if they think fit *positively* to enact a law, there is no power which can controul them. When the main object of such a law is clearly expressed, and the intention manifest, the judges are not at liberty, altho' it appears *unreasonable*, to reject it: for this were to set the *judicial* above the legislative, which would be subversive of all government.[164]

In the end, the court split the baby by holding that the law of nations served as a defense when considering orders of the British commander, but not when considering orders of officials of the British commissary.[165] Commissary officers were civilians and usurped the authority of the military commander when they permitted Waddington and Pierrepont to operate a brew house on Maiden Lane. Rutgers could recover damages for the years 1777 to 1780 (when the property was held pursuant to the commissary's orders), but not 1780 forward (when the property was held pursuant to the commander's orders). Judge Duane rejected Hamilton's treaty argument in toto.[166]

Judge Duane exercised some legal gymnastics to reach this result. He also likely faced political pressure as evidenced by an open letter in the *New York Packet and American Advertiser*. In this letter, published after the *Rutgers* decision, Melancton Smith and other influential New Yorkers noted that a power in the courts to control the legislature would be "absurd in itself."[167] The job of the courts, the letter lectured, was "to declare the laws, not to alter them."[168] If courts struck an act of the legislature, they violated principles of separation of powers and endangered the liberties of the people.[169] According to Smith, a court exercising judicial review "confound[s] legislative and judicial powers."[170] In addition to irking Smith and his followers, Duane's efforts at statutory construction also earned him a rebuke from the legislature and the threat of impeachment. The legislature did not agree that the words of the statute yielded an absurd result.[171]

The threats and stinging criticism of Judge Duane's opinion, however, seem misplaced because he did not strike down the Trespass Act nor did he claim a power to do so. The *Rutgers* opinion was true to Blackstone and to American respect for the legislative branch; Judge Duane did not accept Hamilton's theory of judicial review. He also did not realize the significance of popular sovereignty and its effect on the judiciary. Judge Duane in 1784 operated under the British constitution's assumptions about parliamentary/legislative supremacy. His statutory construction did defeat the purpose of full compensation for patriots and thus started a political firestorm. This firestorm revealed much distrust of judicial power and the preference for legislative power. New Yorkers were not yet ready to accept expanded judicial authority.

Kamper v. Hawkins (1793)

In 1792, Virginia passed a statute giving state general court judges the power "of granting injunctions to stay proceedings on any judgment" obtained in the general courts and to "proceed to the dissolution or final hearing of all suits commencing by injunction."[172] An injunction is a court order prohibiting a person from taking a certain act or ordering a person to undo a wrong.[173] *Kamper* involved the constitutionality of the legislature's granting of equitable jurisdiction to the state's general court judges. The legislature's statute permitted the general court judges to grant injunctions and to hear suits commenced by injunction.[174] At this time in American law, there was sharp distinction between legal and equitable remedies, with injunctions allotted to the equitable camp. Thus, only judges sitting in chancery courts — courts of equity — could grant injunctions and hear suits seeking injunctive remedies. Virginia followed this distinction and, until the 1792 statute, jurisdiction over suits seeking injunctive relief was reserved for the state chancery court.[175]

Peter Kamper filed a motion in the law courts for an injunction to stay proceedings on a judgment against him obtained by Mary Hawkins. The motion was heard in Dumfries by Judge Spencer Roane, who adjourned proceedings so that the en banc general court could decide the case. Inasmuch as Hawkins apparently challenged the statute on grounds that it circumvented constitutional provisions requiring judges be appointed by the joint ballot of both houses of the legislature followed by an executive commission for good behavior, Roane sought help in tackling this issue.[176]

The case was heard on November 17, 1793. The judges present included some of Virginia's finest legal minds: St. George Tucker, John Tyler, James Henry, Spencer Roane, and William Nelson. All five judges issued separate opinions on the propriety of judicial review and the validity of the statute.

Judge Nelson began his opinion by making a distinction between free and arbitrary governments. "[I]n the former limits are assigned to those to whom the administration is committed; but the latter depends on the will of the departments or some of them."[177] Turning to the legislative department, Judge Nelson asserted that the legislature obtains its very "*existence* from the Constitution"; therefore, the legislature is inferior to the written document.[178] Because the legislature is inferior to the constitution, it follows that the legislature cannot alter the document — such power, in Judge Nelson's view, resided in the people of Virginia.[179] "Who then can change it? — I answer, the PEOPLE alone."[180]

He candidly admitted that some Virginians believed that the judiciary assumed the power of the legislature or placed itself above the legislature when exercising judicial review.[181] In response to this objection, Judge Nelson averred that he did not consider the judiciary to be "champions of the

people, or the Constitution, bound to sound the alarm" when the legislature exceeded its powers.[182] But, if the courts were presented with actual cases or controversies between litigants, the courts were obligated to rule.[183] This review of legislation, Judge Nelson asserted, was no "novelty."[184] He observed that often "one statute is virtually repealed by another, and the judiciary must decide which is the law, or whether both can exist together."[185] After this discussion of judicial review, Judge Nelson held that the statute was unconstitutional because it attempted to overturn constitutional requirements for the appointment of judges.[186]

Next, Judge Spencer Roane considered the statute. Judge Roane began by observing that the case had originated in his court and that he had referred it to the general court because of the issue's import.[187] He further commented that in the lower court he had "doubted how far the judiciary were authorized to refuse to execute a law, on the ground of its being against the spirit of the Constitution."[188] On further reflection, Judge Roane noted, he had changed his opinion: "I now think that the judiciary may and ought not only to refuse to execute a law expressly repugnant to the Constitution; but also one which is, by a plain and natural construction, in opposition to the fundamental principles thereof."[189] In other words, the judiciary should strike laws violating express provisions and those violating the spirit of the document.

In support of his new opinion, Judge Roane declared that since the rupture with Great Britain, the people were "the only sovereign" power and that the legislature was subordinate to them and the constitution.[190] Whereas the people had a right to alter the constitution "by a convention, or otherwise," the legislature enjoyed no such power.[191] The legislature might pass a measure purporting to amend the constitution, but such an act of the assembly has no force because "the legislature have not the power to change the fundamental laws."[192] Judge Roane rejected the notion that judges should "shut their eyes" and decline to refer to the highest law of all: the constitution.[193]

To hold otherwise would permit the legislature to infringe upon the constitution "and the liberties of the people" would be "wholly at the mercy of the legislature."[194] Having established the principles of judicial review, Judge Roane agreed that the statute was contrary to the constitution. "I am of opinion, that the clause in question, is repugnant to the fundamental principles of the Constitution" because "judges of the general court have not been balloted for and commissioned as judges in chancery, pursuant to" the state's fundamental law.[195]

Judge Henry was the third judge to discuss the 1792 statute. He began his opinion by observing that the issue before the court was both delicate and important.[196] It was "as important as any which can ever come before a court."[197] He then recounted some history of the Revolution, observing that George III's actions in the 1770s "had produced a total dissolution of the social band" and that deputies of the people of Virginia proceeded "to prepare that form of government for us they judged best."[198]

Prior to the Revolution, Judge Henry observed, Americans were "taught that Parliament was *omnipotent*, and their powers beyond control."[199] With the Virginia Constitution, this legislative power was limited because the constitution was "founded on the authority of the people."[200] By focusing on the shift from parliamentary sovereignty to popular sovereignty, Judge Henry offered that "it might free the mind from a good deal of embarrassment in discussing several questions where the duty, and the power of the legislature is considered."[201] Judge Henry emphasized that judges, the governor, council members, and legislators were all servants of one master: the people. Accordingly, the people's constitution is superior to the agents exercising the powers of government.

Turning to the statute, Judge Henry could not reconcile it with the constitutional provisions for judicial appointments. To uphold the statute, he observed, "would be a solecism in government,—establishing the will of the legislature, servants of the people, to control the will of their masters." Such an outcome could not be permitted. "[M]y opinion is that the district court of Dumfries be advised to over-rule the motion for an injunction in this cause."[202]

Judge Tyler was the fourth judge to deliver an opinion in *Kamper*. Like his colleagues, he led off with fundamentals. He described George III as an "invading tyrant" who severed "the bands of civil government."[203] With the old system destroyed, Virginians established a "great contract of the people."[204] The Virginia Constitution was "paramount law" because of the people's sanction.[205] He much preferred the principles of popular sovereignty to parliamentary sovereignty, which he described as "an abominable insult upon the honour and good sense of our country."[206] In post-revolutionary Virginia, only "the God of Heaven and our constitution" could claim true omnipotence.[207]

He doubted that any branch of government could lawfully ignore the enumerated rights of the people or the plan of government outlined in the constitution.[208] If one branch did choose to violate the constitution, it should not expect assistance from another branch "to aid in the violation of this sacred letter."[209] Judge Tyler recognized that all three branches of government have a duty to consider the constitution when exercising their delegated powers. Consequently, he declared it his duty to rule upon the constitutionality of statutes that were presented in cases and controversies.[210] Recognizing the nature of this power, he noted that the alleged "violation must be plain and clear, or there might be a danger of the judiciary preventing the operation of laws which might be productive of much public good."[211] Upon consideration of the extension of equity jurisdiction, Judge Tyler concurred that the statute circumvented constitutional provisions requiring that judges be appointed by the joint ballot of both houses of the legislature followed by an executive commission to validate good behavior.

The last opinion was delivered by Judge St. George Tucker. Similar to his colleagues, Judge Tucker considered the history of the American Revolution and the use of conventions in framing constitutions. In determining the source of ultimate power, Tucker looked to the people and described them as possessing "*sovereign, unlimited,* and *unlimitable* authority."[212] Governments possessed only that authority delegated by the people, Tucker noted, which was in sharp contrast to the British theory of legislative omnipotence.[213] With the source of power established, Tucker declared that Virginia "legislators derive their power from the constitution"; therefore, "they can[not] change it … without destroying the foundation of their authority." As the body charged with expounding laws, Tucker continued, the judiciary is obligated "to take notice of the constitution, *as the first law of the land*; and that whatsoever is contradictory thereto, is *not* the law of the land."[214]

Endorsing judicial power and quoting from *The Federalist Papers*, Tucker described the courts as "an intermediate body between the people and the legislature" designed to "keep the latter within the limits assigned to their authority."[215] In the performance of their duties, courts ascertain the meaning of a constitution "as well as the meaning of any particular act proceeding from the legislative body."[216] But would not such a power place the judiciary above the legislative? According to Tucker, no. It only means that the people are superior to both branches and thus the judges must follow the instructions of the people as found in fundamental law.[217] Obeying the people's constitution, Tucker agreed with his four colleagues and struck the statute expanding equity jurisdiction as a violation of Virginia's fundamental law.

In putting *Kamper* in perspective, one must recognize that it was not an opinion lost in dusty law reports. The case report was published in Philadelphia in 1794. The editor described the case's import as involving "the dearest rights and interests of the community, by its creating a ground of nice and critical enquiry between the legislative and judicial departments" of Virginia.[218] Believing that *Kamper* had implications outside of Virginia, the editor included a copy of the federal Constitution with the case report because the opinions of the five judges apply "not only to the respective States, but to the co-relative departments of the federal government."[219]

Examining *Caton*, *Rutgers*, and *Kamper*, we can trace the development of judicial review in the United States. Having grown up under the British constitution, American judges were hesitant to embrace the power of the judiciary to pass on the constitutionality of legislation. In 1782, Judge Edmund Pendleton described the existence of judicial review as "a deep, important, and I will add, tremendous question"[220] that he hoped no court would ever have to decide. Judge Duane embraced legislative supremacy and refused to follow the arguments of Alexander Hamilton because it would be subversive to government for anyone to attempt to control the sovereign legislative branch. Pendleton and Duane were reared on Blackstone and struggled with breaking from the British tradition.

George Wythe, on the other hand, seemed far ahead of his time. By 1782, he had accepted that judiciary was a coequal branch of government. Wythe believed that the courts, as a coequal branch of government, could strike a law as contrary to the Constitution. By the early 1790s, Wythe's view was widely accepted in Virginia. The *Kamper* judges all embraced a form of judicial review. Interestingly, all of the *Kamper* judges mentioned the doctrine of parliamentary sovereignty and how this had been replaced by popular sovereignty in Virginia. They cogently detailed the constitutional earthquake caused by popular sovereignty. With the demise of legislative omnipotence, courts were required to "take notice" of the constitution when deciding cases and controversies. Constitutional law was no longer reserved for the legislature; America was not Britain.

At the beginning of the American Revolution, few could have foreseen the rise of the judiciary. Viewing the courts as a tool of executive power, some states in their new constitutions did not even accord the judiciary a position as a branch of government. Americans knew that power could be abused; however, they did not look to the judiciary to interpose to protect individual rights. Instead, the people put their trust in juries and institutional safeguards such as bicameralism, delaying veto, term limits, and frequent elections.

The acceptance of popular sovereignty eventually served to elevate judges as equals with the executive and legislative branches regarding constitutional interpretation. Once judges understood that they were agents of the people — just like governors or state representatives — they slowly abandoned the shackles imposed by legislative sovereignty. As cases or controversies were brought in court, judges had to examine statutes to determine whether they could be squared with fundamental law, i.e., the peoples' constitutions. If a statute was not congruent with the constitution, the judges were duty-bound to declare it void.

CHAPTER 5

Jefferson, Marshall, and Marbury

The Supreme Court's decision in *Marbury v. Madison* (1803)[1] is revered by American lawyers and citizens as laying "the foundation for the American rule of law."[2] Generations of scholars and judges have cited *Marbury* for the proposition that the Supreme Court is the final arbiter of the Constitution — the one branch to which the executive and legislative branches must defer in matters of constitutional interpretation.[3] Once the judiciary has spoken, we are taught, neither the president nor Congress can offer a competing interpretation in the performance of their constitutional duties.[4] The matter is settled unless the Supreme Court revisits the issue.

Although judicial review[5] naturally flows from principles of popular sovereignty, judicial supremacy does not.[6] In fact, the modern concept of judicial supremacy would shock the Founding generation, including John Marshall himself. Viewed against the backdrop of the American Revolution and the explanations of state courts adopting judicial review, an aggrandizing interpretation of *Marbury* cannot stand. *Marbury* was but a federal version of *Kamper v. Hawkins*. It simply affirmed that the judiciary is a coequal branch of government that must consider the Constitution when presented with an actual case or controversy. To read more into *Marbury* undermines popular sovereignty and puts the Supreme Court in a position once occupied by the Stuarts and later the British Parliament.

John Marshall's rise to the Supreme Court and the *Marbury* decision are inseparable from the elections of 1800. Although political parties were anathema to the Framers of the Constitution, in the 1790s American statesmen began to divide themselves into two parties: the Federalists and

Republicans.[7] The former was led by Alexander Hamilton and the latter by Thomas Jefferson and James Madison. The rival parties had different visions for the federal union. The Federalists favored commercial interests, a pro–British foreign policy, and a liberal interpretation of the Constitution meant to energize the national government. The Republicans championed agriculture, a pro–French foreign policy, and a strict construction of the Constitution meant to limit national power. Whereas the Federalists generally distrusted the people and believed their voices should only be heard at the ballot box, the Republicans believed that ordinary people — yeomen farmers and tradesmen — were capable of governing themselves and that their agents in government should respect the people's wishes. Federalists favored the power of the union; Republicans preferred that of the states and localities.

With George Washington universally regarded as a national hero, the results of the first two presidential elections were certain. So long as Washington wanted the job, the presidency was his. Republicans disagreed with some of his Hamilton-inspired policies, but the Republican leadership could not fathom opposing the choice of Washington as president. As the election of 1796 approached, Washington decided that two terms were enough and that he was ready to leave public life. On Hamilton's advice, Washington did not announce his retirement until the last minute to prevent the Republicans from mounting an extended campaign. Any campaign, of course, would be mounted by promoters of the candidates. In the 1790s, it was unseemly for a person to seek office; therefore, the candidate pretended to be disinterested and awaited a call to public service.[8]

When the votes were tallied, John Adams edged Jefferson by three electoral votes and became the country's second president. Jefferson, as the runner-up, became Adams' vice president. Jefferson stated that he preferred this outcome because Adams "has always been my senior from the commencement of our public life."[9] Madison, disappointed that Adams prevailed, nonetheless hoped that Jefferson would be a positive influence on the president and steer him away from the policies of Hamilton. Adams and Jefferson had long been collaborators — e.g., serving on the committee that drafted the Declaration of Independence, working as diplomats in Europe, and occupying posts in Washington's first administration. The successful collaboration and vaunted friendship, however, was destined to end.[10]

Jefferson was repulsed by many of the initiatives of Adams and the Federalists. He found especially odious the Alien and Sedition Acts of 1798.[11] The acts, intended ostensibly to shore up the home front because of conflict with France, restricted American civil liberties and unduly oppressed foreigners. The Sedition Act punished persons who wrote, uttered, published, or printed "false, scandalous and malicious" statements about the national government with the intent to bring it "into contempt or disrepute."[12] Violators could be imprisoned for two years and/or fined up to $5,000. The Alien Acts, among other things, gave President Adams the power to remove an alien from the United States based on the president's reasonable suspicion that the alien was involved in "secret machinations against the government."[13] Using the Sedition Act, the Federalists prosecuted a number of Republican newspaper editors and even one sitting congressman for questioning the wisdom of the Adams administration.

Revolution at the Ballot Box

As the election of 1800 approached, the Republicans believed that freedom and constitutional government were endangered in the United States. The Federalists, fearing that Jefferson and his cohorts planned to mimic the worst excesses of the French Revolution, supposed that continued Federal rule was the only thing standing between Americans and a Jacobin reign of terror. Federalist clergy described Jefferson as "an open enemy" to Christianity and warned the people that support of the Republicans in the elections "would be mischief to themselves and sin against God."[14] Republican writers countered that many Federalists were wedded to England and that they would sacrifice the interests of America to that of Britannia.

The state legislatures were key to the presidential election. At this time, electoral-college delegates were chosen by the legislatures in 10 of 16 states.[15] The South and West were decidedly for Jefferson, while New England was Adams territory. New York, however, was a "battleground" state. The candidate capturing New York's electoral votes likely would win the presidency. Republicans employed Aaron Burr and his New York political machine to deliver the state. Burr had a great grasp of New York politics and was popular with small business owners. He had been instrumental in creating the Bank of Manhattan Company, which was the only financial institution that would provide capital to lesser merchants and entrepreneurs. Using his connections, Burr delivered the legislature — and thus the state's electoral votes — to Jefferson.

Hamilton, aghast that the legislature had fallen into Republican hands, sought to undo the harm to his party. Writing to New York governor

John Jay, Hamilton suggested that the lame-duck Federalist legislature be reconvened and that a new election law be passed that would ensure all of New York's presidential electors were staunch Federalists. Hamilton understood that such a proposal was out of the ordinary, but stated that "in times like these in which we live, it will not do to be overscrupulous."[16] Jay refused to be party to such machinations and did not reconvene the Federalist legislature.

Despite his fear of Republican rule, Hamilton did Adams no favors in the election of 1800. He distrusted Adams and designed a plan to elevate Federalist Charles Cotesworth Pinckney to the presidency. Hamilton urged Federalist electors to support equally Adams for president and Pinckney for vice president. He calculated that Pinckney's home state, South Carolina, would ignore this instruction and give its full support to Pinckney. (Under the original Constitution, there were no "tickets" for president and vice president; the electors simply put two names on the ballot and submitted them. The person with the greatest number of votes, and a majority of the electors, became president. The person having the next highest total became vice president). Thus, under Hamilton's plan, Pinckney would become president and a disgraced Adams would be demoted to vice president. Adams knew the equal-support scheme meant him ill and retaliated by dismissing Secretary of War James McHenry and Secretary of State Timothy Pickering, both of whom were loyal to Hamilton and kept him informed about Adams' administration. Once he learned of Adams' decision, Hamilton instructed McHenry and Pickering to bring with them official documents that would cast Adams and Jefferson in an unfavorable light.

In a further effort to undermine Adams in Federalist circles, Hamilton wrote *Letter from Alexander Hamilton, Concerning the Public Conduct and Character of John Adams, Esq., President of the United States.* Hamilton blasted Adams in this 54-page pamphlet and mailed copies to influential Federalists.[17] The pamphlet criticized everything from Adams' handling of foreign policy to his decision not to appoint Hamilton commander of the armed forces after Washington's death. The latter charge made Hamilton appear spiteful and haughty. One of the copies fell into Republican hands and Jeffersonian newspaper editors reprinted some of the most scurrilous passages.

The Republicans rewarded Burr for his work in New York by making him Jefferson's vice presidential candidate.[18] Once all the ballots were counted, Jefferson and Burr tied with 73 electoral votes each, with Adams receiving 65, and Pinckney receiving 64. The tie between Jefferson and

Burr could have been prevented had one elector cast his vote for someone other than Burr. But many feared that the election would be close and hence the Republican electors were skittish about throwing away any votes. The solution to the tie under the original Constitution was to submit both Jefferson's and Burr's names to the sitting House of Representatives, which was solidly Federalist. The House, voting by states, would then choose one or the other as president. Importantly, "a Majority of all the States shall be necessary to a Choice."[19]

The Federalists, determined to keep Jefferson out of the White House, cast their ballots for Burr. On the first ballot Jefferson won eight states and Burr six, with Maryland and Vermont evenly divided. This meant that Jefferson was one state shy of the nine necessary to make him president. Had it not been for the efforts of Maryland representative Joseph Hopper Nicholson, the Federalists would have been one state closer to electing Burr. A loyal Republican, Nicholson was bed ridden with illness and had himself carried several miles through snow so he could be present in the House to vote. With Nicholson's presence, Maryland remained divided and was thus prevented from going in Burr's column.

Ballot after ballot yielded eight states for Jefferson, six for Burr, and two states divided. With the gridlock, the Federalists planned how they could retain the presidency. Writing to Madison, Jefferson recounted that many Federalists "openly declare that they will prevent an election, and will name a President of the Senate, *pro tem.* by what they say would only be a stretch of the constitution."[20] The Federalists, Jefferson speculated, would then give the government to this official or John Jay or John Marshall. A Federalist, writing as "Horatius," argued that Adams and the outgoing Federalist Congress should pass a statute naming an officer of the United States government to be president. Horatius rested his argument on the removal clause, which provides that "the Congress may by Law provide for the Case of Removal, Death, Resignation or Inability, both of the President and Vice President, declaring what Officer shall then act as President, and such Officer shall act accordingly, until the Disability be removed, or a President shall be elected."[21] Horatius believed that once Adams and Jefferson left office, they were legally unable to serve and thus Congress was authorized to act.[22] Horatius emphasized that the person appointed to be president should be an officer of the government. Although Horatius did not explicitly say so, this pointed to John Marshall as the logical choice because he, as secretary of state, was the highest commissioned officer in the government.[23]

Rather than seeing the Federalists "strangle the election of the people,"

Madison suggested that Jefferson and Burr summon the newly elected Congress, in which the Republicans had a majority, to choose between the two.[24] Madison recognized that such a proceeding would not "be strictly regular," but that "the irregularity will be less in form than any other adequate to the emergency."[25] The other options suggested by the Federalists, Madison said, were "substantial violations of the will of the people, the scope of the Constitution, and of the public order and interest."[26]

The people, ensuring their voice would be heard, descended on Washington. Mobs threatened revolt if the Federalists did not vote for Jefferson. Virginia and Pennsylvania readied their militias for action if the Federalists attempted to install Jay or Marshall as president. With the situation becoming tense, Jefferson reached out to President Adams, who informed him that if he promised to retain Federalists working in the civil service, maintain the navy the Federalists had built up, and preserve the national debt, then the House would elect him.

Jefferson refused to go into office handcuffed, but Republicans eventually communicated to Federalist leaders that he was not inclined to dismiss the civil service for political reasons. Upon hearing this news, James Bayard, Delaware's sole representative, urged his fellow Federalists to relent. On the 36th ballot in the House, Bayard submitted a blank ballot rather than vote for Burr as he had previously done. Federalists from Maryland and Vermont abstained, which permitted their Republican colleagues to add the two states to Jefferson's column. South Carolina joined Bayard and abstained. As a result, Jefferson garnered ten states to Burr's four and became president.

Packing the Courts

Not content with attempts to steal the presidential election, Federalists engaged in other questionable conduct designed to thwart the people's decision to change course. In mid–December 1800, President Adams received a letter from Chief Justice Oliver Ellsworth announcing his decision to resign from the Supreme Court. Rather than leaving this appointment to his successor, who would assume office in less than three months, Adams dashed off a letter to John Jay. Adams informed Jay of Ellsworth's decision and beseeched him to accept a nomination to the high court. Adams explained to Jay that "the firmest security we have against the effects of visionary schemes and fluctuating theories, will be a solid judiciary."[27] Without waiting to hear from Jay, Adams sent his name to the Senate, which promptly confirmed him as the third chief justice of the United States. Citing health concerns and the lowly stature of the Supreme Court, Jay politely declined the nomination.

Adams received Jay's letter in mid-January and now had less than two months before his presidency came to an end. Adams knew he had far less than two months to take action. In January, Congress began working on a bill reorganizing the federal judiciary. Under the Judiciary Act of 1789, Congress had created three levels of federal courts: a Supreme Court, eleven circuit courts, and 13 district courts. The circuit courts consisted of two justices of the Supreme Court and one district judge from the state in which the circuit court was presiding. While today federal circuit courts are appellate courts, under the Judiciary Act of 1789, the circuit courts were the main trial courts.[28] District court jurisdiction was limited to admiralty suits, small federal crimes, customs cases, and suits brought by the federal government in which the amount in controversy exceeded $100.[29]

Under the Judiciary Act of 1801, which was under debate when Jay declined his nomination, Supreme Court justices were freed from circuit court duty. In place of the Supreme Court justices riding circuit, Congress created 16 new circuit judges. Because of the reduced workload for Supreme Court justices, the act cut the number of justices from six to five at the next vacancy.[30] Inasmuch as the Federalists controlled both the House and Senate, Adams knew the judiciary bill would soon become law. He also knew that if he appointed someone to Ellsworth's seat before the bill was passed, the next president would have to wait for two justices to leave office before he could make an appointment. Adams had to act fast. He had no time to wait for the mails to inform him whether a nominee would accept or reject. He needed a sure thing.

Adams turned to John Marshall, his trusted advisor and secretary of state. During the election of 1800, Marshall had worked to keep the Federalist party from disintegrating. Marshall's credentials dated back to the Revolutionary War. He served with Washington at Valley Forge and went on to study law under George Wythe at William and Mary. Marshall became a prominent lawyer and ably defended the proposed federal constitution at the Virginia ratifying convention. In the 1790s Marshall served in the federal Congress, as a commissioner to France, and in Adams' cabinet. He was also an antagonist of Thomas Jefferson. Marshall and Jefferson traced their roots to the Randolphs of Virginia, but Marshall's maternal grandmother had been disowned by the family while Jefferson's ancestors received full benefit of the Randolph name and resources. Marshall resented the family advantage enjoyed by Jefferson and never liked his cousin Thomas.

Adams forwarded Marshall's nomination to the Senate on January 20, 1801. The Hamiltonian wing of the Federalist Party was outraged. Marshall had opposed the Sedition Act of 1798 and thus was not pure enough for the High Federalists. A delegation of senators approached Adams and urged him to withdraw Marshall's name. They suggested that Adams instead appoint someone with more impeccable Federalist credentials. Adams refused to be bullied and stuck by Marshall. Realizing that an Adams Federalist was better than no Federalist at all, Hamilton's partisans relented and the Senate confirmed Marshall on January 27, 1801.

President Adams signed the Judiciary Act of 1801 into law on February 13, 1801—less than one month before he was to leave office. Rather than let the Jefferson administration fill the 16 new circuit judge slots, Adams asked Marshall to stay on as secretary of state to help him with the nominations.[31] Marshall also helped Adams with appointments pursuant to an Act Concerning the District of Columbia, under which Adams could name three more judges and a host of justices of the peace, clerks, marshals, and other minor officials.[32] This act was signed into law on February 27, 1801, with only four days remaining in the life of the Adams administration.

In the last month of the Adams presidency, Adams and Marshall submitted 217 nominations to the Senate.[33] This number included judgeships, military positions, and various other judicial and legal officers. Federalists applauded filling the spots before Jefferson took office. Writing as "Falkland," Fisher Ames described the judiciary as a "rampart against the foes of all right." Ames emphasized that Federalist judges were needed to defeat "jacobin juries" and their "perversion of the law."[34] Gouverneur Morris saw the appointments as creating an "anchor" for fellow Federalists struggling against "a heavy gale" of Republican sentiment.[35] Serving as the president of the Senate, Vice President Jefferson watched the parade of nominations, realized that the Federalists had refused to accept defeat at the ballot box, and observed that "they have retired into the judiciary as a stronghold."[36]

While many of the nominees were qualified, Adams and Marshall made some very questionable decisions as they rushed to pack the courts. For instance, Oliver Wolcott had never practiced law in his life, left the federal Treasury Department under a cloud of suspicion, but yet was nominated for a judgeship. Philip Barton Key had fought for the British during the Revolution, but he earned a nomination for his embrace of Federalism. Finally Adams and Marshall had no qualms about nominating close family members for seats on the bench. Marshall secured places for two of his brothers-in-law and Adams assisted his nephew.[37]

With Jefferson scheduled to take the oath of office at noon on March 4, 1801, Adams and Marshall worked long hours on their judiciary project. Unfortunately for a few men appointed to positions under an Act Concerning the District of Columbia, Marshall and Adams ran out of time and were unable to deliver their commissions. When Jefferson took office, he discovered the undelivered commissions and forbade any further action on them.[38]

Republican Retaliation

Jefferson and his fellow Republicans took umbrage at the Federalists' 11th-hour passage of the Judiciary Act of 1801 and their efforts to fill every newly created position with their allies. In his first annual message to Congress, Jefferson touted his reduction of the number of federal employees and urged Congress to reduce the number of persons on the federal payroll.[39] He specifically drew attention to the Judiciary Act of 1801: "The judiciary system of the United States, and especially that portion of it recently erected, will of course present itself to the contemplation of Congress."[40]

Shortly after Jefferson delivered his message to Congress, the Supreme Court heard a rule to show cause why a mandamus should not issue to Secretary of State James Madison.[41] Former attorney general Charles Lee brought the proceeding and represented four men: Dennis Ramsay, Robert Hooe, William Harper, and William Marbury. Lee was from a prominent Virginia family, graduated from Princeton, served in the Continental Congress, and held the position of attorney general in both the Washington and Adams administrations. According to affidavits filed with the Court, the four men represented by Lee had been nominated by President Adams and confirmed by the Senate to the office of justice of the peace for the District of Columbia. Their commissions were never delivered and they sought to force Secretary of State Madison to do so. The Court took the matter under advisement and set argument for June 1802, but certain events (described below) caused the case to be delayed.

On January 6, 1802, congressional Republicans responded to President Jefferson's suggestion that they revisit the Judiciary Act of 1801. Senator John Breckinridge of Kentucky introduced a motion to repeal the act.[42] Breckinridge attacked it as "unnecessary and improper."[43] He argued that the creation of 16 new circuit judges was "a wanton waste of the public treasury" inasmuch as state courts could easily handle numerous matters of litigation touching on federal concerns.[44] Breckinridge tackled the issue of whether Congress could repeal the act. Under Article III, "[t]he judicial power of the United States, shall be vested in one Supreme Court and in such inferior courts as the Congress may from time to time ordain and establish."[45] Breckinridge contended that this provision gave Congress the power to create inferior courts as well as to abolish them if Congress so chose. The Constitution did not compel Congress to create lower federal courts, and, if Congress decided to create such courts, the Constitution did not guarantee their existence in perpetuity.

Breckinridge acknowledged that federal judges "shall hold their offices during good behavior" and shall not have their salary diminished while in office.[46] However, he did not read this provision as influencing Congress' discretion to erect or abolish courts. "The construction obviously is, that a judge should hold an existing office, so long as he did his duty in that office; and not that he should hold an office that did not exist, and perform duties not provided by law."[47] To read this section differently, Breckinridge reasoned, would prohibit Congress from correcting errors or making improvements in the structure of the federal judiciary.

Senator Steven Thomson Mason of Virginia supported Breckinridge's motion. Mason also read Article III to permit Congress "from time to time, to create, to annul, or to modify the courts, as the public good may require."[48] To prove his point, Mason asked what would hypothetically happen if a judicial district of the United States was conquered by an enemy or ceded to another nation. Would the federal district judges for that former state or territory be entitled to pay from the federal treasury even though their courts no longer existed? It would be foolish, Mason concluded, to claim that such judges must stay on the payroll.

The Federalists countered that Breckinridge's motion was an attack on fundamental law. Uriah Tracy of Connecticut described the proposed repeal as "the total destruction of our Constitution."[49] The Federalists emphasized issues of judicial independence and service during good behavior. Senator Jonathan Mason of Massachusetts warned that if the Republicans could repeal an entire law erecting courts, then they could also "repeal the law so far as it applies to a particular district and thus get rid of an obnoxious judge."[50] If Congress can remove an office, it can nullify the good behavior provision and thus threaten judicial independence.

Opponents of repeal also observed that the Judiciary Act of 1801 was a great improvement on the original statute. For members of the Supreme

Court, riding circuit was physically taxing and time consuming. Senator Gouverneur Morris of New York quipped that in nominating a man for the Supreme Court, the executive "must seek less the learning of a judge than the agility of a post-boy."[51] Without so much time taken up on poor roads, more cases could be heard and decisions timely given. Moreover, under the Judiciary Act of 1789, justices of the Supreme Court could hear appeals on cases where they served on the trial court. A judge ought not sit in review of his own decision nor should his colleagues on the Supreme Court be faced with the prospect of overruling a fellow justice.

While the Federalists were correct that the 1801 act made many needed changes, Republicans refused to ignore the circumstances of its passage. Senator Robert Wright of Maryland reminded the Federalists that "the judiciary law of the last session had arisen from a disposition to provide for the warm friends of the existing administration."[52] Mason of Virginia averred that the act was motivated by "an immoderate thirst for Executive patronage."[53] In the end, it was the spirit in which the act was passed — and not its merits — that resulted in repeal.

After repealing the 1801 act, the Republicans passed the Judiciary Act of 1802.[54] Under both the 1789 and 1801 acts, the Supreme Court held two sessions per year. The 1802 act decreed that the Court should meet but once a year in February. This meant that the Court could not convene to hear a challenge to the repeal of the 1801 act until February 1802 — 14 months would pass between terms. The 1802 act also created six circuits within each of which a Supreme Court justice would reside. The act contemplated a justice and a district judge sitting together as a circuit court twice per year. Although the act reinstated circuit riding, the travel required would be less than it had been under 1789 act.

Federalist leaders approached Chief Justice Marshall and Associate Justice Samuel Chase and urged them to refuse to resume circuit riding duty. If the Supreme Court justices agreed, the Federalists would then instruct the circuit judges appointed under the 1801 act to convene court as if the repeal had not happened. Marshall discussed the matter with his colleagues and they decided to return to the circuit (the pugnacious Chase preferred a confrontation but went along with Marshall).[55]

In the Supreme Court

High Federalists, however, could not be dissuaded from attacks on the repeal act and tried to force the Supreme Court to rule via test cases.

One such case arose in Richmond, Virginia, where Chief Justice Marshall was sitting as a circuit judge pursuant to the 1802 act. John Laird had won a judgment against Hugh Stuart in one of the circuit courts that had been abolished by the 1802 act. Charles Lee, defending Stuart against execution of the judgment, argued to Marshall that Supreme Court justices could not sit as circuit judges because the justices only held commissions for the high court. Lee also contended that the repeal of the circuit judge positions was unconstitutional. Marshall ruled against Stuart and the case was appealed to the Supreme Court. In a brief opinion authored by Justice William Paterson, the Supreme Court declined to revisit the repeal of the 1801 act. Paterson found no problem with a case being transferred from an abolished circuit court to another circuit court that included a Supreme Court justice. He also noted that circuit riding by justices was established under the first Judiciary Act and should not be questioned at such a late date.[56]

In the same term that he presented appellate arguments in *Stuart*, Lee introduced evidence and made arguments in *Marbury v. Madison* (1803).[57] William Marbury, whose name will be forever associated with the Marshall Court, was a prominent Federalist from Georgetown. He served on the board of directors for the Bank of Columbia and acted as the naval agent for the Port of Georgetown. Shortly into Jefferson's first term, Secretary of War Henry Dearborn removed Marbury from his naval agent position because of cost overruns related to the construction of a new warship. Marbury undoubtedly resented the combination of his firing and the withholding of his justice of the peace commission. He hoped the Federalist Court would teach Mr. Jefferson a lesson.

Because *Marbury* was brought in the Supreme Court's original jurisdiction, the Court sat as a six-person trial court. President Jefferson declined to send counsel to the hearing, so Lee was unopposed. Nonetheless, he faced a hurdle: proving the existence of the commissions. The Republican-controlled Senate had declined to assist Lee with documentary evidence as had Madison's State Department. Oddly enough, the Chief Justice was the most knowledgeable about the commissions' existence, but he presided over the trial. Marshall's personal involvement in the underlying facts and his failure to recuse himself led legal scholar Bruce Ackerman to observe that "[i]f there is another case in the annals of the Supreme Court that reveals such a grotesque form of judicial impropriety, I have yet to come across it."[58]

Jacob Wagner and Daniel Brent, clerks from the State Department, were the first witnesses called by Lee. Both objected to being sworn and asserted executive privilege. They told the Court that it would be improper for them to disclose any facts related to the business of the State Department. In response, Lee asserted that the clerks wear two hats when performing their duties: public ministerial officers and agents of the president. When wearing the first hat, the clerks are independent, accountable officers who may be compelled to do their duties. When donning the second hat, the clerks are accountable to the president alone and cannot be forced to divulge confidences. Lee argued that his questions dealt solely with administrative matters; therefore, the clerks could not assert executive privilege. The Court agreed with Lee and ordered the witnesses to be sworn, but informed them that they could object to a particular question if they believed it touched upon confidential matters.[59]

Wagner testified that because of the passage of time, he could not remember whether he had seen any of the JP commissions in the office. He thought some of the commissions had been recorded, but was unsure which ones. Brent testified that he did not remember the names of persons commissioned to be JPs, but that he believed that Marbury's and Hooe's commissions were made out. He did not recall the recording of any of the commissions signed by President Adams. He did not believe that the commissions were ever sent out and did not know what became of them.[60]

Lee next called Attorney General Levi Lincoln. Lincoln had served as acting secretary of state when Marshall resigned the position. Once Madison arrived in Washington, Lincoln ceased work in the State Department. Similar to the clerks, Lincoln asserted executive privilege. The Court rejected Lincoln's arguments for the same reason that the Court required the clerks to testify. However, the Court postponed proceeding until the next day so Lincoln could consider his answers. Lee gave Lincoln a list of written questions to facilitate the process.

When the Court reconvened, Lincoln said he had only one objection to the written questions: he did not want to disclose what had been done with the undelivered commissions. The Court sided with Lincoln and ruled that the commissions' ultimate fate was irrelevant. Lincoln testified that he had seen commissions for JP. These commissions had been signed by President Adams and affixed with the seal of the United States. He was not aware that any of the commissions had been sent out.[61]

The final piece of evidence introduced by Lee was an affidavit of James Marshall, the Chief Justice's brother. In the closing hours of the Adams Administration, John had asked James to assist in delivering commissions to the midnight judges. In his affidavit, James described how he was unable to deliver all of the commissions given to him by John. He believed at least 12 were left in the secretary of state's office. He recalled that the commissions of Harper and Hooe were among the ones he could not deliver.[62]

Satisfied that he had proven the existence of the commissions, Lee suggested that the Court decide three questions: (1) whether the Court could award a writ of mandamus, (2) if it could, whether the writ could be directed to a secretary of state, and (3) whether the writ could be used to compel Madison to deliver Marbury's commission.[63] Lee then offered arguments on these points and sat down.

The Supreme Court delivered its opinion on February 24, 1803. Chief Justice Marshall wrote the opinion for the unanimous court. In examining Marbury's claim, the Court reversed the order of the issues presented by Lee and framed them as follows: (1) whether Marbury had a right to the commission, (2) if such a right existed, whether the law afforded him a remedy, and (3) if a remedy existed, whether the requested mandamus was the proper remedy.[64] Thus, Marshall planned to examine the merits of the claim before studying the authority of the Court to issue a writ of mandamus to Madison. Typically, a court considers its power to act before tackling the substantive issue of a case. Marshall's approach to the case notifies the reader to be on guard for something out of the ordinary.

Regarding the first inquiry, the Court held that Marbury did have a right to the commission. The evidence revealed that Marbury had been nominated by President Adams and confirmed by the Senate and that his commission had been sealed by the secretary of state.[65] By this process he had a vested right because there was no other solemnity required by law.[66] With the process having moved so far, the executive's power over the appointment terminated.[67] "The point in time," lectured Marshall, "must be when the constitutional power of appointment has been exercised. And this power has been exercised when the last act, required from the person possessing the power has been performed. This last act is the signature on the commission."[68] President Jefferson, according to the Court, improperly interfered with the process when he instructed Secretary of State Madison to hold the sealed commission. The delivery of the commission is not part of the formal appointment process.

In considering the existence of a remedy, the Court recognized that some executive functions are purely political and thus not the subject of judicial scrutiny.[69] "But where a specific duty is assigned by law, and individual rights depend upon performance of that duty," the Court reasoned, "it seems equally clear that the individual who considers himself injured, has a right to resort to the laws of his country for a remedy."[70] If this were not true, the federal government would cease being a government of laws, and the executive would enjoy greater power than the king of Great Britain.[71] Indeed, the "essence of civil liberty consists of the right of every individual to claim protection of the laws."[72] Because delivery of the sealed commission was not a political act, the Court concluded that Marbury, having been deprived of a vested right, had recourse to the courts to seek redress of his injury.[73]

Finally, the Court turned to the question of whether it could issue a writ of mandamus to Secretary of State Madison commanding him to deliver the sealed commission to Marbury. After a discussion of the nature of the writ, the Court observed that its power to issue writs of mandamus originated in section 13 of the Judiciary Act of 1789.[74] Marshall stated that the Constitution grants the Supreme Court original jurisdiction only "[i]n cases affecting Ambassadors, other public Ministers and Consuls, and those in which a State shall be a Party."[75] In all other cases, the Court has appellate jurisdiction subject to congressional regulation.[76] Although the secretary of state is a public officer and suits affecting this officer are part of the Supreme Court's constitutionally mandated original jurisdiction, Marshall focused on the fact that Article III mentions nothing about issuing writs of mandamus as part of the Court's original jurisdiction. In light of such an omission from the Constitution, Marshall concluded that the Court had to consider whether a mere act of Congress could alter original jurisdiction to permit issuance of the writ in cases falling within original, rather than appellate, jurisdiction. This was a hypertechnical — if not a plain wrong — reading of the Judiciary Act of 1789. As Akhil Amar has argued, section 13 of the Judiciary Act "simply provided that if and when the Court already had jurisdiction (whether original or appellate), the justices would be empowered to issue certain technical writs — in particular, writs of prohibition and mandamus."[77] Thus, the 1789 Act did not really expand original jurisdiction.

As so many state courts had done in the two decades prior to *Marbury*, the Supreme Court turned to the first principle of popular sovereignty: "That the people have an original right to establish, for their future government, such principles as, in their opinion, shall most conduce to their own happiness, is the basis, on which the whole American fabric has been erected."[78] Recognizing the people as ultimate sovereigns, the Court described the people as having "original and supreme will."[79] Exercising this supreme power, the people created three departments of government with limited and defined powers.[80] So "that those limits may not be mistaken, or forgotten, the constitution is written."[81] Again recognizing the majesty of the people, the Court averred that "the constitution controls any legislative act repugnant to it."[82] The Court specifically denied that Congress could alter the people's Constitution by a mere ordinary act of legislation.[83] From this discussion of ultimate sovereignty, it naturally followed "that an act of the legislature, repugnant to the constitution, is void."[84]

If the Constitution is paramount, must the courts simply follow the direction of the legislature and give effect to its enactments? Such a proposition, according to the Court, was "an absurdity too gross to be insisted on."[85] "[O]f necessity," the Court continued, the judiciary must "expound and interpret" the law.[86] Often courts are faced with conflicting statutes and they "must decide on the operation of each" to adjudicate the case or controversy presented.[87] Hence, the Court declared that "[i]t is emphatically the province and duty of the judicial department to say what the law is."[88] With sovereignty no longer vested in the legislative body, "courts are to regard the constitution" when performing their judicial duties.[89] To do otherwise would "controvert the very foundation of all written constitutions" and give the people's agent (i.e., Congress) a power greater than the principal.[90] It would give the legislature "a practical and real omnipotence."[91]

The Court then set about giving examples of its duty to refer to the Constitution when adjudicating, specifically discussing conditional prohibitions against bills of attainder, ex post facto laws, and the levying of duties on exported goods.[92] The clearest example given dealt with treason. The Constitution provides that "[n]o Person shall be convicted of Treason unless on the Testimony of two Witnesses to the same overt Act, or on Confession in open Court."[93] What if Congress decreed that "*one* witness, or a confession *out of* court, sufficient for conviction, must the constitutional principle yield to the legislative act?"[94] To give effect to such an enactment, the Court concluded, would be a violation of the judges' oath.[95] Although members of Congress violated their oath if they attempted to alter the law of treason by mere statute, nothing required judges to join in the violation.[96] Hence, Congress' attempt to alter original jurisdiction by statute failed and the Court refused to issue the writ of mandamus.

Marbury, then, was simply the federal version of *Kamper*.[97] Both cases examined whether an act of the legislature could expand court jurisdiction in the face of a constitutional provision to the contrary and both reached the same result. In *Kamper*, we are treated to five separate opinions and more in-depth reasoning on what was a novel issue at the time. But the essential holding of the cases was the same: the judiciary is put on par with the legislative branch. Critically, neither *Kamper* nor *Marbury* declared the judiciary greater than the legislature.

Such an understanding is borne out by contemporary reaction to the *Marbury* opinion. Although Jefferson's Republicans and Marshall's Federalists believed themselves to be in a battle for the survival of sound government in America, the Republican newspapers expressed little hostility toward the opinion.[98] James Madison, the defendant in the case, paid even less attention to the decision or its ramifications. Madison put not a single comment in writing about the decision.[99] Jefferson's objections to the opinion were grounded in Marshall's criticism of his decision to deny Marbury his right to the commission (issues one and two discussed in the opinion).[100] The Republicans' failure to criticize the Court's discussion of judicial review is a strong indicator that there was little or no disagreement on this third point of the opinion.[101] Jefferson was a champion of the people and principles of popular sovereignty that denied the legislature the exclusive right to interpret or modify the Constitution.[102] Similar to the reasoning of so many state judges on the subject, Jefferson believed all three branches had a duty to regard the Constitution when performing their duties.[103]

Jefferson's theory of constitutional interpretation is best explained in his September 11, 1804, letter to Abigail Adams. In responding to Mrs. Adams' criticism of Jefferson's decision to pardon the men convicted under the Sedition Act, Jefferson averred that "nothing in the Constitution has given [the judges] a right to decide for the Executive, more than the Executive to decide for them" on the constitutionality of the Sedition Act.[104] Alluding to principles of separation of powers, Jefferson observed that both branches "are equally independent in the sphere of action assigned to them."[105] Although he believed that the Sedition Act was unconstitutional, he conceded that "[t]he judges, believing the law constitutional, had a right to pass a sentence of fine and imprisonment."[106] Likewise, "the Executive, believing the law to be unconstitutional, was bound to remit the execution of it."[107] Jefferson summed up his understanding of the Constitution as follows:

> That instrument meant that its co-ordinate branches should be checks on each other. But the opinion which gives to judges the right to decide what laws are constitutional, and what are not, not only for themselves in their own sphere of action, but for the Legislature & Executive also, in their spheres, would make the judiciary a despotic branch.[108]

Jefferson realized that the coordinate branches would occasionally disagree on matters of constitutional interpretation. Rather than any one branch having the power to decide for the others, he envisioned the people acting through the ballot box or in convention making the final decision. In Jefferson's draft of his first annual message to Congress, he explained his departmentalist theory in a manner similar to his 1804 letter to Mrs. Adams. After discussing his response to the Sedition Act, he stated that the Constitution "has provided for it's own reintegration by a change of persons exercising the functions of those departments."[109] To Jefferson, this is exactly what happened in the 1800 election (Revolution of 1800): "the Revolution of 1800 was as real a revolution in the principles of our government as that of 1776 was in its form; not effected indeed by the sword, as that, but by the rational and peaceable instrument of reform, the suffrage of the people."[110]

As early as 1783, Jefferson believed that a convention of the people was the proper body to settle disputes of interpretation. In his 1783 draft of a constitution for Virginia, Jefferson provided that any two branches of the government by a two-thirds vote in each branch could summon a constitutional convention for altering or correcting breaches of the constitution.[111] Forty years later, Jefferson continued to believe that the people acting in convention were the final arbiters of the Constitution.[112]

The election of 1800 was hotly contested. Both sides feared that the election of their rivals would cloud the future of the Republic. The allegations made were foul, and men stooped to ever-lower levels to gain an advantage. Founding father Alexander Hamilton tried to persuade New York governor John Jay to recall a lame-duck legislature for the sole purpose of passing a law to deny Jefferson electoral votes. Hamilton then went on to harm his own party by vilifying John Adams. When Jefferson and Burr tied, Federalists refused to accept defeat and hatched schemes to elevate Marshall or Jay to the presidency.

Against the background of the election, the Federalists passed the Judiciary Act of 1801. Although the Act made needed changes to the judicial structure, such as relieving Supreme Court justices of circuit riding, the true aim of the act was unmistakable. Defeated at the polls and unsure whether Jefferson could be denied the White House, the Federalists created a new level of courts and packed them with their allies. If ever a group deserved the moniker "sore loser," it was the Federalist Party.

Out of the flurry of nominations made in February and March 1801, the *Marbury* case arose. Far from laying the foundation for judicial supremacy, the *Marbury* opinion is inimical to the modern Court's position as final arbiter of the Constitution. Separated from the history of the Revolution and pioneering court decisions of the 1780s and 1790s, *Marbury* has been misread for decades. Rather than establishing the Court as the final interpreter of the Constitution, the decision is much more modest. Built upon principles of popular sovereignty, *Marbury* recognized that the legislature does not enjoy ultimate power. Because Americans rejected the British concept of legislative supremacy, all of the people's agents have a duty to interpret the Constitution. Judges, just like legislators and executives, are servants of the people. Thus, the courts have an equal right — not a supreme right — to interpret the Constitution. In this regard, Marshall's analysis bears a closer resemblance to Jeffersonian departmentalism than current constitutional theory.

CHAPTER 6

Curbing the Courts

If James I could examine modern America, he would lament that we have abandoned monarchy and that ultimate sovereignty no longer rests in the executive branch. He would rejoice, however, to know that divine-right theory still thrives. Judges, James would conclude, are now God's lieutenants on earth. To borrow a phrase from Roger Maynwaring, James' chaplain, judges are inferior to none, to no man, to no multitudes of men, to no angels or order of angels. Once the Supreme Court rules, the president, Congress, and the states are bound to follow the Court's exegesis of the Constitution. Just as the people of Jacobean England were expected to quietly submit to the king's will in the name of order, so must the American people accept the courts' constitutional interpretations. If the people begin to grumble, the likes of Sandra Day O'Connor, stepping into the role of James I's Anglican clergy, sternly warn that threats to judicial independence will undermine the foundations of civil society.[1]

Faced with these dire warnings, the people and their representatives flaccidly accept that unelected federal judges should make policy determinations. Moderns no longer understand, to quote Raoul Berger, that the Framers "drew a line between the judicial reviewing function, that is, *policing* grants of power to insure that there were no encroachments beyond the grants, and legislative policymaking *within* those grants."[2] For Americans raised in the post–Warren Court era, judicial policymaking is the norm. The people recognize that, although their representatives may pass laws, the courts will have the final say on the policies behind those laws. The courts make the ultimate decision on such diverse matters as affirmative action in awarding contracts or in school admissions, restrictions on abortion, the medicinal use of marijuana, homosexual marriage, and capital punishment. Although reasonable people have different views on these subjects, the opinions of the judges become "constitutional law." As such, the judges' policy preferences are forced on the people. Debate is quashed and democracy atrophies.

So how did *Marbury* and the courts' ability to take note of the Constitution evolve into judicial supremacy? No simple answer exists. One factor, however, must be the growing number of years between the revolutionary generation and its progeny. As *Kamper* makes clear, the transformation from legislative sovereignty to popular sovereignty was critical to our forefathers. The locus of sovereignty was the driving principle of the American Revolution. Today, modern Americans think of the Revolution as a tax protest movement and do not have a clue about the struggle for sovereignty. They assume that courts, at least since 1803, have enjoyed the final word on the constitutionality of state and federal statutes.

The Unitary State

Also to be factored in is the rise of the unitary state. A centralized, unchecked state, for both English and American Whigs, meant the end of free government. In England this aversion of consolidated power evidenced itself as MPs battled the excesses of the Stuarts. They feared that James II sought to remake the English monarchy along the pattern of Louis XIV's absolutism. With the rise of parliamentary sovereignty, Englishmen believed that absolutism had been defeated and that English liberty was secure. In the 1760s and 70s, American Whigs challenged this assumption. They saw Parliament as an artificial body just as greedy for power as the Sun King.

Consequently, the first charter of American union, the Articles of Confederation, was careful to limit the power of the Confederation government. The Articles simply sought to promote common state interests and to protect state sovereignty.[3] The former goal was directed at the war with Britain and the achieving of independence. The latter goal aimed to prevent the Confederation Congress from imitating the excesses of the British central government. Although the Articles have been much maligned by historians, they achieved both of the broad goals of the union.

Americans won their independence from one of the greatest superpowers of the eighteenth century. With the Treaty of Paris, Great Britain recognized the independence and sovereignty of the 13 states. As for the

Confederation government, it was limited by sundry provisions. For example, congressional delegates were elected annually and subject to term limits. The Articles required the assent of nine of the 13 members before Congress could take action on significant matters such as borrowing money or raising troops. Congress could not tax citizens directly and instead had to make requests of the states for funds. Rather than entrusting power to a single executive when it was out of session, a committee consisting of one delegate from each state kept the government running while the others were back at home taking care of personal affairs.

The Articles, of course, were not perfect. The Confederation government lacked certain critical powers. The system of state requisitions often produced revenue shortfalls, especially after Cornwallis surrendered to General George Washington in October 1781. Without a steady stream of revenue, the Confederation had difficulty paying its debts and, because of the dismal shape of public credit, would have been unable to obtain loans if an emergency had arisen. Foreign powers were reluctant to deal with the Confederation Congress because it could not ensure that states and individuals would respect treaty obligations. Congress also lacked the power to persuade foreign powers to comply with existing duties or to respect American rights.

These shortcomings were accentuated by several events in the mid-1780s. First, the British refused to vacate key fortifications because the states ignored treaty provisions prohibiting impediments to creditors' recovery of debts. British merchants faced state legislation that effectively nullified the debts owed and they quickly complained to Parliament. In responding to protests from the British government, Congress was unable to persuade the states to repeal the debt-relief legislation. Second, independence did not bring the prosperity expected by the commercial states of the union. Merchants envisioned new markets opening up and handsome profits to be earned. They did not foresee natural trading partners such as Britain and France imposing discriminatory restrictions on American trade. Without a power to regulate foreign commerce, Congress could not respond with its own restrictions to force a resolution. Third, in 1784, Spain had closed the Mississippi to American commerce. Citizens in the western part of the United States depended on the river to bring their goods to market. Spain's actions threatened the livelihood of thousands and also discouraged American expansion into the wilderness. Finally, when debt-ridden Massachusetts farmers revolted and closed courthouses throughout the state to prevent confiscation of their property, Congress was unable to raise money or forces to assist Massachusetts in restoring order. The state's government eventually quelled the rebellion, but this episode persuaded many that the union needed a more vigorous national government.

The Philadelphia Convention convened in May 1787 and drafted a plan of government that was partly federal and partly national. In addition to invigorating powers that the Confederation Congress already possessed, the proposed Constitution added powers such as the regulation of commerce and taxation. Under the theory of the new Constitution, the people of each state delegated certain government functions to the national government and other functions to their state governments. In the *Federalist Papers*, Madison described the two governments (state and federal) as "but different agents and trustees of the people, instituted with different powers, and designed for different purposes."[4] To quell fears about excessive centralization, Madison further explained that the federal government would principally operate on "external objects" such as war, peace, negotiation, and foreign commerce.[5] Where the federal government had no grant of authority, the states could continue to freely govern themselves absent an explicit restriction in the Constitution of 1787 or the state's own constitution. Thus, in most matters affecting the daily lives of the people, the state governments were to predominate.[6]

Madison also expected that the federal and state governments would clash and thereby serve as a limitation on power. This was succinctly explained in *Federalist No. 51*:

> In the compound republic of America, the power surrendered by the people, is first divided between two distinct governments, and then the portion is allotted to each, subdivided among distinct and separate departments. Hence a double security arises to the rights of the people. The different governments will control each other; at the same time that each will be controlled by itself.[7]

Accordingly, the states were not to occupy a second-class position in the union, but were expected to serve as a check on the new national government.

From the inception of the federal government, men quarreled over just how far the few and defined powers of the national government extended. All supporters of the Constitution sought to energize the national government, but their understandings differed on the potency of the infusion. Looking back to the ratification debates, Anti-Federalists such as Brutus (probably Robert Yates) seem prophetic when protesting that the new government's powers were "very general and comprehensive, and … may receive a construction to justify the passing almost any law."[8] In the 1790s and early 1800s and over the protests of strict constructionists, nationalists gave short shrift to the idea of strictly enumerated powers and championed vague "implied powers." Via implied powers and loose construction of specific grants, the federal government chartered a national bank, spent money on various public works projects, passed general criminal statues, and slowly garnered more authority over the states and individuals. The national portion of union waxed while the federative component waned.

Issues of national power coupled with African slavery led to a war between the states and the military victory of proponents of a strong central government. The United States would no longer be a partly national and partly federative union, but a perpetual nation-state dedicated to intellectual propositions. Nationalists such as Abraham Lincoln created a myth whereby the Declaration of Independence was *the* founding document of the United States.[9] The poetic language of the Declaration's opening lines was abstracted from the remainder of the document and became, to Lincoln and his progeny, the North Star of all governmental action. When promotion of equality, liberty, and happiness — by positive national action — becomes the mandate of a government's existence, there is very little that strict constitutional enumerations of powers or restrictive amendments can do to halt the aggrandizement of the State. To the extent a proposed action furthers the nebulous propositions of *the* founding document, this American general will or "higher law" must be accomplished.[10] Parchment barriers, no matter how unequivocal, are brushed aside.

The national elites ceased to view America as a grouping of self-governing communities and states united for certain definite objectives. Instead, the Union and the central government were seen as no different from the great European powers. The question was no longer whether the national government had a delegated power to accomplish a particular objective, but which means would the national government use to achieve the desired result.

Northern victory and the Reconstruction Amendments to the Constitution made national citizenship paramount and, to a large extent, nationalized protection of many individual liberties.[11] Madison's expectation that the states would check the national government was undone. In the aftermath of the Civil War, the states were not immediately transformed into mere administrative subdivisions of Washington, D.C., but a change of climate had occurred whereby the federal government would soon determine state policy on banal matters from highway construction to education. The states ultimately ceased to be independent laboratories of democracy, and instead were pressed into the service of the national government as it enforced the general will. The unitary state had arrived.

Substantive Reasonableness

As power gravitated to the national government, the federal courts assumed a more aggressive role in American society. To large extent, this judicial transformation was accomplished via four words: "due process of law." A due process clause appears in both the Fifth and Fourteenth amendments to the United States Constitution. The amendments prohibit the federal and state governments from depriving persons of life, liberty, or property without due process of law. The idea of due process dates back to chapter 39 of the Magna Carta, which provides that "[n]o freeman shall be taken, imprisoned, or disseized, or outlawed, or exiled, or in any way harmed — nor we will go upon or send upon him —*save by the law of the land*."[12] By the end of the fourteenth century, Englishmen viewed "due process of law" and "law of the land" as interchangeable phrases.[13] Sir Edward Coke, in his *Institutes*, unambiguously equated law of the land with "the due course and processe of Law."[14] By the time the colonists arrived in North America, due process meant that before the government could punish a person for some act or omission, government had to resort to the courts and use "established and nondiscriminatory procedures" under "pre-existing laws."[15]

Blackstone highlighted this understanding in his *Commentaries*. When discussing the personal rights, he devoted a separate section to the portion of personal liberty marked by the freedom of movement. According to Blackstone: "This personal liberty consists in the power of loco-motion, of changing situation, or removing one's person to whatsoever place one's own inclination may direct; without imprisonment or restraint, unless by due course of law."[16] Right after this statement, Blackstone goes on to discuss the writ of habeas corpus and how no English subject can be long detained before he must be brought before a judge. Thus, Blackstone viewed "due course of law" as related to judicial proceedings in which the individual's right of movement was at stake. He does not mix this aspect of personal liberty with legislative action.

Standing on the shoulders of Coke and Blackstone, Alexander Hamilton was clear about the scope of due process when writing in the late 1780s: "The words 'due process' have a precise technical import, and are only applicable to the process and proceedings of courts of justice; they can never be referred to an act of the legislature."[17] Although a firm believer in judicial review, Hamilton did not recognize a judicial power to consider the substantive reasonableness of the acts of the people's elected representatives.

Early treatise writers supported this understanding. For example, St. George Tucker, who participated in the *Kamper* decision, in his influential *View of the Constitution of the United States* examined the Fifth Amendment's due process clause and instructed that due process "is by indictment or presentment of good and lawful men, where such deeds be done in due manner, or by writ original of the common law." Tucker further stated that due process "must then be had before a judicial court, or a judicial magistrate."[18]

In his 1825 treatise, William Rawle also discussed due process. Rawle was a prominent lawyer, having studied at the prestigious Middle Temple in London, and had been appointed by President Washington as United States attorney for Pennsylvania. Rawle saw the due process clause as intimately connected with the other procedural guarantees contained in the Bill of Rights, such as grand jury presentment, the right to counsel, and the right to confront witnesses at trial. According to Rawle: "It follows from all the antecedent precautions, that 'no one can be deprived of life, liberty, or property, without due process of law,' and the repetition of this declaration is only valuable as it exhibits the summary of the whole, and the anxiety that should never be forgotten."[19] Hence, Rawle saw the due process clause as having no independent significance other than as an exclamation point on other procedural guarantees.

For the next century, most judges and lawyers agreed that due process referred only to certain procedural guarantees that must be followed in court proceedings.[20] Of course, there were aberrations. For instance, in 1856, the New York Court of Appeals struck down a prohibition statute by reading a substantive component into the state's due process provision. Angry that many owners of bulk quantities of alcohol would lose money with the onset of state prohibition, the judges in *Wynehamer v. People* (1856)[21] extended the idea of due process to encompass legislation. Due process, the court insisted, did not permit the legislature to render worthless casks of wine and barrels of beer that had been acquired when there were few restrictions on the use or sale of alcohol.

The Supreme Court's evisceration of the privileges and immunities clause of the Fourteenth Amendment also contributed to the due process clause becoming a catch-all for judicial power. Section 1 of the Fourteenth Amendment prohibits the states from making or enforcing laws "which shall abridge the privileges and immunities of citizens of the United States." It is unclear exactly what Congress meant by this provision, but many certainly believed that the Bill of Rights, which did not originally circumscribe state action, would be applied to the states. For example, Senator Jacob Howard of Michigan specifically argued in debates that the privileges and immunities protected by the proposed Fourteenth Amendment included "the personal rights guaranteed and secured by the first eight amendments of the Constitution."[22] With the Bill of Rights applied to the states, Senator Howard asserted that the states would be prohibited "from passing laws trenching upon those fundamental rights and privileges which pertain to citizens of the United States."[23] Representative John Bingham of Ohio, the chief architect of the amendment, emphasized that section 1 was crafted "to enforce the bill of rights as it stands in the Constitution today."[24] Bingham even published a pamphlet on the Fourteenth Amendment that was subtitled *In support of the proposed amendment to enforce the Bill of Rights.*[25]

In 1873, the Supreme Court, in *The Slaughter-House Cases* (1873),[26] limited "privileges and immunities" to such things as petitioning the national government and protection of the writ of habeas corpus.[27] A consequence of this decision, as noted by Justice Clarence Thomas, was that "litigants seeking federal protection of fundamental rights turned to the remainder of §1 in search of an alternative fount of such rights."[28] Thus, lawyers crafted arguments that "due process of law" meant more than use of the legal process in courts. They argued that "due process" incorporated the Bill of Rights and that it inherently limited the power of the state and federal legislatures.

For a short while, the Supreme Court resisted the inventive arguments based on due process. However, in the late 1800s, the Court latched onto the idea of substantive due process when reviewing state laws enacted to protect workers from the unpleasant side effects of the Industrial Revolution. Corporate lawyers, attempting to free their clients from state restrictions, argued that laws circumscribing business operations deprived corporations of due process because the laws were arbitrary. The classic judicial statement accepting substantive due process is *Lochner v. New York* (1905).[29] *Lochner* dealt with a New York statute prohibiting bakers from working more than 60 hours per week and/or 10 hours per day. The state argued that the statute was a simple exercise of the police power — the reserved power to pass general legislation for the health, safety, and welfare of the people. The high court, however, held that the statute deprived bakers of liberty without due process of law. Asserting that bakers were not "wards of the state," the Court found "no reasonable ground for interfering with the liberty of person or the right of free contract by determining the hours of labor, in the occupation of baker."[30] The Court rejected the idea that reasonable legislators could conclude that working long hours near hot ovens was unhealthy and thus should be regulated. In short, the *Lochner* Court substituted its judgment for that of New York's elected representatives.

The Court also used the idea of substantive due process to strike down minimum wage laws. In *Adkins v. Children's Hospital* (1923),[31] the Court considered congressional legislation that fixed minimum wages for women working in the District of Columbia. At the beginning of its analysis, the Court claimed that it would give the statute "every possible presumption" of constitutionality.[32] The Court also made clear that if a statute was contrary to the people's Constitution, it had no choice but to strike the law. The Court denied that it exercised "a substantive power to review and nullify acts of Congress" because "no such substantive power exists."[33] Despite this disclaimer, the Court proceeded to evaluate the policy considerations behind the act and made a compelling case—were it part of the legislature—that minimum-wage laws are an improper interference with labor markets.

The Court protested that the statute "exacts from the employer an arbitrary payment for a purpose and upon a basis having no causal connection with his business, or the contract or work the employee engages to do."[34] By legislating a "living wage," Congress brushed aside the principle that "the amount paid and some service to be rendered shall bear to each other some relation of just equivalence."[35] Analogizing the purchase of labor to the purchase of groceries, the Court explained that one cannot demand from the butcher or baker more meat and bread than one has paid for. Just because a person needs or wants more food does not compel the grocer to give him an additional bag of provisions. Based on the Fifth Amendment's due process clause, the Court held that the statute was "the product of a naked, arbitrary exercise of power that cannot be allowed to stand."[36]

The Court continued to carefully scrutinize economic legislation into the 1930s. Between 1934 and 1936, the Court struck 16 New Deal statutes on substantive due process grounds. The Court's aggressive review of legislation prompted President Franklin Delano Roosevelt to concoct a court-packing plan. In 1937, FDR addressed Congress and lamented that the justices were "laboring under a heavy burden."[37] Noting that, in the most recent term, the Court had allowed "private litigants to prosecute appeals in only 108 cases out of 803 applications," the president suggested "the enlargement of the capacity of all the federal courts."[38] He also complained that many federal judges were over 70 years old and that the courts needed an "infusion of new blood."[39] Such an infusion would "vitalize the courts and better equip them to recognize and apply the essential concepts of justice in the light of the needs and the facts of an ever-changing world."[40]

Legislation was crafted that permitted the president to appoint an additional judge for every sitting judge over age 70 who had not retired within six months after the judge's 70th birthday. The legislation also prohibited the Supreme Court from having more than 15 members, thus permitting the president to add no more than six justices. The court-packing plan was controversial and lost steam when the Supreme Court overruled *Adkins* with *West Coast Hotel v. Parrish* (1937),[41] the so-called "switch in time that saved nine." Based on pressure applied by FDR and the retirements of several older justices, the Court got out of the substantive due process business when examining economic legislation.[42] The Court, however, was not willing to part with substantive due process in all cases.

In 1938, the Court decided *United States v. Carolene Products Co.* (1938),[43] in which it held that due process did not prohibit Congress from stopping the shipment of filled milk (i.e., compounded with fat or other oils not milk products) in interstate commerce. Because the legislation was rationally related to public health concerns, the Court declined to subject it to exacting review. In footnote four of the opinion, the Court made clear that it would use heightened scrutiny when reviewing legislation restricting the political process or affecting "discrete and insular minorities."[44] Substantive due process still lived and would continue to cause controversy in the years to come.

Perhaps the most familiar modern substantive due process case is *Roe v. Wade* (1973),[45] in which the Court struck down a Texas restriction on abortion as violative of due process of law. The Court then crafted a trimester system governing abortion regulations. In the first trimester, the Court decreed, decisions regarding abortion must be left to the woman and her physician. During the second trimester, restrictions reasonably related to the mother's health are permitted. Finally, once the fetus is viable, the state may regulate and/or prohibit abortion except when the procedure is necessary to preserve the life or health of the mother.

Roe is unabashedly a clear instance of judicial policymaking. While the Court's framework, for many Americans, is a reasonable outline for abortion legislation, it is alien to the Constitution. The justices simply transferred their personal opinions about abortion into the realm of constitutional law. The Court dismissed the suggestion that reasonable people can disagree on when life begins, the meaning of life, and the extent that pregnancy is a personal matter between the woman and her physician. Instead of deferring to elected representatives, the Court made abortion the special province of the judicial branch.

The Judiciary Unchecked

Despite the controversy surrounding *Roe*, the Court continues to act as a super-legislature. A recent example of the Supreme Court's foray into public policy is *Kennedy v. Louisiana* (2008).[46] At issue was whether capital punishment is permissible for crimes that do not result in death. Patrick Kennedy had been sentenced to death for the aggravated rape of his eight-year-old stepdaughter. The act was so vicious that the child required emergency surgery. Doctors opined that her injuries were the most severe they had ever seen from a sexual assault. At the scene, police found pools of the girl's blood throughout the Kennedy residence.

The Bill of Rights contemplates that society may inflict the death penalty so long as the perpetrator receives due process of law.[47] Despite this clear constitutional provision permitting capital punishment, some members of the Supreme Court have opined that "the death penalty is in all circumstances cruel and unusual punishment forbidden by" the Eighth Amendment.[48] The Eighth Amendment simply states that "[e]xcessive bail shall not be required, nor excessive fines imposed, nor cruel and unusual punishments inflicted." The latter clause was meant to apply to torture and the like[49] — not to the death penalty, which is expressly allowed under the Fifth Amendment.

The *Kennedy* Court examined the death penalty for child rape through the lens of the Eighth Amendment. The Court observed that "extreme cruelty is not merely descriptive, but necessarily embodies a moral judgment."[50] The Court did not shy away from examining moral judgments made by legislatures that have chosen to punish the rape of a child with death. In striking down the death penalty for child rape, the Court based its decision on two factors: (1) an alleged national consensus, and (2) "our own independent judgment."[51] Regarding the first factor, the Court observed that in only six states is child rape a capital crime. The Court ignored that such a small number resulted not from a consensus against the death penalty, but from state interpretation of prior Court decisions wherein the justices, in dicta, averred that the death penalty is unconstitutional absent the death of the victim.⁵² Based on signals from the Court dating back to the 1970s, the national and state legislatures chose to avoid protracted litigation and the risk that the Supreme Court would undo their work. Thus, the "consensus" was the result of the Court's previous decisions, not the result of a free debate across America.

While the Court obfuscated on the first factor, at least the justices were honest that the second factor was simply the sum total of their personal opinions and policy preferences. The justices candidly explained that, in their opinion, the goal of retribution "does not justify the harshness of the death penalty here." To them, the rape of a child does not equate with the loss of a life. "It is not at all evident," lectured the Court, "that the child rape victim's hurt is lessened when the law permits the death of the perpetrator."⁵³ Of course, if lessening the hurt of the victim is the goal of punishment, then in very few cases — capital or noncapital — will this goal be met. The Court further reasoned that because the trial process might require the child to relive terrible events, more harm might be done to the child in the long run. The Court also opined that child victims are not the most accurate historians; therefore, a child's statement should not be used to inflict the death penalty. Finally, the Court worried that if death is permitted for child rape, the victim and family members will be more likely to shield the perpetrator from discovery. "These considerations lead us to conclude, *in our independent judgment*, that the death penalty is not a proportional punishment for the rape of a child."⁵⁴

Many of the policy arguments raised by the Court do have some merit. Legislators should consider such matters as the toll a trial will have on a victim and the trustworthiness of child testimony. But policy should be left to the legislatures. Before deciding to impose the death penalty for child rape, Congress and the state legislatures can hold hearings and take testimony from child psychologists, penologists, law enforcement, victims, and others. The legislators can then debate the merits of applying the death penalty to child rape. Inasmuch as capital punishment is constitutionally permissible and is not akin to forbidden punishments such as torture, it is within the purview of our elected representatives to determine the range of punishment for an individual who chooses to have forcible intercourse with a minor.

Considering the mental and physical damage inflicted on a child victim, a legislature does not act unreasonably to punish the perpetrator with death after due process has been given. Nor does a legislature act unreasonably if it concludes that life imprisonment, rather than death, is the appropriate punishment for the rapist. By writing their opinions into law, the Court steps outside of the judicial role and usurps the functions of the people's elected representatives. The Court no longer is a neutral umpire, but instead becomes a participant — the ultimate participant — in the policy debate.[55]

Following the lead of the Supreme Court, the lower federal courts have no hesitancy to wade into the waters of public policy. Gay marriage is the most recent hot-button issue about which the lower courts have claimed the final say. In *Perry v. Schwarzenegger* (2010), U.S. District Judge Vaughn R. Walker held that California's Proposition 8, which amended the state constitution to define marriage as union between a man and a woman, violated the due process and equal protection clauses of the Fourteenth Amendment to the federal Constitution.[56] In essence, Judge Walker ruled that there is no rational reason to limit marriage to opposite-sex couples. He redefined marriage to mean "a couple's choice to live with each other, to remain committed to one another and to form a household based on their own feelings about one another and to join in an economic partnership and support one another and any dependents."[57]

Judge Walker purportedly subjected Proposition 8 to rational basis review. To pass this test, a state law need only be "rationally related" to a "legitimate government interest." Under Supreme Court case law, so long as there is any reasonably conceivable state of facts that could provide a rational basis for the classification, the law must be upheld. The most obvious legitimate government interest is the preservation of public morals. Under the Tenth Amendment, the states retain broad authority known as the "police power." Absent a state constitutional provision restraining this power, the states and localities may pass laws and regulations to promote the comfort, safety, morals, and health of the people. State laws prohibiting such matters as gambling, polygamy, prostitution, and public drunkenness are enacted pursuant to the police power. A ballot initiative limiting marriage to heterosexual couples, one would conclude, should fall squarely within the ambit of the police power and be upheld.

Prior to 2003, this would have been true. In that year, a six to three majority of the Supreme Court invalidated a Texas statute criminalizing homosexual sodomy. The decision in *Lawrence v. Texas*, authored by Justice Anthony Kennedy, held that Judeo-Christian "ethical and moral principles" may not form the basis of state legislation.[58] The fact that a majority of citizens has "traditionally viewed a particular practice as immoral is not a sufficient reason for upholding a law prohibiting the practice."[59] All persons, according to Justice Kennedy, may define their own concepts "of existence, of meaning, of the universe, and of the mystery of human life," without regard to contrary views firmly established and engrained in American experience.[60]

Justice Kennedy further opined that "[p]ersons in a homosexual relationship may seek autonomy for [marriage, contraception, family relationships, childrearing, etc.] just as heterosexual persons do."[61] In other words, Justice Kennedy signaled that the courts should reexamine traditional notions about marriage and strike state laws based on ancient moral codes.

In light *of Lawrence*, Judge Walker demanded that the defenders of Proposition 8 define a secular purpose furthered by the traditional definition of marriage. They responded that Proposition 8 promotes "naturally procreative sexual relationships and channel[s] them into stable, enduring unions for the sake of producing and raising the next generation."[62] Californians could also rationally deduce that a family structure with married opposite-sex parents is the best social environment in which to bear children. Californians could further conclude that the raising of children by same-sex couples — prohibited by nature from being the biological parents of a child — cannot furnish children with a parental authority figure of each gender. At a minimum, such purposes appear rational and lack a moral component declared impermissible by *Lawrence*.

Judge Walker, however, still found fault with the possible secular purposes behind Proposition 8. "Children," Judge Walker lectured, "do not need to be raised by a male parent and a female parent to be well-adjusted, and having both a male and a female parent does not increase the likelihood that a child will be well-adjusted."[63] Judge Walker further determined that gender roles in marriage were an unnatural concoction of the State's previous efforts to perpetuate a patriarchal society. Now in our more enlightened age, we know that "the exclusion [of same-sex couples from marriage] exists as an artifact of a time when the genders were seen as having distinct roles in society and marriage. That time has passed."[64] He therefore pronounced that "[g]ender no longer forms an essential part of marriage."[65] Men and women are much like pennies, fungible units having identical roles and functions.

Judge Walker's reasoning leaves open many other possibilities for "marriage." His definition of marriage refers to "couples," but why should marriage be limited to two people? *Perry* teaches that marriage is only a matter of affections. If polygamists want access to marriage, how can a state use its police power to stop them? Because there is nothing magical about gender, one can hardly argue that there is anything special about the number two.

Similarly, why should consanguinity pose an obstacle to a father and daughter who desire to marry? If they believe a marital union is the mechanism for their self-actualization, then how can they be denied a marriage license? Dad and daughter must define for themselves the concepts "of existence, of meaning, of the universe, and of the mystery of human life." One cannot fall back on Biblical prohibitions against these relationships since the Bible, according to *Lawrence*, may not be used to support a statute. *Lawrence* is also clear that a majority opinion that an act is immoral may not be used to bind the minority. If the majority's moral code may not be used as a frame of reference, can any moral code be used? If not, then are there any limitations that may be placed on efforts at self-actualization?

Perry is perhaps the greatest affront to popular sovereignty seen in decades. Judge Walker plainly averred, "That the majority of California voters supported Proposition 8 is irrelevant."[66] If the people cannot enshrine into fundamental law the traditional definition of marriage accepted by generations of Americans, then what can they do? Absent a blessing from a federal judge, there are few consequential measures that can be enacted without a danger that an unelected official will undo the act of the people or their representatives.

Judge Walker and others would do well to heed the wisdom of Justice Potter Stewart and Justice Hugo Black. Justice Stewart rightly believed that the judicial function does not extend to determining whether a "law is unwise, or even asinine."[67] Justice Black was even more pointed: "There is no provision of the Constitution which either expressly or impliedly vests power in this Court to sit as a supervisory agency over acts of duly constituted legislative bodies and set aside their laws because of the Court's belief that the legislative policies adopted are unreasonable, unwise, arbitrary, capricious or irrational."[68] Watching the Court become more aggressive in reviewing legislation in the 1950s and 1960s, Black feared that "a great unconstitutional shift of power to the courts" was underway.[69] He predicted that this would "be bad for the courts and worse for the country."[70]

In essence, the federal judiciary has resurrected the suspending power championed by James II. This power was so reviled by Englishmen that the seven bishops chose imprisonment over the king's favor when ordered to read the Declaration of Indulgence to their congregations. The bishops would not concede that the king enjoyed the unilateral power to void entire statutory schemes. With the Glorious Revolution, Englishmen took aim at the suspending power via the English Bill of Rights, which averred that "the pretended power of suspending laws or the execution of laws by regal authority without the consent of parliament is illegal."[71]

If anyone doubts the ascendance of the courts to the status of ultimate sovereign wielding a suspending power, they need only examine the judicial confirmation process. Between 1945 and 1980, a nominee to the Supreme Court, on average, was confirmed within 47 days of his nomination.[72] Lower court nominees, prior to 1980, were often confirmed in "less than a month, certainly no more than two."[73] Today, nominees for the courts of appeals must wait more than a year for confirmation and district court judges expect at least a five- or six-month delay.[74] Nominees for the high court face a media circus: Senate staffers and interest groups sifting through every article or postcard written by the nominee, and grandstanding senators performing for TV cameras and attempting to trick the nominee into disclosing how he will vote on particular issues.[75]

Interest groups, politicians, and the public battle over judicial nominations like never before. They do not see judges as disinterested servants deciding disputes between private parties. Instead, as aptly described by former attorney general John Ashcroft, courts now "mediate long-standing disputes between interest groups and the Government."[76] Left-leaning elites cheer the expanded role for the courts because of a distrust of the people and a justified expectation that the Supreme Court will give them policy successes that they could not otherwise achieve through the political process.[77] When arguing for judicial activism, they point to decisions such as *Brown v. Board of Education* (1954),[78] which declared state-sponsored "separate but equal" public schools unconstitutional. What they ignore is that even with segregation, real reform did not occur through the courts, but rather through other organs of society (e.g., desegregation of the armed forces and professional baseball, and eventually legislative enactments).[79] True and meaningful reform rarely occurs outside a victory in the marketplace of ideas. Court-decreed policy preferences do not produce true conviction either in the mind of the losing party or in the minds of the public.

Judicial supremacy is incongruent with the development of sovereignty in Anglo-American history. It is a step back from both the American Revolution and the Glorious Revolution. Acceptance of a judicial policy-making function nullifies the victories of English Whigs and the American revolutionaries. We erase from memory the work of John Lilburne, Algernon Sidney, and Thomas Jefferson. In their places, we elevate the Stuarts and George Grenville. With the problem of judicial supremacy identified, we must ask what can be done to curb the courts and to return the people to their proper position as ultimate sovereigns.

Judicial Self-Restraint

The threat of judicial activism is not new. Judicial review, while entirely consistent with popular sovereignty, has always posed a danger that overzealous judges will do more than take notice of the Constitution. As unelected agents of the people, serving during good behavior, federal judges have a heightened duty to cautiously exercise their powers. If the president, senators, or representatives exceed their powers or choose policies inconsistent with the people's preferences, these agents can be voted out of office. But there is no such accountability for judges. New cases arise for decision and no sleep is lost over the people's disapprobation.

Writing in 1893, Harvard Law Professor James B. Thayer warned the courts about dabbling with judicial supremacy. At that juncture in American history, the Supreme Court had just begun to hint that it was open to using the due process clauses of the Fifth and Fourteenth amendments to gage the reasonableness of legislation.[80] Recognizing the movement toward substantive due process, Thayer addressed the Congress on jurisprudence and law reform and spoke about the necessity for judicial restraint. Thayer argued that the people's representatives should be allowed "a range of choice; and that whatever choice is rational is constitutional."[81] The judicial power, according to Thayer, does not extend to policy considerations.[82] In the realm of competing policies, legislative choice should be "unfettered."[83] A duly enacted law, Thayer continued, ought not be questioned by the courts unless "it is so obviously repugnant to the constitution that when pointed out by the judges, all men of sense and reflection in the community may perceive the repugnancy."[84]

In making his argument, Thayer was simply restating the "doubtful-case rule" articulated by James Wilson at the Philadelphia Convention and by Judge Tyler in *Kamper v. Hawkins*.[85] John Marshall also expressed this rule in *Marbury v. Madison*. In giving examples when a court should refuse to sanction a legislative enactment, Marshall observed that the Constitution prohibits a treason conviction absent the testimony of two witnesses to the same overt act, or a confession by the accused in open court.[86] What should the courts do, Marshall asked, if Congress passed a law declaring that the testimony of one witness was sufficient or that a confession outside of court is enough to sustain a conviction? Because such a statute is obviously repugnant to the Constitution, a court should refuse to give it legal effect.

Marshall also pointed out that the Constitution forbids the placing of duties on articles exported from a state.[87] "Suppose a duty on the export of cotton, of tobacco, or of flour; and a suit instituted to recover it. Ought judgment to be rendered in such a case?"[88] Of course not—such a case is so against the text of the Constitution that no reasonable man would disagree as to the repugnancy of the law.[89]

The doubtful-case rule requires great self-restraint, a quality in opposition to the modern judicial trend. It is a principle that should be reexamined by judges enjoying life-tenure during good behavior. Judges must grasp that policy preferences should be left to agents who are accountable to the people. If the people's agents serving in the legislature make a decision not outside the bounds of reason, the courts must let that decision stand. If it is an unwise or even an asinine decision, the courts must leave it to the people to make the correction. Unless the bench and bar compel a concerted effort to revive the doubtful-case rule, the judiciary will likely face populous efforts that will be much less to their liking.

Removal of Judges

Considering that Thayer's 1893 call for judicial restraint has gone largely unheeded, alternative curbs on judicial power should be explored. In so doing, Americans should consider the advice of Edmund Pendleton given in 1801. Pendleton was a distinguished lawyer from the Old Dominion. Although he did not come from a prominent family, his hard work and natural ability led to leadership positions on Virginia's High Court of Chancery and Supreme Court of Appeals. He also served as the president of the Virginia ratifying convention in 1788.

After the elections of 1800, Pendleton was pleased that the people had tossed the Federalists out of office and given Jefferson's Republicans control of the White House and Congress. Pendleton, however, sought lasting reform that would outlive a mere change in administrations. This senior statesman urged the people to "seize an opportunity to erect new barriers against folly, fraud, and ambition."[90] He hoped for amendments to fix the Constitution "upon principles capable of restraining passions."[91] One of the amendments suggested by Pendleton dealt with the removal of judges. According to him, the Constitution should subject "the judges to removal by the concurring vote of both Houses of Congress."[92]

As a former jurist, Pendleton valued judicial independence. He also justly feared that aggressive judges might use their powers to usurp the decisions of the people's elected representatives. As discussed in Chapter 4, Pendleton was hesitant about exercising judicial review when deciding *Commonwealth v. Caton*. Separation-of-powers concerns caused him to question whether a court could nullify an act of the legislature. Having seen judicial review develop in Virginia and other states, he believed that an additional check was needed on the unelected federal judiciary.

The Constitution does permit removal of judges for high crimes and misdemeanors, but Pendleton's amendment would extend this power to removal for matters such as abuse of judicial authority. If judges decline to follow the advice of Thayer to exercise restraint, then the people's representatives should have the authority to remove the judges. Requiring a majority of both the Senate and the House of Representatives would ensure that this power would not be used cavalierly. Only when the offending judge has raised the ire of majorities in both chambers of the legislature will he be subject to removal.

Critics will likely raise concerns that such a power could be abused, for example, by a Republican president and Congress removing Democratic judicial appointees without cause. While this is possible, the real danger is not abuse of the power, but rather disuse. As Professor William J. Quirk has noted, a "Happy Convention" exists in which Congress gladly punts the most controversial issues to the courts for resolution.[93] The Supreme Court decides cultural, social, and moral issues that animate the public (e.g., abortion), and Congress retains the powers that it wants such as borrowing and spending. Congress spends to help "keep its members in office, but it out-sources its responsibilities."[94] Although occasionally members of Congress make noise about the Court overstepping its bounds, one wonders whether the modern Congress would have it any other way.

Pendleton's removal proposal is no panacea, but it should be considered. If unelected servants such as judges scoff at judicial restraint, then elected representatives should have some recourse. While there is a danger that the removal power itself could be abused one day, the judicial power is in fact being abused today. The simple threat of removal could spark a revival of judicial restraint as judges weigh the consequences of their policymaking.

Overriding the Court

If one is uncomfortable with Pendleton's proposal to alter the Constitution's good-behavior provision for judicial tenure, another option would be giving the other branches of the national government a veto power over Court decisions. Inasmuch as both Congress and the president are elected by the people and thus are accountable to the people, they would be the natural holders of this veto power. If, for example, our elected representatives disagreed with the Court's policy decision that child rape may not be punished by the death penalty, then a majority of both houses of Congress, with the concurrence of the president, could nullify the Court's decision. Judges would not be deprived of their offices for their jaunt into the realm of policy, but rather the Court's policy decisions would be voided. Thus, the people would have some protection from an unrestrained Court, but valued (perhaps overvalued) principles such as judicial independence would not be affected.

This option is akin to reviving the idea of a council of revision discussed in Chapter Four. The difference is that that the target is not the legislature as it was for the councils in Pennsylvania and New York, but the federal courts. This is not to say that Congress has stayed within its delegated powers and needs no rebuke. Congress has certainly unconstitutionally augmented its powers, but the people at least have some recourse at the ballot box. With the high court acting as a legislature, but avoiding any possible sanction at the polls, this revisionary power must be lodged somewhere in accountable bodies.

Supporters of a council of revision at the Philadelphia Convention believed that the judges should participate in such a council to aid the executive in checking the power of the legislative branch. The likes of James Madison and James Wilson feared that the president on his own would not be powerful enough to effectively resist Congress.[95] The judges would add their weight to the balance and assist in combating congressional usurpations. Madison and Wilson obviously did not anticipate a transfer of sovereignty to the courts so that the judicial branch would be in need of a counterweight or check. Opponents of judges serving on a council of revision grounded their objections in popular sovereignty. Elbridge Gerry reminded the delegates that a policymaking position on the council would "make the Expositors of the Laws, the Legislators which ought never to be done."[96] Nathaniel Ghorum agreed with Gerry and observed that "[a]s Judges they are not to be presumed to possess the peculiar knowledge of the mere policy of public measures."[97] If judges became involved in policymaking, Luther Martin warned, they would lose "the confidence of the people."[98] By rejecting a council of revision that included judges, the delegates endorsed Gerry's and his colleagues' admonitions about judicial policymaking. They rejected any expansion of the judicial role.

Today, the expositors are policymakers and the option of a joint presidential and congressional override of the Court's "legislation" simply recognizes the new reality of the modern federal power structure. While

Congress' hands are indeed soiled, our first objective should be to undo the current predicament of judicial supremacy and then consider issues with the elected branches. Hence, a veto by the elective branches over the Court's most egregious decisions would go far in curtailing the current judicial ascendency.

The Role of Juries

A consequence of modern judicial power is that jurors are typically instructed that they must follow all facets of the law as given to them by the judge. Jurors are relegated to finding facts while the judges are the masters of the law. The typical instruction goes something like this: "It is your duty to follow my instructions and conscientiously apply the law as I give it to you to the facts as you find them in order to arrive at your ultimate verdict. If you should have a different idea of what the law is or even what you feel it ought to be, you must disregard your own notions and apply the law as I give it to you."

Of course, this notion that jurors have nothing to do with determining the law surfaces long before the beginning of a trial. During the jury selection process, potential jurors in federal court typically fill out a questionnaire that is reviewed by the judge and the lawyers. In most districts, the potential jurors are asked the following:

> Under the law, the facts at issue in the trial are for the jury to determine. The law applicable to the charges in the case is something on which the court will instruct you. You are required to accept the law as the judge explains it to you regardless of any opinions you might have as to what the law is or should be. Would you have any difficulty following that instruction?

If a member of the jury pool expresses any hesitation about blindly accepting the judge's explanation of the law, he will be struck for cause. He will not be allowed to sit on the jury and hear evidence in the case.

This is a far cry from the trust reposed in jurors in the early Republic. The charge given by Chief Justice John Jay in *Georgia v. Brailsford* (1794) is a good example. Although advising the jury that it should respect the court's rendition of the law, Jay made clear that the judges were not the final arbiters of the law. "But it must be observed that by the same law," Jay instructed, "which recognizes this reasonable distribution of jurisdiction, you have nevertheless a right to take upon yourselves to judge of both ... the law as well as the fact in controversy."[99] Because judges have training in the law, lay persons should accord the judges' statements of law the deference that they deserve. However, principles of popular sovereignty dictate that ordinary Americans have the right to judge the content of substantive law.

If Congress were to pass a sedition statute (as it has done on multiple occasions in the past) making it a crime to criticize the policies or actions of the national government, a jury should have the power to declare the statute void on First Amendment grounds. A juror robotically following the judge's sedition charge commits a far greater crime than the criminal defendant who has the audacity to speak his mind about important political questions. If the law is obviously repugnant to the Constitution, jurors should follow the example of John Lilburne's jury or the Parsons' Cause jury (discussed in Chapter 4) and defend First Principles.

Americans are correct to desire a check on legislative power in the judicial branch. Rather than focusing on the presiding judge, we should turn our attention to the jury and the role it was intended to play in policing the bounds of legislative authority.

Judicial Selection

In considering methods to curb judicial power — or at least institute some accountability — judicial selection also should be reconsidered. Currently, federal judges are nominated by the president and assume office upon Senate approval. Because of the hoopla surrounding federal judicial appointments, this mode of selection is the most familiar to Americans. What many fail to realize is that most judges in the United States (i.e., state court judges) are selected by other methods such as elections, legislative appointment, and merit selection.[100] No state currently uses the federal model to select judges.[101]

In 1940, Missouri became the first state to adopt merit selection for its judges.[102] Under the so-called "Missouri Plan," an independent commission composed of lawyers and citizens recommends to the governor a list of suitable candidates for judgeships. The governor appoints a judge from the list of candidates and sometime later a retention election is held by which the voters permit the judge to continue in office or terminate his tenure. In 1977, President Carter experimented with merit selection panels for circuit judges.[103] The panels were hardly independent inasmuch as the president appointed all members of the panels. The panels were tasked to "recommend for nomination as circuit judges persons whose character, experience, ability, and commitment to equal justice under the law, fully qualify them to serve in the Federal judiciary."[104] President Reagan abandoned the selection panels when he assumed office in 1981.

The retention election feature of the Missouri Plan is its most attractive and dubious feature. On its face, a retention election holds judges accountable and gives the people a voice in judicial selection. In practice, judges seldom are dismissed from office in retention elections. Research indicates that "[o]f the 6,306 state court judges who were up for retention between 1964 and 2006, only fifty-six (less than 1%) were defeated."[105] Retention elections typically spark little public interest, and often the public is short on information about the judge's jurisprudence that might otherwise be available in a contested election.[106] This toothlessness of retention elections is one reason that proponents of complete judicial independence praise the Missouri Plan.[107]

Of course, if a high-profile decision and retention elections happen to coincide, there can be some effectiveness in the system. For example, shortly after the Iowa Supreme Court sanctioned homosexual marriage in April 2009, a retention election was held and three justices lost their seats. This was the first time since Iowa's merit selection system began in 1962 that a member of the Iowa Supreme Court was rejected by the voters.[108] Because of the extensive media coverage of the case in Iowa and throughout the nation, the people possessed the necessary information to evaluate the performance of the justices and overwhelmingly rebuked them for their infidelity to the text of the state constitution.

Another criticism of the Missouri Plan is that the politics surrounding judicial selection are moved from public view to committee rooms. The involvement of the organized bar in the Missouri Plan framework creates, according to scholars, "a somewhat subterranean process of bench and bar politics."[109] The plaintiffs and defense bars vie behind the scenes to put their candidates on the bench. The Missouri Plan teaches that politics will always be a part of any judicial selection process. It also raises the question of whether the politics should be left to interest groups with the people excluded altogether.

The infirmities of the Missouri Plan counsel consideration of judicial elections. The election of judges has a long history in America. Every state that entered the union between 1846 and 1912 provided for some form of judicial elections.[110] Scholars have noted that "[b]y the time of the Civil War, 24 of 34 states had established an elected judiciary with seven states adopting the system in 1850 alone."[111] Today, 33 states select all or a portion of their judges using some form of popular election.[112]

Opponents of judicial elections bristle at the notion that judges should be responsive to electoral politics. "If judges are subject to competitive elections," argues Sandra Day O'Connor, "they cannot help being aware that if the public is not satisfied with the outcome of a particular case, it could hurt their re-election prospects."[113] Exactly. That is the point. Before a judge decides to write into law his personal opinion concerning legitimate policy preferences, he ought to know that the ultimate sovereigns can hold him accountable. The judge is but another agent of the people — just like a governor and a representative. The federal system of judicial selection treats judges as superior to ordinary citizens and other public servants. This breeds an attitude in the federal judiciary that they are anointed to rule over their inferiors. In the words of Theodore Roosevelt, "The judge has no more right than any other official to be set up over the people as an irremovable and irresponsible despot."[114]

Contrary to popular myth, judicial elections do not eviscerate reasonable versions of judicial independence. Scholars have long noted that "[c]omplete independence would permit judges to be reckless in their use of the law as a tool of power."[115] Judicial abandonment of the doubtful-case rule and the propensity for judges to make policy decisions demonstrate just how dangerous complete independence can be. Moreover, this book does not argue that after every decision a judge should be subject to a retention election, but rather that all of the people's agents should be held accountable. Some form of popular involvement in judicial selection would provide that accountability.

What about the risk that the judges will ignore clear constitutional provisions because they fear the loss of their livelihood? To the extent that this is a real concern, the rules for the vesting of federal judicial retirement benefits could be altered to address this. Currently, to earn retirement benefits, a judge must meet the "Rule of 80." Under this rule, a judge who is between the ages of 65 and 70, whose age and years in service total 80, receives an annuity equal to the salary he was receiving at the time he retired.[116] This formula could be changed to provide that a judge who is voted out of office or removed from office (other than for an impeachable offense) is entitled to the same benefits as a judge who retires upon satisfying the Rule of 80. Consequently, we easily eliminate the fear that judges will ignore the Constitution for the sake of a paycheck.

Of course, direct election of federal judges would be a big change in the current system. Perhaps some middle ground could be reached that retains something of the current system with an added element of popular participation. Because this would be a great experiment, I suggest that we begin reform of the selection process with the Supreme Court and then consider whether to extend the reforms to all lower federal courts. At base, I urge that the Constitution be amended (1) to provide term limits for Supreme Court justices, and (2) to give the people a voice in the choice of justices.

Life tenure for members of a Court that claims ultimate sovereignty is a recipe for oligarchy. A permanent class of Platonic Guardians is inimical to a country founded upon popular sovereignty.[117] A justice's knowledge that after eight or ten years he must set the robe aside and return to private life would have a salutary effect. He would lose his entitlement to a lifetime of sycophantic lawyers kowtowing and praising his wisdom in hopes of receiving favorable rulings. The justice would face the prospect of a return to private life where he is but one of the people.

The idea of term limits for agents of the people is not radical or new. Once the colonies declared independence, many of the new state constitutions mandated rotation in office.[118] Believing that power can corrupt even the best citizens, Americans reasoned that term limits were one means by which liberty could be protected. The Articles of Confederation limited terms so that "no person shall be capable of being a delegate for more than three years in any term of six years."[119] In the fourth resolution of the Virginia Plan, Edmund Randolph proposed that members of the first branch of the national legislature should "be incapable of reelection for the space of ____ after the expiration of their term of service."[120] Madison's *Notes* indicate that the Philadelphia Convention declined to adopt this portion of the Virginia Plan "as entering too much into detail for general propositions."[121]

Considering the judiciary's refusal to respect the doubtful-case rule and Congress' contentment with the Court deciding hot-button issues, term limits are a crucial part of judicial reform. Critics will counter that while rotation in office might be suitable for elected representatives, the judiciary's unique role as an impartial arbiter settling disputes requires life tenure during good behavior. The problem with this argument, as outlined above, is that judges are no longer neutral umpires. They are participants in the cultural wars.[122] It is as if a major league umpire went from calling balls and strikes to dictating starting line ups, pitching changes, and decisions to hit and run. The umpire would become a participant in the game rather than a neutral official ensuring that both teams adhere to the same rules.

Term limits are essential. But in addition, the people are entitled to a voice in the choice of policymakers. I suggest that the Constitution's current selection method be altered as follows. Upon the existence of a vacancy on the Supreme Court, the president, the House majority leader, and the House minority leader each submit the name of a candidate to fill the vacancy. The three nominees (it could be two or one depending on the political climate) would be listed on the ballot for the next regularly scheduled federal election (every two years), and the people would vote for one of the nominees to serve on the Supreme Court. The nominee with a plurality of votes (in cases of three nominees) or a majority of votes (in cases of fewer than three nominees) assumes the vacant seat on the high court.

Typically, this system would result in two names being offered to the people as nominees for the open slot. The party controlling the White House would likely submit a single candidate. Strategically, President Obama and Nancy Pelosi would not want two Democrats on the ballot to compete for votes against a solitary Republican. However, this system does ensure that if a president is wedded to cronyism, his party in the House has an opportunity to offer the people a better qualified choice to serve on the Court. Bottom line: the people would have some say in who wields ultimate federal judicial authority.

In sum, there is nothing magical about the current constitutional framework for choosing judges. No state follows the federal system in this regard. Judicial term limits of eight or ten years coupled with the opportunity for the people to choose among a slate of candidates would create accountability and control. Now, when the Supreme Court makes public policy the people have no recourse. Term limits and popular involvement in judicial selection would shift the balance of power from the Court to the people. The justices could still give the people decisions such as *Kennedy*, but the members of the Court would have a definite term, and voters, in choosing replacements, could select new justices who would correct the abuses of previous Courts.

Jurisdiction Stripping

Most Americans would be surprised to know that Congress has the authority to strip the Supreme Court of jurisdiction to hear certain cases. The Constitution notes that the Court has both original and appellate jurisdiction. The former is the Court's right to hear a case for the first time. The latter is the Court's power to review decisions of lower courts. The Constitution specifies that "[i]n all cases affecting ambassadors, other public ministers and consuls, and those in which a state shall be party, the Supreme Court shall have original jurisdiction."[123] In all other cases in which the Court may exercise judicial power "the Supreme Court shall have appellate jurisdiction, both as to law and fact, with such exceptions, and under such regulations as the Congress shall make."[124]

Under a plain reading of the Exceptions Clause, so long as a matter does not fall within the Court's limited grant of original jurisdiction, Congress can alter or abolish the Supreme Court's power to hear a case. The debates at the Philadelphia Convention are not extremely helpful when interpreting the exceptions clause. The Committee on Detail drafted the exceptions clause and we do not have a record of the Committee's deliberations. However, statements made during the state ratification debates support a broad reading of the clause.

For example, when responding to Patrick Henry's attack on the creation of the federal judiciary, friends of the Constitution in the Virginia convention pointed to the exceptions clause as a powerful weapon in the hands of the people's representatives. John Marshall highlighted Congress' authority over the Court's appellate jurisdiction: "Congress is empowered to make exceptions to the appellate jurisdiction, as to law and fact, of the Supreme Court. These exceptions certainly go as far as the legislature may think proper for the interest and liberty of the people."[125] Similarly, in *Federalist No. 81*, Alexander Hamilton avowed "that the supreme court will possess an appellate jurisdiction, both as to law and fact, in all cases referred to them, but subject to any exceptions and regulation which may be thought advisable."[126]

In 1868 the Supreme Court also gave a broad reading of the exceptions clause. *Ex Parte McCardle* (1868)[127] dealt with a newspaper editor who was imprisoned by federal military authorities for his criticism of Reconstruction policy. Confined under the Military Reconstruction Act of 1867, McCardle sought a writ of habeas corpus challenging his imprisonment. The lower court denied relief and McCardle appealed to the Supreme Court. Before the Court decided the case, Congress repealed the statute granting the Court appellate jurisdiction to hear the case.

McCardle's lawyer argued that Congress's motive for stripping jurisdiction was improper. He pointed out that Congress simply wanted to stop the Court from deciding the case so Reconstruction could not be hindered. He further doubted whether Congress could constitutionally tamper with the Supreme Court's jurisdiction. The Court brushed aside these concerns and disclaimed a power "to inquire into the motives of the legislature."[128] It recognized congressional power to make exceptions to appellate jurisdiction and dismissed the appeal: "It is quite clear, therefore, that this court cannot proceed to pronounce judgment in this case, for it has no longer jurisdiction of the appeal."[129]

Despite the text, explanations of the text, and *McCardle*, some scholars argue that Congress cannot divest the Court of jurisdiction over classes of cases such as abortion or capital punishment for child rapists.[130] They suggest that the Supreme Court must sign off on any stripper act and, when reviewing Congress's efforts, subject the act to strict scrutiny. Such restrictions on exercise of congressional authority nullify the exceptions clause and maintain the Court's position as ultimate sovereign. Liberal scholars cannot imagine a system under which the Supreme Court must obey the people's elected representatives. They refuse to accept that the Constitution permits Congress to create or abolish lower federal courts and to limit the Supreme Court's power with regard to its original jurisdiction. They speculate about congressional abuses of power and threats to liberty.

The real danger to the people comes not from what Congress might do, but instead comes from what the Court does do. As a policymaking body with no accountability, the Court threatens the people's right to self-government when, as in *Kennedy*, it declares off-limits a punishment that is constitutionally permissible. Moreover, considering the issues raised by the "Happy Convention," danger comes not from abuse of the exceptions clause, but from congressional neglect of this delegated power. Congress has a duty to protect the people from a runaway Court, but it has taken no action. Our representatives should resurrect the exceptions clause and use it to curb some of the Court's usurpations.

In the past 400 years the theory of sovereignty has evolved. We have gone from the divine right of kings to parliamentary sovereignty to popular sovereignty to judicial supremacy. Judicial review, a natural result of popular sovereignty, has metamorphosed into something akin to James I's beloved divine right of kings. An unelected Supreme Court (or at least five members thereof) claims a final say on the meaning of the people's Constitution. Affirmative action, abortion, medical marijuana, marriage, capital punishment, and a host of other issues are the province of the courts. The Supreme Court is the most powerful policymaking body in America. It is decidedly the most unaccountable policymaking body. The president, Congress, state legislators, governors, and many state judges all must face the people at election time. If elected officials have abused their powers or made unwise policy decisions, the people can rebuke them and replace them with other agents. Not so with Supreme Court justices. In the name of judicial independence, the Court supposedly protects us from ourselves. Lost on the champions of judicial supremacy is the fact that we have no one to protect us from the Court.

Americans must act to reclaim their Constitution from the Supreme Court. The first step is a realization that judicial supremacy is not a sacred Founding principle highlighted by John Marshall in *Marbury v. Madison*. All Marshall did was recognize that the courts, unlike courts in the British system, have a right to take notice of the Constitution when deciding a case or controversy. The Constitution does not belong to the legislature any more than it belongs to the judiciary. When Congress passes a law that is obviously repugnant to the Constitution, judges must refuse to give the law effect in the case before them. However, when the law is within the gamut of a reasonable interpretation of a grant of power, the Court should leave the correction, if any, to the people when exercising the franchise.

A refusal to adhere to the doubtful-case rule forces citizens and their elected representatives to exercise other options such as removal of activist judges, congressional nullification of Court decisions, jury nullification, alternative means of judicial selection, and use of the exceptions clause. While none of these options is a cure-all for our problems, some combination of them might curtail the Court's policy experimentation and restore the people to their place as the ultimate sovereigns.

Appendix A

The Agreement of the People, as Presented to the Council of the Army (October 28, 1647)

The political upheaval of the English Civil War provoked much thought about the first principles of government. Until the 1640s, the collective consciousness of the English people knew only rule by a divinely anointed monarch governing with the assistance of a council or Parliament. In the fall of 1647, the Levellers offered England a much different foundation for civil society. The Levellers asserted that ultimate authority resided in the people themselves. Institutions of government, under the Leveller theory, were but agents of the people and could only exercise delegated powers with the consent of the people. The Levellers described government as a "tyranny" if it exercised power without the free consent of the governed. The people, the Levellers explained, possessed supreme power and could withdraw delegated powers from their agents if the agents exceeded the bounds of the original grant. This bold statement for popular sovereignty was memorialized in the Agreement of the People. At base, the Agreement was a proposed written constitution in which the people delegated powers and protected fundamental rights. Although the Agreement and its advocacy of popular sovereignty did not triumph in England, the spirit of the Agreement would take root in North America in the 1770s and 1780s.

An Agreement of the People for a firm and present peace upon grounds of common right.

Having by our late labours and hazards made it appear to the world at how high a rate we value our just freedom, and God having so far owned our cause as to deliver the enemies thereof into our hands, we do now hold ourselves bound in mutual duty to each other to take the best care we can for the future to avoid both the danger of returning into a slavish condition and the chargeable remedy of another war; for, as it cannot be imagined that so many of our countrymen would have opposed us in this quarrel if they had understood their own good, so may we safely promise to ourselves that, when our common rights and liberties shall be cleared, their endeavours will be disappointed that seek to make themselves our masters. Since, therefore, our former oppressions and scarce-yet-ended troubles have been occasioned, either by want of frequent national meetings in Council, or by rendering those meetings ineffectual, we are fully agreed and resolved to provide that hereafter our representatives be neither left to an uncertainty for the time nor made useless to the ends for which they are intended. In order whereunto we declare:—

That the people of England, being at this day very unequally distributed by Counties, Cities, and Boroughs for the election of their deputies in Parliament, ought to be more indifferently proportioned according to the number of the inhabitants; the circumstances whereof for number, place, and manner are to be set down before the end of this present Parliament.

II

That, to prevent the many inconveniences apparently arising from the long continuance of the same persons in authority, this present Parliament be dissolved upon the last day of September which shall be in the year of our Lord 1648.

III

That the people do, of course, choose themselves a Parliament once in two years, viz. upon the first Thursday in every 2d March, after the manner as shall be prescribed before the end of this Parliament, to begin to sit upon the first Thursday in April following, at Westminster or such other place as shall be appointed from time to time by the preceding Representatives, and to continue till the last day of September then next ensuing, and no longer.

IV

That the power of this, and all future Representatives of this Nation, is inferior only to theirs who choose them, and doth extend, without the consent or concurrence of any other person or persons, to the enacting, altering, and repealing of laws, to the erecting and abolishing of offices and courts, to the appointing, removing, and calling to account magistrates and officers of all degrees, to the making war and peace, to the treating with foreign States, and, generally, to whatsoever is not expressly or impliedly reserved by the represented to themselves: Which are as followeth.

1. That matters of religion and the ways of God's worship are not at all entrusted by us to any human power, because therein we cannot remit or exceed a tittle of what our consciences dictate to be the mind of God without wilful sin: nevertheless the public way of instructing the nation (so it be not compulsive) is referred to their discretion.

2. That the matter of impresting and constraining any of us to serve in the wars is against our freedom; and therefore we do not allow it in our Representatives; the rather, because money (the sinews of war), being always at their disposal, they can never want numbers of men apt enough to engage in any just cause.

3. That after the dissolution of this present Parliament, no person be at any time questioned for anything said or done in reference to the late public differences, otherwise than in execution of the judgments of the present Representatives or House of Commons.

4. That in all laws made or to be made every person may be bound alike, and that no tenure, estate, charter, degree, birth, or place do confer any exemption from the ordinary course of legal proceedings whereunto others are subjected.

5. That as the laws ought to be equal, so they must be good, and not evidently destructive to the safety and well-being of the people.

These things we declare to be our native rights, and therefore are agreed and resolved to maintain them with our utmost possibilities against all opposition whatsoever; being compelled thereunto not only by the examples of our ancestors, whose blood was often spent in vain for the recovery of their freedoms, Buffering themselves through fraudulent accommodations to be still deluded of the fruit of their victories, but also by our own woeful experience, who, having long expected and dearly earned the establishment of these certain rules of government, are yet made to depend for the settlement of our peace and freedom upon him that intended our bondage and brought a cruel war upon us.

Appendix B

Kamper v. Hawkins (November 16, 1793)

> *The rise of judicial review in the United States cannot be understood outside of the context of popular sovereignty. But for the acceptance of popular sovereignty, the courts today might not be co-equal branches of government. The mists of time and modern judicial supremacy have obscured the role of popular sovereignty in the development of the American courts. Law school studies of judicial review begin with* Marbury v. Madision *(1803), which is alleged to have established the judiciary as the final arbiter of constitutional law. If one is ignorant of state cases from the 1780s and 1790s, the standard interpretation of* Marbury *seems plausible. However, if we read* Marbury *in light of pioneering state decisions, something like scales might fall from our eyes.*
>
> *In* Kamper v. Hawkins *(1793), we are treated to five separate opinions written by some of the greatest judicial minds in the Old Dominion and the early Republic. These opinions take great care to trace the American rejection of parliamentary supremacy and to discuss popular sovereignty's transformative effect on the judiciary. In* Kamper, *we learn why judicial review is a necessary component of the American systems of government and also why courts cannot be the final arbiters of constitutions.*

The adjournment of this case originated in novelty and difficulty, touching the constitutionality, or judicial propriety of the judges of the District Court, carrying the following clause of an act of the General Assembly into execution, which was conceived to be opposed to, or in direct violation of the Constitution of the Commonwealth of Virginia.

The title and clause of the said act are thus: "An act reducing into one, the several acts concerning the establishment, jurisdiction, and powers of District Courts." (Passed December 12, 1792.)

"Sect. XI. Each of the said district courts in term time, or any judge thereof in vacation, shall, and may have and exercise the same power of granting injunctions to stay proceedings on any judgment obtained in any of the said district courts, as is now had and exercised by the judge of the high court of chancery in similar cases, and the said district courts may proceed to the dissolution or final hearing of all suits commencing by injunction, under the same rules and regulations as are now prescribed by law for conducting similar suits in the high court of chancery."

The Record, Arguments, and Decision, here follow.

At a District Court, held at Dumfries, the twenty-third day of May, one thousand seven hundred and ninety-three — Present, the Honourable Spencer Roane, Esq.

Upon a motion for an injunction to stay the proceedings on a judgment obtained at the last term held for this district, by Mary Hawkins, against the said Peter Kamper, under an act of assembly, entitled, "an act reducing into one, the several acts concerning the establishment, jurisdiction, and power of district courts."

The court is of opinion, that the said question should be adjourned to the General Court for novelty and difficulty, as to the constitutionality of the said law in this behalf. Whereupon,

At a General Court held at the capitol in the city of Richmond, on Saturday the ninth day of November, in the year of our Lord, one thousand seven hundred and ninety three — Present, Saint George Tucker.

And from thence continued by adjournments until Saturday, November 16, 1793. — Present, St. George Tucker, John Tyler, James Henry, Spencer Roane, and William Nelson, jun. esquires, judges.

The honorable the judges, delivered their respective opinions touching the case aforesaid, in the following manner:

JUDGE NELSON:

This is a motion for an injunction, adjourned from the District Court of Dumfries on the constitutionality of the eleventh section of the district court law,* which gives the district court in term time, or a judge thereof in vacation, the same power of granting injunctions to stay proceedings on any judgment obtained in a district court, and of proceeding to the dissolution or final hearing of suits commencing by injunction, under the same rules and regulations as are now prescribed to the high court of chancery.

I shall consider the question under *two* points.

First. Whether, if this clause be contrary to the constitution of this commonwealth, it can be executed.

---

*Passed in 1792.

And, *Secondly*, Whether it be contrary to the constitution.

I. As to the first point, although it has been decided by the judges of the court of appeals, (whether judicially or not is another question,) that a law contrary to the constitution is *void*—I beg leave to make a few observations on general principles.

The difference between a free and an arbitrary government I take to be—that in the former limits are assigned to those to whom the administration is committed; but the latter depends on the will of the departments or some of them. Hence the utility of a written constitution.

A *Constitution** is that by which the powers of government are limited.

It is to the *governors*, or rather to the departments of *government*, what a *law* is to individuals—nay, it is not only a *rule* of *action* to the branches of government, but it is that from which their existence flows, and by which the powers, (or portions of the right to govern,) which may have been committed to them, are prescribed—It is their commission—nay, it is their *creator*.

The calling this instrument the *constitution* or *form* of *government*, shews that the framers intended it to have this effect, and I shall presently endeavour to obviate the objection arising from the want of their appointment in form.

The present question is whether an act of the legislature contrary to it, be valid?

This is the paper by which the *delegates* and *representatives* of the people, viewing with concern the deplorable situation to which this country must have been reduced unless some *regular adequate mode* of civil *polity* had been speedily adopted, did *ordain* and *declare* the *future form* of government to be as there set forth.†

This is the paper which divides the government into three distinct departments, with one exception.‡

This is the very paper under which there are two branches of legislature now assembled.

This is the very paper under which they are to meet once every year, or oftener.

This is the very paper which gives them their style—of the General Assembly of Virginia.

---

*In the American edition of the Encyclopædia, "*Constitution* in matters of policy, signifies the form of government established in any country or kingdom. *Constitution* also denotes an ordinance, decision regulation, or law made by authority, superior ecclesiastical or civil."

That the word constitution in the title of the instrument under consideration, is not synonymous with ordinance or law, (as seems to be the opinion of the able author of "Notes on Virginia,") but is used in the former sense, is evident from its being called "the constitution, or form of government, &c."

†See second section of the Constitution.

‡That justices of the County Courts are eligible to either House of Assembly.

This is the very paper which calls one house the house of Delegates, and the other the Senate.

This is the very paper which declares that the former shall consist of two representatives from each county, chosen by freeholders, &c.

This is the very paper which fixes the number of the senate to twenty-four — which defines the number that shall compose a house of senate, — under which the state is to be divided into twenty-four districts.

Which declares that each county shall vote for a senator, who besides other qualifications shall be twenty-five years of age; — that a comparison of polls shall be made by the sheriffs, who are to return the person having the greatest number of votes.

That a certain number are to be displaced by rotation.

That writs may issue from each house for supplying vacancies. — And —

That all laws shall originate in the house of delegates subject to amendment by the senate, except money bills.

I ask then, whether the legislature do not sit under the constitution?

The answer in the affirmative to me is inevitable.

But it may be objected that, although the legislature would be bound by a fundamental regulation, made by a convention or other body delegated expressly for such a purpose, the body who formed this, not having been thus specially appointed, — this act possesses not sufficient sanctity; but is an act equal only to those of a common legislature, because some acts passed in the same session are confessedly so.

Here let it be remembered that the question is not whether the *people* can change it; but whether the legislature can do so.

As to the powers of the convention, this body seems to have been appointed, not only to see that the commonwealth sustained no injury, but also to consult in general for the public good, and in such a crisis as that at which our government was formed, those who are delegated have authority more extensive than a legislature appointed under a government, one object of which is to restrain that as well as the other departments, — whereas in the former case the people alone can decide whether these powers have been strained too far.

As to some acts of the same session being temporary and others revocable by the legislature. —

I answer, that the subject-matter of them will evince which are intended to be of this nature, and if any were designed to be permanent, they must be so until changed by the people, unless indeed calling these *ordinances* and the other a *Constitution*,* sufficiently manifest a design that *this* should be of higher authority than *those*.

---

*See note, p. 24.

It is confessedly the assent of the people which gives validity to a Constitution.

May not the people then, by a subsequent acquiescence and assent, give a Constitution, under which they have acted for seventeen years, as much validity, at least *so long as they acquiesce* in it, as if it had been previously expressly authorized?

The people have received this as a Constitution. The magistrates and officers down to a constable (for even the mode of *his* appointment is directed) have been appointed under it.

The people have felt its operation and acquiesced.

Who then can change it?—I answer, the PEOPLE alone.

But it has been supposed that the *legislature* can do this.

To decide this question, I have already stated that the legislature derive their *existence* from the Constitution.

It may be answered that those members who passed the law under contemplation were elected under the act of 1785.

But who held the election? Who was to decide in case of an equality of votes? and, who certified the persons elected?—The *sheriff* under the law. Who appointed the sheriff?—The executive.—By what authority?—Under the fifteenth article of this Constitution, which the legislature from their acts acknowledge to be inviolable.

If then the legislature were elected at an election holden by, and were returned by a sheriff, who derives his commission from the Constitution, does not that body derive its existence from the same source?

And can the legislature impugn that charter under which they claim, and to which by their acts they themselves have acknowledged an obligation?—I apprehend not, nor can any argument against this position be drawn from an acquiescence in some acts which may be unconstitutional.

1st, Because we may presume, that if there be any such, their unconstitutionality has not yet been discovered by the legislature, which, if it had been done, (from the instance before recited, and some other instances) we have reason to think, would have produced a similar declaration from that body.—And

2dly, Because no individual may have yet felt the operation of them, and consequently they have not been brought to investigation.

But the greatest objection still remains, that the judiciary, by declaring an act of the legislature to be no law, assumes legislative authority, or claims a superiority over the legislature.

In answer to this,—I do not consider the judiciary as the champions of the people, or of the Constitution, bound to sound the alarm, and to excite an opposition to the legislature.—But, when the cases of individuals are brought before them judicially, they are bound to decide.

And, if one man claim under an act contrary to the Constitution, that is, under what is *no* law, (if my former position, that the legislature cannot impugn the Constitution, and consequently that an act against it is void — be just,) must not a court give judgment against him?*

Nor is it a novelty for the judiciary to declare, whether an act of the legislature *be in force* or *not in force*, or in other words, whether it be a *law* or *not*.

In many instances one statute is virtually repealed by another, and the judiciary must decide which is the law, or whether both can exist together.

The only difference is, that in one instance that which was once in existence is carried out of existence, by a subsequent act virtually contrary to it, and in the other the prior *fundamental law* has prevented its *coming into existence* as *a law*.

With respect to the idea that for the judiciary to declare an act of the legislature void, is to claim a superiority to the legislature, — if the legislative authority is derived from the constitution, and such a decision be a judicial act (as I have endeavoured to prove) this objection seems to be refuted.

For the reasons which I have given, I am of opinion that the fundamental act of government controls the legislature, who owe their existence and powers to it; — this concludes the first point — That if the clause under consideration be unconstitutional it is *void*.

II. The second point — whether it be unconstitutional, is next to be considered.

By the fourteenth section of the Constitution, "the two houses of assembly shall, by joint ballot, appoint judges of the supreme court of appeals, and general court, *judges* in chancery, judges of admiralty, &c."

I was at first inclined to think that the insertion of the word *judges* between the *general court* and *chancery*, evinced an intention that the judges of the general court and those in chancery should be distinct persons; but perhaps it would be unjustifiable to rest such an opinion on so critical a construction.

However, this opinion is supported by the sixteenth and seventeenth sections.

---

*There are but three lines of conduct, one of which must be pursued on such an occasion, — either

    1st, To refuse to decide the question at all, which would be a dereliction of duty; or

    2dly, To wait for the legislature to decide whether the act be unconstitutional, which would be contrary to that article in the Constitution, which declares, that "the legislative, executive, and judiciary departments shall be separate and distinct, so that neither exercise the powers properly belonging to the other." — Since to decide whether the plaintiff or the defendant under the existing laws have a right, is a judicial act, and to decide whether the act be a void law as to a right vested or in litigation, is in fact to decide which of the parties have the right.

    There remains therefore when the question occurs, but one thing to be done by the judiciary, — which is,

    3dly, To decide that the act is void, and therefore that the claimant under it cannot succeed.

By the sixteenth, the governor and others offending against the state, by mal-administration, corruption, &c. are impeachable before the general court. And,

By the seventeenth, the judges of the general court are to be impeached before the court of appeals. This might prove then that a judge of the general court could not, according to the Constitution, be a judge of the supreme court of appeals, because all officers (except the judges of the general court,) are to be tried before the general court; but judges of the general court, are to be tried before the court of appeals — and the Constitution intended to prevent a man being tried in that court of which he is a member; because in causes which might give rise to an impeachment, the judges of a court might act jointly, and the influence of partiality, or an *esprit du corps*, was to be guarded against.

However, to decide whether a judge of the general court could be a judge of the court of appeals, would be extrajudicial, as that question is not before the court; but this research enables me to decide the question that is before the court — that is, whether the same person can, under the Constitution, be a judge in chancery, and a judge of the general court? I think that he cannot, for these reasons —

A judge in chancery is to be tried before the general court. — A judge of the general court cannot be a judge in chancery, because a judge in chancery must be tried before the general court; but if a judge of the general court be a judge in chancery, then he (a judge of the general court) will be tried in the general court, which is against the seventeenth article, which declares that a judge of the general court shall be impeached before the court of appeals.

My inference is, that a judge in chancery, and a judge of the general court, were intended under the Constitution to be distinct individuals.

This is one reason against the law; but there are others also of force. Whoever is appointed a judge in chancery under the Constitution, must be elected by joint ballot, and commissioned by the governor; neither of which requisitions have been complied with.

On the whole, I am for certifying to the court below, that the motion for an injunction be overruled, the clause under which it is prayed being unconstitutional.

JUDGE ROANE:

This great question was adjourned by me from the district court of Dumfries. I thought it necessary to obtain the opinion of this court, for the government of the several district courts, who might otherwise have differed in their construction of the clause in question, and the administration of the law in this instance been consequently partial.

My opinion then was, upon a short consideration, that the district courts ought to execute this law; for I doubted how far the judiciary were authorized to refuse to execute a law, on the ground of its being against the spirit of the Constitution.

My opinion, on more mature consideration, is changed in this respect, and I now think that the judiciary may and ought not only to refuse to execute a law expressly repugnant to the Constitution; but also one which is, by a plain and natural construction, in opposition to the fundamental principles thereof.

I consider the people of this country as the only sovereign power.—I consider the legislature as not sovereign but subordinate; they are subordinate to the great constitutional charter, which the people have established as a fundamental law, and which alone has given existence and authority to the legislature. I consider that at the time of the adoption of our present Constitution, the British government was at an end in Virginia: it was at an end, because among many other weighty reasons very emphatically expressed in the first section of our Constitution, "George the Third, heretofore entrusted with the exercise of the kingly office in this colony, had abandoned the helm of government, and declared us out of his allegiance and protection."

The people were therefore at that period, they were at the period of the election of the Convention, which formed the Constitution, absolved from the former kingly government, and free, as in a state of nature, to establish a government for themselves. But admitting for a moment that the old government was not then at an end, I assert that the people have a right by a convention, or otherwise, to change the existing government, whilst such existing government is in actual operation, for the ordinary purposes thereof. The example of all America in the adoption of the federal government, and that of several of the states in changing their state constitutions in this temperate and peaceable manner, undeniably proves my position. The people of Virginia, therefore, if the old government should not be considered as then at an end, permitted it to proceed, and by a convention chosen by themselves, with full powers, for they were not restrained, established then a Constitution.

This convention was not chosen under the sanction of the former government; it was not limited in its powers by it, if indeed it existed, but may be considered as a spontaneous assemblage of the people of Virginia, under a recommendation of a former convention, to consult for the good of themselves, and their posterity. They established a bill of rights, purporting to appertain to their posterity, and a constitution evidently designed to be permanent. This constitution is sanctioned by the consent and acquiescence of the people for seventeen years; and it is admitted by the almost universal opinion of the people, by the repeated adjudications of the courts of this commonwealth, and by very many declarations of the legislature itself, to be of superior authority to any opposing act of the legislature. The celebrated Vattel in a passage of his, which I will not fatigue this audience by quoting, denies to the ordinary legislature the power of changing the fundamental laws, "for, (says he,) it is necessary that the Constitution of the state be fixed."

But if the legislature may infringe this Constitution, it is no longer fixed; it is not this year what it was the last; and the liberties of the people are wholly at the mercy of the legislature.

A very important question now occurs, viz. whose province it is to decide in such cases. It is the province of the judiciary to expound the laws, and to adjudge cases which may be brought before them — the judiciary may clearly say, that a subsequent statute has not changed a former for want of sufficient words, though it was perhaps intended it should do so. It may say too, that an act of assembly has not changed the Constitution, though its words are expressly to that effect; because a legislature must have both the power and the will (as evidenced by words) to change the law, and it is conceived, for the reasons above mentioned, that the legislature have not power to change the fundamental laws. In expounding laws, the judiciary considers *every* law which relates to the subject: would you have them to shut their eyes against that law which is of the highest authority of any, or against a part of that law, which either by its words or by its spirit, denies to any but the people the power to change it? In cases where the controversy before the court does not involve the private interest, or relate to the powers of the judiciary, they are not only the proper, but a perfectly disinterested tribunal; — e. g. if the legislature should deprive a man of the trial by jury — there the controversy is between the legislature on one hand, and the whole people of Virginia (through the medium of an individual) on the other, which people have declared that the trial by jury shall be held sacred.

In other cases where the private interest of judges may be affected, or where their constitutional powers are encroached upon, their situation is indeed delicate, and let them be ever so virtuous, they will be censured by the ill-disposed part of their fellow-citizens: but in these cases, as well as others, they are bound to decide, and they do actually decide on behalf of the people; for example, though a judge is interested privately in preserving his independence, yet it is the right of the people which should govern him, who in their sovereign character have provided that the judges should be independent; so that it is in fact a controversy between the legislature and the people, though perhaps the judges may be privately interested. The only effect on the judges in such case should be, to distrust their own judgment if the matter is doubtful, or in other words to require clear evidence before they decide in cases where interest may possibly warp the judgment.

From the above premises I conclude that the judiciary may and ought to adjudge a law unconstitutional and void, if it be plainly repugnant to the letter of the Constitution, or the fundamental principles thereof. By fundamental principles I understand, those great principles growing out of the Constitution, by the aid of which, in dubious cases, the Constitution may be explained and preserved inviolate; those land-marks, which it may be necessary to resort to, on account of the impossibility to foresee or provide for cases within the spirit, but without the letter of the Constitution.

To come now more immediately to the question before the court; can those who are appointed judges in chancery, by an act of assembly, without ballot, and without commission during good behaviour, constitutionally exercise that office?—The fourteenth article of the Virginia Constitution recites "that the people have a right to uniform government; and therefore, that no government separate from, or independent of, the government of VIRGINIA, ought to be erected or established within the limits thereof." Here then is a general principle pervading all the courts mentioned in the Constitution — from which, without an exception, we ought not to depart. If those may be judges who are not appointed by joint ballot, but by an act of assembly, the senate have in that instance more power than the Constitution intended; for they control the other branch, by their negative upon the law, whereas if they mixed with that branch in a joint ballot, a plurality of votes of senators and delegates would decide.

If there can be judges in chancery who have no commission during good behaviour, their tenure of office is absolutely at the will of the legislature, and they consequently are not independent. The people of Virginia intended that the judiciary should be independent of the other departments: they are to judge where the legislature is a party, and therefore should be independent of it, otherwise they might judge corruptly, in order to please the legislature, and be consequently continued in office. It is an acknowledged principle in all countries, that no man shall be judge in his own cause; but it is nearly the same thing, where the tribunal of justice is under the influence of a party. If the legislature can transfer from constitutional to legislative courts, all judicial powers, these dependent tribunals being the creatures of the legislature itself, will not dare to oppose an unconstitutional law, and the principle I set out upon, viz. that such laws ought to be opposed, would become a dead letter, or in other words, this would pave the way to an uncontrolled power in the legislature. The constitution requires the concurrence of the legislature to appoint, and the executive to commission a judge: — but an appointment by act of assembly, will invest with this high power one who has not the sanction of the executive; and will throw a new office upon a man, without the liberty of declining such appointment, if he thinks proper. For these reasons, and others which it would be tedious to enumerate, I am of opinion, that the clause in question, is repugnant to the fundamental principles of the Constitution, in as much as the judges of the general court have not been balloted for and commissioned as judges in chancery, pursuant to the fourteenth article of the Constitution.

Mr. ROANE then said, "Although it is not in my opinion now necessary to decide, whether the offices of a judge in chancery and of the general court, may be united in the same person or not, supposing a constitutional appointment to have been made of the same person to each — yet in as much as this question is in some measure involved in the one just discussed, I will give my present impressions upon it, leaving myself free to decide hereafter the one way or the other, should it come judicially before me.

The constitution has declared that the three departments of government should be separate and distinct.— There are great political evils which would arise from their union;— for example, if according to Montesquieu, the members of the legislature were also members of the judiciary, the same man would as a legislator make a tyrannical law, and then as a judge would enforce it tyrannically. This union, it is evident, would produce a complete despotism.

It is therefore a fundamental principle not only of our constitution, but acknowledged by all intelligent writers, to be essential to liberty, that such a union should not take place.

But is there any great political evil resulting from the same person being a judge in chancery, and of the general court?

Is there any constitutional impediment?— It would be wise in the legislature to keep the offices separate; for an union of several functions in one person, will put it out of his power to be perfect in either, and the commonwealth will be better served by dividing than by accumulating the public duties.

But it has been said, and I confess with great force, that in as much as the judges in chancery are to be tried, on impeachment, before the general court, if the judges of the general court are also judges in chancery, they in their latter character must be tried before themselves in their former, and consequently there will be a defect of an impartial tribunal. I can only answer this objection by saying, that the former court of appeals was composed of the judges of the general court, court in chancery, and admiralty.— The legislature might have so organized the *said courts* as to have had nine-tenths of the court of appeals members of the general court.

The judges of the general court are by the constitution to be tried before the court of appeals, i.e. *under that organization*, before themselves;— and the judges of appeals before the general court, which would produce the same dilemma.

This case then is precisely similar to the case before us. And yet the judges of the court of appeals did in the remonstrance of May, one thousand seven hundred and eighty-eight, declare "that the forming the court of appeals, so as to consist of all the judges, is *no violation* of the constitution;" thereby overruling the objection which must have occurred in that case as well as in this.

Upon the whole I must say, that however inconvenient and unwise it might be to unite these distinct offices in the same person;— however in the case that has been supposed, there might be a defect of an impartial tribunal to try an offending chancellor upon an impeachment;— still not seeing any express provision in, or fundamental principle of, the constitution, restricting the power of the legislature in this respect; and grounding myself upon the above recited opinion of the former court of appeals as to the constitutionality of the union of offices which then existed in that body;— my present impressions are, that there is no constitutional impediment, plainly apparent, against uniting the two offices in the same person.

JUDGE HENRY:

This is an adjourned case from the Dumfries District, and the question (*new and difficult*) referred to this court is,— Ought the district judges to exercise that branch of chancery jurisdiction committed to them by the last district law, of hearing and deciding all causes brought before them by injunction according to the rules prescribed by law for conducting similar suits in the high court of chancery.

The difficulty and novelty of this case is, that the law in question requires of the common law judges, to exercise chancery jurisdiction, and that without a legal appointment, and without a commission.

The discussion of this subject is no less delicate than it is important.— It is important as it brings in question the rights of the legislature on one of the particular subjects committed to them by the plan of government: it is delicate, as the judges are compelled to examine their powers, their duties, and the regularity of their appointments, and therefore, they may be considered, in some sense, as judges in their own cause.— But be the subject as delicate as can be supposed possible, and as important as any which can ever come before a court, it is now before us, and I embrace the opportunity, now offered me for the first time, of publicly declaring my opinion.

The importance of the subject requires a particular attention, and thorough examination. We will then have recourse to the revolution and some of the history.

In the year 1776, the people of this country chose deputies, to meet in general convention, to consult of, and take care for, their most valuable interests. These deputies seem to have been complete representatives of the people, and vested with the most unlimited authority. Accordingly, having taken a careful review of the state of their country, they found a number of instances of misrule in the then existing government, and that our prince, by abandoning the helm of government, and declaring the people to be out of his allegiance and protection, had produced a total dissolution of the social band.

When this was found to be our unhappy situation, our deputies proceeded, (as of right they might), to prepare that form of government for us they judged best.

Accordingly, a plan of government was agreed upon, promulged, and accepted by the people, which has been uniformly acquiesced under from that day to this time. But previous to the promulging the plan of government, these deputies declared that certain rights were inherent in the people, which the public servants who might be intrusted with the execution of this government, were never to be permitted to infringe;—for example, the legislative branch were declared to be restrained from interfering with the right of trial by jury in criminal cases; from meddling with the rights of conscience, in matters of religion; and each of the three branches into which the government was to be divided was declared incompetent to any of the duties of either of the other two.

The judiciary, from the nature of the office, and the mode of their appointment, could never be designed to determine upon the equity, necessity, or usefulness of a law; that would amount to an express interfering with the legislative branch, in the clause where it is expressly forbidden for any one branch to interfere with the duties of the other. The reason is obvious, not being chosen immediately by the people, nor being accountable to them, in the first instance, they do not, and ought not, to represent the people in framing or repealing any law.

There is a proposition which I take to be universally true in our constitution, which to gentlemen whose ideas of parliament, and parliamentary powers, were formed under the former government, may not be always obvious; it is this—We were taught that *Parliament* was *omnipotent*, and their powers beyond control; now this proposition, in our constitution, is limited, and certain rights are reserved as before observed;—if this were always kept in mind, it might free the mind from a good deal of embarrassment in discussing several questions where the duty, and the power of the legislature is considered.

Our deputies, in this famous convention, after having reserved many fundamental rights to the people, which were declared not to be subject to legislative control, did more;—they pointed out a certain and permanent mode of appointing the officers who were to be intrusted with the execution of the government. Though the choice of the officers was intrusted to the wisdom of the legislature, yet the manner of conducting this choice was fixed; hereby declaring in the most solemn manner, the public will and mind of the people to be, that the laws when made, should be executed by officers chosen and appointed, as therein is directed, and not otherwise; whereas under the former government, the legislature seemed to have had no bounds to their authority but the negative of the crown, and the public officers were appointed and displaced at the pleasure of the governing powers which then were.

I come now to the particular case before the court. Kamper applied to the district court of Dumfries, for an injunction to a judgment obtained at law in that court by Hawkins, under the law which directs the district judges to hear and determine all suits commencing by injunction, under the same rules and regulations as are now prescribed by law, for conducting similar suits in the high court of chancery.

The permanent will of the people, expressed in the constitution, is that the legislature, by joint ballot of both houses, shall appoint judges of the supreme court of appeals and general court, judges in chancery, &c. to be commissioned by the governor, and to hold their offices during good behaviour.

It is alleged by some of my brethren, that the legislature are not warranted in appointing the same men to be judges both at common law and in chancery. The words of the plan of government are, "they shall appoint judges of the high court of appeals and general court, judges in chancery, &c." These words, *judges in chancery*, are supposed to design different persons from the judges of the general court, and an argument to inforce this opinion is drawn from sect. 16 and 17, where it is provided, that any judge of the general court, offending against the state, may be prosecuted in the high court of appeals; but a chancery judge offending must be prosecuted in the general court; therefore it is alleged, a common law judge cannot be a chancery, nor a chancery a common law judge in our government.

This question has heretofore been alleged as one of the reasons of the high court of appeals for declining to execute a very important law of the land;—without saying any thing about the propriety or impropriety of that business, it is sufficient for my present purpose to observe, that the question did not then come before the court in a judicial manner,—it was taken up as a general proposition, and when published, contained an appeal to the people; this looked like a dissolution of the government,—therefore I cannot view it as an adjudged case, to be considered as a binding precedent.

It is much to be wished that the question had been then decided, by calling a convention of the people. But unfortunately the legislature neither yielded the point nor insisted, but adopted an expedient.—They new-modelled the courts.—The question then went to sleep, but the legislature preserved the principle; they appointed judges of the high court of appeals, with unlimited jurisdiction, both in law and equity; they appointed judges of the general court, and a judge in chancery.

If the common law and chancery jurisdiction ought not to be united in the same persons in the first instance, I do not see how it can be justified in the appellate jurisdiction. If the form of government has provided that justice at common law ought to be administered by one set of men, and in chancery by another, it seems to me to follow as a necessary inference, that the appellate, as well as the original jurisdiction, ought to be separate and distinct, and that those gentlemen who now exercise the appellate jurisdiction have admitted the legislative construction of the form of government formerly objected to.

But I do not rest the question on this ground. Where I am not bound by regular adjudications of the superior court, I cannot rest on other men's opinions. I must and will think for myself.

Our government is declared to be founded on the authority of the people.

The people, in convention, have ordered that a legislature shall be chosen, a governor and council shall be chosen, judges shall be appointed.—All these different characters are servants of the people, have different duties, and are amenable to them. When the legislature were intrusted with the appointment of judges, I can find no particular characters, or any description of men, declared to be ineligible, but those holding legislative or executive authority, who are forbidden to interfere. To the discretion of the legislature is committed the choice of the judges, who shall fill all the superior courts, and therefore, if they have chosen, or shall hereafter choose to appoint the same set of men to administer justice to the people, both at common law and in chancery, I cannot find any thing in the form of government to restrain them. They are to appoint judges in chancery, at their discretion; and for me to say I cannot act as a chancery judge in any case, because if I should offend, I am to be prosecuted for such an offence before my brethren in the general court, seems to be a strange reason for me to assign for declining the office.

I am therefore very clear and decided in my opinion, that the legislature were fully authorized by the form of government, to appoint the district judges to exercise a chancery jurisdiction in the case before us, and I do cheerfully embrace this public opportunity of declaring my hearty approbation of the measure, and my willingness to act when the appointment is regularly made.

This brings me to the second point in the case. Have the legislature made the appointment in the manner prescribed by the form of government?

I wish most seriously I could give an affirmative answer to this question. It is provided by the form of government, so often alluded to, that judges in chancery shall be chosen by joint ballot of both houses, shall be commissioned by the governor, shall hold their office during good behaviour, and to secure their independence and remove them from all temptation to corruption, their salaries shall be adequate and fixed.—If a chancellor in any case must be chosen by ballot, be commissioned and hold his office during good behaviour, surely it is proper, it is necessary in all cases, that every judge shall be so chosen, shall be so commissioned, and hold his office so long as he behaves well. The business of hearing causes originating in that court by injunction, is of a permanent nature. To exercise this duty without the appointment and commission prescribed by the constitution, would be an exercise of a power according to the will of the legislature, who are servants of the people, not only without, but expressly against the will of the people. This would be a solecism in government,—establishing the will of the legislature, servants of the people, to control the will of their masters, if the word may be permitted. Till the appointment is made agreeable to the directions of the constitution, I cannot think myself duly authorized to take upon me the office.

Before I conclude, I wish to embrace the present opportunity of saying something about what may be called inconsistency in my conduct.—It is well known I sat in the former court of appeals, not being particularly balloted for and commissioned. I have latterly obeyed the commands of the legislature, by sitting in the special court of appeals without any such appointment or commission.

When I was appointed a judge of the court of admiralty, there was a standing law of the land, that every such judge should of course be a judge of the court of appeals, and an oath of office in both courts was prescribed. When I was balloted for, I considered myself as having a general appointment to both the courts, and acted accordingly: and had a commission been applied for as a judge of the court of appeals, it is probable, it might have been granted. However, the legislature, on reviewing this subject, availing themselves of what was then in their opinion judged to be an incomplete appointment, thought themselves authorized to garble the commission, and dismiss one half of the judges, without either giving them notice, or assigning any reason, assuming a right from their own omission, if it was one, to dismiss their judges. — If the legislature were authorized to take this step at that time, it surely furnishes all succeeding judges, as they value their reputation and their independence, to see that their appointment be regular, before entering upon the duties of their office, in future.

This dismission was submitted to, though, in a short time afterwards, the legislature seem to have forgotten the principle on which they grounded the dismission of the judges; for when public convenience seemed to require a special court of appeals in cases where a majority of the judges of that court should be interested, they commanded the judges of the general court to attend in such special court, without either an appointment or commission, which command I have more than once obeyed: and I freely acknowledge, that I consider this special court, with respect to me, who have been neither appointed nor commissioned since the passing of that law, as unconstitutional; but it is temporary. The case cannot often happen; it is exceedingly disagreeable to be faulting the legislature; and, perhaps, one particular mischief had better be submitted to, than a public inconvenience. These were my reasons for sitting in this special court.

It is most devoutly to be wished, that the present subject, now become the topic of public discussion, may be fully and generally understood, by the legislature, by the judiciary, and by the public at large, that there be no more of these unhappy differences of opinion between any of the different departments of government.

It remains only for me to add, that where I have been appointed and commissioned, I obey with alacrity, — when a new appointment shall be made, and a commission be directed, authorizing me to exercise the office of a judge in chancery, in any case whatever, I shall then have it in my power to exercise the right of every other free man, — to accept or refuse, — though I have no difficulty in declaring, were the appointment perfect, that I might hold during good behaviour, I should have no objection to enter upon the discharge of those new duties;—but until that it is done, in justice to the public, whose rights are concerned, and to myself, as an individual, I must decline the duty prescribed by the law in question, not being as yet such a judge in chancery as the people have said shall exercise that kind of jurisdiction.

Of course, my opinion is that the district court of Dumfries be advised to over-rule the motion for an injunction in this cause.

JUDGE TYLER:

I am saved much trouble in the investigation of this case, by the gentlemen whose opinions have been already delivered with so much propriety and sound reason, as it respects the question of the validity of the Constitution.

It is truly painful to me to be under the necessity of saying any thing in support of it at this day; but since I am reduced to this necessity, I must be indulged with a few observations on the subject.

I know it has been the opinion of some critical and speculative gentlemen of considerable merit and abilities too, that our form of government was not authorised by the people, inasmuch as no instructions were given by the people to the convention at the time the Constitution was established.

To investigate this subject rightly, we need but go back to that awful period of our country when we were declared out of the protection of the then mother country—and take a retrospective view of our situation, and behold the bands of civil government cut asunder, and destroyed:—No social compact, no system of protection and common defence against an invading tyrant—in a state of nature, without friends, allies, or resources:—In such a case what was to be done?

Those eminent characters to whom so much gratitude is, and for ever will be due—whose names are enrolled in the annals of America, recommended a convention of delegates to be chosen for that purpose; who were to meet together for the express design of completely protecting and defending the rights, both civil and religious, of our common country.—The delegates were so elected and convened.—What power had the people therefore that was not confided to their representatives? All their rights, all their power, all their happiness, all their hopes and prospects of success, were most indubitably entrusted to their care.—They were not betrayed.—The people did not say to their representatives, so far shall ye go, and no farther.—Happy, indeed, for this country, that no such restraint was laid on them.

In order to protect and defend the common cause then, a system of social duties was formed.—Without this what obedience could have been expected, and how could a regular defence have been made?

A great variety of departments were established, and those who were to execute them must have been made responsible to some regular power:—And all this was to complete the great work of liberty.

Has not this policy been sufficiently ratified by time and action? And if it were possible to doubt, under these circumstances, has it not been sealed with the blood of this wide extended empire? And shall its validity be now questioned? For what purpose? To revert back to our former insignificancy? It cannot be.

Before I proceed to say any thing on the adjourned case now under contemplation, I will beg leave to make a few observations on the opinion that some gentlemen have taken up, of the impropriety of the judiciary in deciding against a law which is in contradiction to the Constitution.

A little time and trouble bestowed on this subject, I am sure, would enable any person, endowed with common understanding, to see the fallacy of such sentiments.

What is the Constitution but the great contract of the people, every individual whereof having sworn allegiance to it? — A system of fundamental principles, the violation of which must be considered as a crime of the highest magnitude. — That this great and paramount law should be faithfully and rightfully executed, it is divided into three departments, to wit: the legislative, the executive, and judiciary, with an express restraint upon all, so that neither shall encroach on the rights of the other. — In the Bill of Rights many things are laid down, which are reserved to the people — trial by jury, on life and death, liberty of conscience, &c. Can the legislature rightfully pass a law taking away these rights from the people? Can the judiciary pass sentence without a conviction of a citizen by twelve of his peers? Can the executive do any thing forbidden by this bill of rights, or the constitution? In short, can one branch of the government call upon another to aid in the violation of this sacred letter? The answer to these questions must be in the negative.

But who is to judge of this matter? The legislature only? I hope not. — The object of all governments is and ought to be, the faithful administration of justice. — It cannot, I hope, be less the object of our government, which has been founded on principles very different from any we read of in the world, as it has ingrafted in it a better knowledge of the rights of human nature, and the means of better securing those rights. — And were I inclined to borrow a sentiment from any man, in support of my opinion, (not as authority, but merely argumentative) I should make use of the following one from the celebrated Hume, in his essay on our government, — viz. "We are therefore to look upon all the vast apparatus of our government, as having ultimately no other object, or purpose, but the distribution of justice, or in other words, the support of the judges. King, and parliaments, heads and armies, officers of the court and revenue, ambassadors, ministers, and privy-counsellors, are all subordinate in their end to this part of administration." — Hence it may reasonably be inferred, that if the commonwealth itself is subordinate to this department of government at times, so therefore will necessarily be the acts of the legislature, when they shall be found to violate first principles, notwithstanding the supposed "*omnipotence of parliament,*" which is an abominable insult upon the honour and good sense of our country, as nothing is omnipotent as it relates to us, either religious or political, but the *God of Heaven* and our constitution!

I will not in an extrajudicial manner assume the right to negative a law, for this would be as dangerous as the example before us; but if by any legal means I have jurisdiction of a cause, in which it is made a question how far the law be a violation of the constitution, and therefore of no obligation, I shall not shrink from a comparison of the two, and pronounce sentence as my mind may receive conviction.—To be made an agent, therefore, for the purpose of violating the constitution, I cannot consent to.—As a citizen I should complain of it; as a public servant, filling an office in one of the great departments of government, I should be a traitor to my country to do it. But the violation must be plain and clear, or there might be danger of the judiciary preventing the operation of laws which might be productive of much public good. These premises being admitted, as I think they must, I will now draw a comparison of the law before us with the constitution. The constitution declares there shall be judges in chancery, judges of the general court, &c.; and the first question that occurs is this—Can the office of a judge in chancery and common law be rightfully vested in the same persons, provided the appointment be regular?—To which I answer, I see no incompatibility, in the exercise of these offices, by the same persons—for although they be distinct offices, possessing distinct powers, they do not necessarily blend and run together, because they are placed in the same hands. The judge who knows the powers and duties of both, will well know how to keep them apart—like the rays of the sun, they radiate from one common centre, and may run parallel for ever, without an interference.—But to this, an ingenious and subtile argument is offered, and taken from the 17th article of the constitution, wherein it is directed, that when the judges of the general court are impeached, the court of appeals shall set in judgment—but all other officers of government, shall be impeached before the general court. Therefore, the constitution meant to keep the offices distinct, in distinct hands, because it is possible that they may try one another, and perhaps form a combination, in favour of the fraternity. This is too nice a deduction, and is a better argument in favour of an amendment of the constitution, than of the question under consideration. We cannot supply defects; nor can we reconcile absurdities, if any there be; this must be done by the people; and were we about the business of amendments duly authorised, it might be well to consider this point. But I cannot see why a judge in chancery, if he be a judge also of the general court, may not be tried by the court of appeals; for if he be convicted of such a crime, as he ought to be displaced from office in either capacity, he would hardly be allowed to hold the other; nor do I see why the judges of the general court, cannot try their brothers in chancery.

The legislature having a knowledge of this case, chose to trust the powers in our hands, as in the case of the high court of appeals who possess both chancery and common law powers, and are yet impeachable before the general court, who ought not to have a stronger sympathy or fellow-feeling for each other than for all the judges. In this case we find the same possible inconvenience, but it is barely possible to suppose that justice and the law will not be the object of a court's decision, let who will be the culprit, or object of trial. We find the county courts possess these powers, and I do suppose, if the doctrine contended for, on this point, was sound, they would not have been suffered to have rested from the beginning of the revolution to this day, in those courts; and without arrogating much to ourselves, we may be allowed to hope the trust would be at least as well executed in our hands.—I have nothing to say with respect to the policy of the measure, that will speak for itself; and moreover, it belongs to the legislature to decide.

The next inquiry we are to make, brings us pointedly to the comparison of the law now under contemplation, and the constitution; and how does it stand? The constitution says that judges in chancery shall be appointed by jointballot of both houses of assembly, and commissioned by the governor during good behaviour—and for the most valuable purposes; to secure the independence of the judiciary.—Contrary to this express direction, which admits of no doubt, implication or nice construction, that bane to political freedom, the legislature has made the appointment by an act mandatory, to the judges, leaving them not at liberty to accept or refuse the office conferred, which is a right every citizen enjoys, in every other case—a right too sacred to be yielded to any power on earth. But, were I willing to do it as it relates to myself, as a judge I ought not; because it would frustrate that most important object before-mentioned—intended by the constitution to be kept sacred, for the wisest and best of purposes—to wit, that justice and the law be done to all manner of persons without fear or reward.

For how would the rights of individuals stand when brought in contest with the public, or even an influential character, if the judges may be removed from office by the same power who appointed them, to wit, by a statute appointment as in this case, and by a statute disappointment as was the case in the court of appeals. Might not danger be apprehended from this source when future times shall be more corrupt? And yet, thank Heaven, the time has not arrived, when any judge has thus degraded his office, or dignity as a man, by a decision governed by fear or any other base motive; and I hope a long time will yet elapse before this will be the case. But our constitution was made, not only for the present day, but for ages to come, subject only to such alterations as the people may please to make. Let me now compare the law and the constitution in the other point; that of the want of a commission during good behaviour, and the reasons will fully or forcibly apply—when I receive the commission, I see the ground on which I stand. I see that my own integrity is that ground, and no opinions, but such as are derived from base motives, can be sufficient to remove me from office — in which case whensoever an appeal is made to me by an injured citizen, I will do him justice, as far as my mental powers will enable me to discover it, without any apprehensions of an unjust attack — that if the proudest sovereign on earth was in contest with the lowest peasant, that creeps through this vale of sorrow, yet should the arm of justice be extended to him also.

To conclude, I do declare that I will not hold an office, which I believe to be unconstitutional; that I will not be made a fit agent, to assist the legislature in a violation of this sacred letter; that I form this opinion from the conviction I feel that I am free to think, speak, and act, as other men do upon so great a question; that as I never did sacrifice my own opinions for the sake of popularity in the various departments I have had the honour to fill, however desirable popular favour may be, when obtained upon honorable principles; so now that I am grown old I cannot depart from those motives which I have both in public and private life made my standard — I concur therefore most heartily with my brothers, who have gone before me, in the last two points, that the law is unconstitutional and ought not to be executed; the injunction therefore must be over ruled — and this opinion I form not from a view of the memorials, nor from writers who knew not the blessings of free government, but as they were seen and felt through the prospect of future times, but from honest reason, common sense, and the great letter of a *Free Constitution*!

JUDGE TUCKER:

This question was an adjourned case from the district court of Dumfries, and arose upon the act of 1792, for reducing into one the several acts concerning the establishment, jurisdiction, and powers of the district courts.

Sect. third of that act declares it to be the duty of two of the judges of the *general court* to attend each district court at their respective terms; and the said two judges shall constitute a court for such district, &c.

Sect. eleventh provides "that each of the said district courts, in term-time, or *any judge thereof*, in vacation, shall, and may have, and exercise the *same power* of granting injunctions, to stay proceedings on any judgment, obtained in any of the said district courts, as is now had, and exercised by the *judge* of the *high court of chancery*, in similar cases, and the said district courts, may proceed to the dissolution, or final hearing of all suits, commencing by injunction, under the same rules, and regulations, as are now prescribed by law for conducting similar suits in the high court of chancery."

Upon this clause, a motion was made in Dumfries district court, May 23, 1791, for an injunction to stay proceedings on a judgment obtained in that court, and was adjourned hither for novelty and difficulty.

The question which it is now incumbent on this court to decide, seems to me to be shortly this — whether a *judge of the general court* of this commonwealth, can constitutionally exercise the functions of a *judge in chancery*? This calls upon us for a recurrence to fundamental principles, a duty which our bill of rights* expressly imposes upon all the servants of the commonwealth. And this renders it necessary not only to investigate the *principles* upon which our government is founded, but the *authority* by which it was established; inasmuch as there are doubts in the breasts of many, whether our *constitution* itself is any more than an act of the ordinary legislature, revocable, or subject to alteration by them, in any manner, and at any time.

In considering this question, I shall first state my own impressions, arising from the text of the constitution, and the spirit of our government, only unsupported by any former judicial opinions on the subject — and, secondly, as founded on the authority and decision of the court of appeals.

I. In stating my own impressions, I shall consider:

1st, Whether the constitution, or form of government of this commonwealth, be an act of the ordinary legislature, and, consequently revocable, or subject to alteration by the same authority; or something paramount thereto?

2dly, Whether, according to that constitution, the functions of a *judge of the general court*, and a *judge in chancery*, were intended to be distinct; or might be blended in the same person?

1st, Whether the constitution be an act of the ordinary legislature; or something paramount thereto?

It will be remembered by all those who are conversant with the history of the rise and progress of the late glorious revolution, that the measures which led to the final consummation of that important event, although they originated, in most instances, with the legal and constitutional assemblies of the different colonies, made but a small progress in that channel, particularly in this state. The dissolution of the constitutional assemblies, by the governors appointed by the crown, obliged the people to resort to other methods of deliberating for the common good. — Hence the first introduction of conventions: bodies neither authorized by, or known to the then constitutional government; bodies, on the contrary, which the constitutional officers of the then existing governments considered as illegal, and treated as such. Nevertheless, they met, deliberated, and resolved for the *common good*. They were the *people*, assembled by their deputies; not a *legal*, or *constitutional assembly*, or *part* of the *government* as then organized. — Hence they were not, nor could be deemed the ordinary legislature; that body being composed of the governor, council, and burgesses, who sat in *several distinct chambers* and *characters*: while the other was composed of a *single* body, having neither the character of governor, council, or legitimate representative among them: they were, in effect, *the people themselves*, assembled by their delegates, to whom the care of the commonwealth was especially, as well as unboundedly confided.

---

*Bill of Rights, Art. 15.

To prove this distinction still farther. The power of convening the *legal* assemblies, or the ordinary constitutional legislature, resided solely in the executive: they could neither be chosen without writs issued by its authority, nor assemble when chosen, but under the same authority. The conventions, on the contrary, were chosen, and assembled, either in pursuance of recommendations from congress, or from their own bodies, or by the discretion, and common consent of the people. They were held, even whilst a legal assembly existed. Witness the convention, held in Richmond in March, 1775: after which period, the legal, or constitutional assembly, was convened in Williamsburgh, by the governor, lord Dunmore; and continued sitting until finally dissolved by him in June or July, 1775. — No other legal assembly was ever chosen, or convened under the British government.

The convention then was not the ordinary legislature of Virginia. It was the body of the people, impelled to assemble from a sense of common danger, consulting for the common good, and acting in all things for the common safety. It could not be the legitimate legislature, under the then established government, since that body could only be chosen under the permission, and assembled under the authority of the crown of Great Britain.

But although the exercise of the authority of the executive government under the crown of Great Britain ceased altogether with the dissolution of that assembly in June, 1775, yet a constitutional dependence on the British government was never denied, until the succeeding May, nor dissolved until the moment of adopting the present constitution, or form of government; an event, which took effect by the *unanimous voice* of the convention, (elected after the final dissolution of the general assembly, as above mentioned, and assembled in Williamsburgh,) on the 29th of June, 1776, after six weeks deliberation thereon,* and eight days before the declaration of independence by the congress of the United States. This was not then the act of the ordinary legislature that dissolved the bands of union between us. It was the voice of the people themselves, proclaiming to the world their resolution to be free; to be governed only by their own laws; and to institute such a government, as, in their own opinion, was most likely to produce peace, happiness, and safety to the individual, as well as to the community.

It seems to me an observation of great importance, that the *declaration of independence* by *this state*, was *first made* in that instrument which *establishes our constitution*. The instant that the declaration of independence took effect, had the convention proceeded no farther, the government, as formerly exercised by the crown of Great Britain, being thereby totally dissolved, there would never have been an ordinary legislature, nor any other organized body,

---

*The convention came to a resolution to instruct their delegates in Congress to move, that body to declare America independent on the 15th of May, 1776, and the *same day* appointed a committee to prepare the draught of the *new constitution*, or *form of government*. See the journals of the convention assembled in Williamsburgh, May, 1776.

or authority in Virginia. Every man would have been utterly absolved from every social tie, and remitted to a perfect state of nature. But a power to demolish the existing fabric of government, which no one will, I presume, at this day, deny to that convention, without authority to erect a new one, could never be presumed. A new organization of the fabric, and a new arrangement of the powers of government, must instantly take place, to prevent those evils which the absence of government must infallibly produce in any case; but more especially under circumstances so awful, and prospects so threatening, as those which surrounded the people of America, at that alarming period. It would therefore have been absurdity in the extreme, in the people of Virginia, to authorize the convention to absolve them from the bonds of one government, without the power to unite them under any other, at a time when the utmost exertions of government were required to preserve both their liberties and their lives: but since they are *both* in *form* and *effect*, only *different clauses of the same act*, and necessary consequences of each other, to question the validity of the one, is to deny the effect of the other. The *declaration of independence*, and the *constitution*, as the ACTS OF THE PEOPLE, must therefore stand, or fall together.

Here let me cite the opinion of an eminent lawyer on the one hand, and of an enlightened politician on the other, on the subject of two national revolutions, the most familiar to us of any, except our own.

"The revolution of 1688," says judge Blackstone, 1 Com. 211, "was not a defeazance of the succession, and a new limitation of the crown by the king, and both houses of parliament: it was the act of the nation alone, upon the conviction that there was no king in being."

"The national assembly of France," says the ingenious M'Intosh, p. 60. "was assembled as an ordinary legislature under existing laws. They were transformed by events into a national convention, and vested with powers to organize a new government. It is in vain that their adversaries contest this assertion by appealing to the deficiency of forms. It is in vain to demand the legal instrument that changed their constitution, and extended their powers. Accurate forms in the conveyance of power are prescribed by the wisdom of the law, in the regular administration of states. But great revolutions are too immense for technical formality. All the sanction that can be hoped from such events is the voice of the people, however informally and irregularly expressed." (Defence of Fr. Revo. 60.)

Our case was much stronger than either of those.

There was at least the shadow of legal, constitutional authority in the convention parliament of England in 1688, as the ordinary legislature; and the national assembly of France was constitutionally assembled under the authority of the government it subverted. The convention of Virginia had not the shadow of a legal, or constitutional form about it. It derived its existence and authority from a higher source; a power which can supersede all law, and annul the constitution itself—namely, the *people*, in their *sovereign, unlimited,* and *unlimitable* authority and capacity.

From what I have said, I am inclined to hope, that it will appear that our constitution was not the act of the ordinary legislature: a few words concerning its operation, authority, and effect, as the act of the people, may not be improper.

"A constitution," says the celebrated Paine, "is not a thing in name only, but in fact. It has not an ideal, but a real existence; and wherever it cannot be produced in a visible form, there is none. A constitution is a thing antecedent to government, and a government is only the creature of a constitution. It is not the act of the government, but of the people constituting a government. It is the body of elements to which you can refer, and quote article by article, and which contains the principles on which the government shall be established, the manner in which it shall be organized, the powers it shall have, &c." See Rights of Man, part I. p. 30.

Vattel, in treating of the fundamental laws of a state, observes, "that a nation may entrust the exercise of the legislative power to the prince, or to an assembly, or to that assembly and the prince, jointly; who have then a right of making new, and of abrogating old laws. It is here demanded, whether if their power extends as far as the fundamental laws, they may change the constitution of the state? to this he answers, we may decide with certainty, that the authority of these legislators does not extend so far, and that they ought to consider the fundamental laws as sacred, if the nation has not in *express terms given them power to change them*. For the constitution of the state ought to be fixed; and since that was first established by the nation, which afterwards trusted certain persons with the legislative powers, the fundamental laws are excepted from their commission. In short, these legislators derive their power from the constitution: how then can they change it, without destroying the foundation of their authority?" Vattel, p. 31.

That the legislature of this commonwealth have regarded our Constitution in this light, will appear from more than one authority. I shall select the preamble of an act passed in May session, 1783, c. 32. Rev. Co. 204. entitled an act to amend an act, entitled an act concerning the appointment of sheriffs, which recites "that the former act was contrary to the Constitution, or form of government," for which reason it was repealed.—A second instance may be found in the acts of 1787, c. 23. which recites "that a former act, entitled an act to extend the powers of the governor and council, Rev. Co. 81. appears to the present general assembly to be contrary to the true spirit of the constitution:" wherefore it was repealed.—Two other instances may be found, the first in the repeal* of the act of 1787, c. 39. for establishing district courts, whereby the *judges of the court of appeals* were required to act as *judges of the*

---

*1787, ch. 67.

district courts: the second, in an act of the last session, 1792, ch. 28. providing for the republication of the laws of this commonwealth, which directs "that the bill of rights, and Constitution, or form of government, shall be prefixed to the code of laws."— Other instances doubtless may be found in our laws, where the legislature have either expressly, or tacitly, recognized the Constitution as paramount to their own legislative acts; so that reasoning, in this instance, is confirmed by precedent.

But here an objection will no doubt be drawn from the authority of those writers who affirm, that the constitution of a state is a rule to the *legislature only*, and not to the *judiciary*, or the *executive*: the legislature being bound not to transgress it; but that neither the executive nor judiciary can resort to it to enquire whether they do transgress it, or not.

This sophism could never have obtained a moment's credit with the world, had such a thing as a written Constitution existed before the American revolution. "All the governments that now exist in the world, (says a late writer,*) except the United States of America, have been fortuitously formed. They are the produce of chance, not the work of art. They have been altered, impaired, improved, and destroyed, by accidental circumstances, beyond the foresight or control of wisdom; their parts thrown up against present emergencies, formed no systematic whole." What the *constitution* of any country *was* or rather *was supposed to be*, could only be collected from what the *government had at any time done*; what had been *acquiesced* in by the people, or other component parts of the government; or what had been *resisted* by either of them. Whatever the government, or any branch of it had *once done*, it was inferred they had a *right* to do *again*. The union of the legislative and executive powers in the same men, or body of men, ensured the success of their usurpations; and the judiciary, having no *written constitution* to refer to, were obliged to *receive* whatever *exposition* of it the legislature might think proper to make. But, with us, the constitution is not an "ideal thing, but a real existence: it can be produced in a visible form:" its principles can be ascertained from the living letter, not from obscure reasoning or deductions only. The government, therefore, and all its branches must be governed by the constitution. Hence it becomes the first law of the land, and as such must be resorted to on every occasion, where it becomes necessary to expound *what the law is*. This exposition it is the duty and office of the judiciary to make; our constitution expressly declaring that the legislative, executive, and judiciary, shall be separate and distinct, so that neither exercise the powers properly belong to the other. Now since it is the province of the legislature to make, and of the executive to enforce obedience to the laws, the duty of expounding must be exclusively vested in the judiciary. But how can any just exposition be made, *if that which is the supreme law of the land be withheld from their view?* Suppose a question

---

*M'Intosh on the Fr. Rev. 115.

had arisen on either of the acts before cited, which the legislature have discovered to be unconstitutional, would the judiciary have been bound by the act, or by the constitution?

But that the constitution is a rule to all the departments of the government, to the judiciary as well as to the legislature, may, I think, be proved by reference to a few parts of it.

The bill of rights, art. 8. provides, that in all capital and criminal prosecutions, the party accused shall be tried by a *jury of the vicinage*, and cannot be found guilty without their *unanimous* consent.

Suppose any future act of the legislature should abridge either of these privileges, what would be said of a court that should act in conformity to such an act?

Again; art. 9. declares that excessive bail ought not to be required. The act* concerning bail, I apprehend, extends not to the superior courts; perhaps not even to the county courts. Is this injunction a mere dead letter, because the legislature have not yet passed a law equally extensive in its obligation?

Art. 10. declares that general warrants are illegal and oppressive, and ought not to be granted. Is this too a dead letter, because we have no act of the legislature to enforce the obligation?

Art. 16. secures the free exercise of our religious duties, according to the dictates of every man's own conscience. Should the legislature, at any future period, establish any particular mode of worship, and enact penal laws to support it, will the courts of this commonwealth be bound to enforce those penalties?

Art. 15. of the constitution, declares that the clerks of courts shall hold their offices during good behaviour, to be judged of and determined in the general court. Can any legislative act give any other court cognizance of such a case? Or can any impeachment be tried in any court of this commonwealth, except this court, and the court of appeals, even should an act of the legislature (as was once contemplated) erect a court for that especial purpose?

From all these instances it appears to me that this deduction clearly follows, viz. that the *judiciary* are *bound* to take notice of the constitution, *as the first law of the land*; and that whatsoever is contradictory thereto, it *not* the law of the land.

And here I shall avail myself of the reasoning of one of the ablest political writers that has appeared in America.†

"Some perplexity respecting the right of the courts to pronounce legislative acts void, because contrary to the constitution, has arisen," he observes, "from an imagination that the doctrine would imply a superiority of the judiciary over the legislative power. It is urged that the power which can declare

---

*1785, ch. 80.
†Pub. v. 2. p. 293.

the acts of another void, must necessarily be superior to the one whose acts may be declared void.

"But there is no position which depends on clearer principles, than that every act of a delegated authority, contrary to the tenor of the commission under which it is exercised, is void. No legislative act therefore, contrary to the constitution, can be valid. To deny this would be to affirm, that the deputy is greater than the principal; that the servant is above his master; that the representatives of the people are superior to the people themselves.

"If it be said that the legislative body are themselves the constitutional judges of their own powers, and that the construction they put upon them is conclusive upon the other departments, it may be answered that this cannot be the natural presumption, where it is not to be collected from any particular provisions in the constitution. It is not otherwise to be supposed that the constitution could intend to enable the representatives of the people to substitute their will to that of their constituents. It is far more rational to suppose that the courts were designed to be an intermediate body between the people and the legislature, in order, among other things, to keep the latter within the limits assigned to their authority. The interpretation of the laws is the proper and particular province of the courts. A constitution is in fact, and must be regarded by the judges, as a fundamental law. It therefore belongs to them to ascertain its meeting, as well as the meaning of any particular act proceeding from the legislative body. If there be an irreconcileable variance between the two, that which has the superior obligation and validity ought of course to be preferred; or, in other words, the constitution ought to be preferred to the statutes; the intention of the people to the intention of their agents.

"Nor does this conclusion by any means suppose a superiority of the judiciary to the legislative power. It only supposes that the power of the people is superior to both; and that where the will of the legislature, declared in its statutes, stands in opposition to that of the people, declared in the constitution, the judges ought to be governed by the latter, rather than the former. They ought to regulate their decisions by the fundamental laws, rather than those which are not fundamental."*

Such is the reasoning of one of the most profound politicians in America. It is so full, so apposite, and so conclusive, that I think it unnecessary to add any thing farther on the subject, and shall now proceed to the second point, viz.

2. Whether, according to the constitution of this commonwealth, a judge of the general court can exercise the functions of a judge in chancery?

---

*"It can be of no weight to say that the courts, on the pretence of a repugnancy, may substitute their own pleasure to the constitutional intentions of the legislature. This might as well happen in the case of two contradictory statutes; or it might as well happen in every adjudication upon any single statute. The courts must declare the sense of the law. The observation, if it proved any thing, would prove that there ought to be no judges distinct from the legislative body." Publius, 295.

There again I must recur to one of the fundamental principles of our government, a principle essentially and indispensably necessary to its existence as a free government, exercised by the immediate authority of the people, delegated to the servants of their own choice, viz. the separation of the legislative, executive, and judiciary departments.

These departments, as I have before observed, our constitution declares shall be for ever separate and distinct. To be so, they must be independent one of another, so that neither can control, or annihilate the other.

The independence of the judiciary results from the tenure of their office, which the constitution declares shall be *during good behaviour*. The offices which they are to fill must therefore in their nature be permanent as the constitution itself, and not liable to be discontinued or annihilated by any other branch of the government. Hence the constitution has provided that the judiciary department should be arranged in such a manner as not to be subject to legislative control. The court of appeals, court of chancery, and general court, are tribunals expressly required by it; and in these courts the judiciary power is either immediately, or ultimately vested.

These courts can neither be annihilated nor discontinued by any legislative act; nor can the judges of them be removed from their offices for any cause, except a breach of their good behaviour.

But if the legislature might at any time discontinue or annihilate either of these courts, it is plain that their tenure of office might be changed, since a judge, without any breach of good behaviour, might in effect be removed from office, by annihilating or discontinuing the office itself.

This has been proved in the case of the former court of appeals.* The moment it was discovered that that court was not constituted according to the directions of the constitution, the legislature, without any charge of a breach of good behaviour by any one of that court, *removed a majority* of the judges from their office, as judges of that court, *by new modelling the court altogether.*

I am far from considering this act of the legislature as unconstitutional, for reasons that I shall hereafter mention.

But it proves that the judiciary can never be independent, so long as the existence of the office depends upon the will of the ordinary legislature, and not upon a constitutional foundation.

The district courts considered as independent of the *general court*, and not a modification of it, are merely *legislative* courts, and consequently may be discontinued, or annihilated, whenever the legislature may think proper to abolish them. And if the judges of those courts held their offices only as judges of the district courts, they might be virtually, and in fact, removed from office, as the judges of the former court of appeals were, by a legislative act, discon-

---

*Virg. Acts vi. 1788, ch. 68.

tinuing the courts, and transferring their jurisdiction to other tribunals, *without any breach of good behaviour.*

Hence arises a most important distinction between *constitutional* and *legislative* courts. The judges of the former hold an office co-existent with the government itself, and which they can only forfeit by a breach of good behaviour. The judges of the latter, although their commissions should import upon the face of them, to be during good behaviour, may be at any time discontinued from their office, by abolishing the courts. In other words, constitutional judges may be an independent branch of the government, legislative judges must ever be dependant on that body at whose will their offices exist.

If the principles of our government have established the judiciary as a barrier against the possible usurpation, or abuse of power in the other departments, how easily may that principle be evaded by converting our courts into legislative, instead of constitutional tribunals?

To preserve this principle in its full vigour, it is necessary that the constitutional courts should all be restrained within those limits which the constitution itself seems to have assigned to them respectively.

What those limits are, may be collected from the 14th article,* which provides for the appointment of "*judges* of the supreme court of *appeals*, and *general court, judges* in *chancery, judges* of *admiralty,*" &c. This specification of judges of *several tribunals*, would lead us of itself to conclude, that the tribunals themselves were meant to be separate and distinct.† This conclusion seems to be warranted by two circumstances, the one extrinsic, the other arising out of the constitution itself. Those who recollect the situation of our jurisprudence, at the time of the revolution, will remember that the union of civil and criminal, common law, and equity jurisdiction, all in the general court, was one of the most obvious defects of that system. In truth, nothing can be more dangerous to the citizen, than the union of criminal courts, and courts of equity. On the European continent, wheresoever the civil law has been adopted, criminal and civil proceedings have been conducted upon the like principles: the defendant in *civil* cases might be examined upon oath by interrogatories, to which if he gave not satisfactory answers he might be committed until he did: this principle being extended to *criminal* cases, was denominated by the moderate term of putting the person accused to the *question*: but inasmuch as the forcing a criminal to accuse himself on *oath*, might prove a *snare to his conscience*, the obligation to answer to the question *was inforced by torture*. To separate for ever, courts, whose principles and proceedings are so diametrically opposite as those of the common and civil law, was,

---

*Const. Virg. art. 14.

†Since every word in that instrument, the constitution of the commonwealth, should be construed to have its effect; a rule applied to all written instruments whatsoever, and more peculiarly applicable, I should presume, to that which expresses the collective, and sovereign will and intention of the people.

I should presume, one of the fundamental principles which the framers of our constitution had an eye to. They, therefore, distributed the powers of the *then existing general court* into three distinct branches, viz. the court of appeals, the court of chancery, and the court of general jurisdiction, at common law. The repetition of the term, judges, shows that it was in contemplation that both the tribunals, and the judges should be distinct and separate. This is farther confirmed by art. 16 and 17*: the former of which provides that impeachments in general shall be prosecuted in *this* court, the latter that impeachments against the judges of *this court*, shall be prosecuted in the *court of appeals*. Nothing, then, can be clearer than that the constitution intended they should be distinct judges of distinct courts. And hence I am satisfied, that the former court of appeals was unconstitutionally organized. This reasoning, I apprehend, will apply no less forcibly to the separation of the general court from the court of chancery. A judge of the general court, if impeached, can be prosecuted in the *court* of *appeals only*; a judge in chancery *only* in the *general court*: if these offices be united in the same person, it must be by separate commissions; a judgment on impeachment in the general court cannot vacate the commission of a judge of that court, because the constitution has assigned another tribunal, where a judge of that court shall be tried; a judgment in the court of appeals cannot vacate the commission of a judge in chancery, because he must be tried, *as such*, in the general court. Hence it seems to me we are driven to conclude that the constitution meant that the two offices shall be separate and distinct. This construction removes every difficulty, the contrary, I apprehend, creates a multitude, and those insurmountable.† In pursuance of this direction, contained in the constitution, the legislature, when it set about organizing the courts, distributed them as above-mentioned. The criminal and common law court, was separated from the court of equity; and both from the court of appeals, in form, though not in reality, until the legislature, by the act of 1788, c. 68. corrected its former error. And thus distinct have they remained, until the act of the last session, which hath not indeed united the constitutional courts, but hath blended them in effect, by assigning the functions of a judge in chancery to the judges of this court; and if carried into effect may lead to the total annihilation of all the courts which the constitution had in contemplation to establish.

I have said before (p. 86,) that the district courts considered as independent of the general court, and not a modification of it, are mere legislative,

---

*Const. Virg. arts. 16 and 17.

†A curious question might here be propounded. Suppose a judge of the general court, holding also a commission as a judge in chancery, and sitting as a judge of a district court, where his functions were united, should receive a bribe from one of the parties to a suit depending there before him: that on the trial at law he shall endeavor to influence the jury, and shall after grant an injunction to the party from whom he received the bribe: must there be two impeachments and two trials, in different courts, in this case; or could one trial, and one judgment, vacate both commissions?

and not constitutional courts. If they are a modification only of the general court, it flows from what I have already said, that the constitution prohibits the exercise of chancery jurisdiction therein. If they be mere legislative courts, it cannot be the duty of any judge of a constitutional court, *merely as such*, to exercise the functions of a judge of these courts: and it is, I conceive, expressly contrary to the duty of a constitutional judge of one court, to exercise the functions of a constitutional judge of another distinct constitutional court.

It appears then immaterial, whether, on the present question, the district courts are to be considered as branches of the general court, or not: yet it would be easy to show, that as they are at present modified and organized, they are nothing more than branches of that court; and not distinct, independent, legislative courts; unless the operation of the act in question should be construed to affect and change their whole system and constitution.

But, if they are mere legislative courts, they may, at any time, be organized at the will of the legislature: legislative judges may be appointed, the tenor of whose commission may import that their office shall be during good behaviour, and yet that office be discontinued whenever the legislature may think fit. If the jurisdiction of the court of chancery can be constitutionally transferred to them, so may that of the general court, and of the court of appeals. In fine these legislative courts may absorb all the jurisdictions, powers and functions of the constitutional courts. These last then must either be suppressed, as useless, which the constitution forbids*; or the judges of them will hold *sinecures* instead of *offices*, which is expressly contrary to the bill of rights, art. 4. Add to this that such an arrangement must ever render the judiciary the mere creature of the legislative department, which both the constitution,† and the bill of rights‡ most pointedly appear to have guarded against.

2. I shall now proceed to take a short view of the subject, as founded upon a solemn decision of the court of appeals, on a similar occasion.

It will not, I presume, be denied that the decisions of the supreme court of appeals in this commonwealth, upon any question, whether arising upon the general principles of law, the operation or construction of any statute or act of assembly, or of the constitution of this commonwealth, are to be resorted to by all other courts, as expounding, in their truest sense, the laws of the land; and where any decision of that court applies to a case depending before any other tribunal, that tribunal is bound to regulate its decisions conformably to those of the court of appeals. This postulatum I conceive to be too obviously founded upon the principles of our government to require an attempt to demonstrate it. Proceeding upon this ground, I shall take up the question upon the authority of a previous decision of that court, on a similar question.

---

*Art. 14.
†Const. V. art. 3.
‡Bill of Rights, art. 5.

In the year 1787, the first act establishing district courts was passed. This act "declared it to be the duty of the judges of the high court of appeals to attend the said courts, allotting among themselves the districts they should respectively attend; three judges to be allotted to each district, any two of whom should constitute a court." Ch. 39. sect. 3.

It should be remembered, that at that time the court of appeals was composed of the judges of the high court of chancery, judges of the general court, and judges of the court of admiralty. The office of the judge of the court of appeals was, at that time, as it were, incidentally annexed to their appointment to a seat on either of the other tribunals.

A part of the duty assigned to the court of appeals by that act was the appointment of clerks to the district courts, which the act required should be done at the next succeeding session of the court of appeals. Ib. Sect. 2.

On the 12th of May following, the court made the following entry upon their records. "On consideration of a late act of assembly, entitled an act establishing district courts, after several conferences, and upon mature deliberation, the court do *adjudge* that clerks of the said courts ought not now to be appointed, for reasons contained in a remonstrance to the general assembly:"— which remonstrance is likewise entered on record, and contains, among other things, the following important passages.

"1. That in discussing the act establishing district courts, the court found it unavoidable to consider, whether the principles of that act do not violate those of the constitution, or form of government, which the people, in 1776, when the former bands of their society were dissolved, established as the foundation of that government which they judged necessary for the preservation of their persons and property; and if such violation were apparent, whether they had power, and it was their duty to declare that the act must yield to the constitution?

"2. That they found themselves obliged to decide, whatever temporary inconveniencies might arise, and in that decision to declare, that the constitution and the act were in opposition, and could not exist together, and that the former must control the latter.

"3. That the propriety and necessity of the independence of the judges is evident in reason, and the nature of their office, since they are to decide between government and the people, as well as between contending citizens; and if they be dependent on either, corrupt influence may be apprehended.

"4. That this applies more forcibly to exclude a dependence on the legislature, a branch of whom, in cases of impeachment, is itself a party.

"5. To obviate a possible objection that the court, while they are maintaining the independence of the judiciary, are countenancing encroachments of that branch upon the departments of others, and assuming a right to control the legislature, it may be observed, that when they decide between an act of the people, and an act of the legislature, they are within the line of their duty, declaring what the law is, and not making a new law.

"6. That although the duties of their office were not ascertained at the time of establishing the constitution, yet in respect thereto, the constitution gives a principle, namely, that 'no future regulation should blend the duties of the judges of the general court, court of chancery, and court of admiralty, which the constitution seems to require to be exercised by distinct persons.'

"7. That the assigning to the judges of chancery and admiralty jurisdiction in common law cases, may be considered as a new office."

These declarations, according to my weak apprehensions, comprehend the present question in the fullest extent. I should therefore be of opinion, upon the ground of this authority, as well as upon the conviction of my own mind, independent thereof, which, unless so fortified, I might have mistrusted, that we ought to certify to the district court of Dumfries "That in the opinion of this court, a judge of the general court cannot constitutionally exercise the functions of a judge in chancery." But the judges who have already delivered their opinions, although some of them appear to dissent from me upon this point, having unanimously concurred in another, viz. That the functions of a judge in chancery can only be exercised by those who may be constituted judges in chancery, in the manner prescribed by the constitution; I shall concur in their unanimous judgment, without offering any reasons on a subject which has been so fully and satisfactorily discussed by them.

Appendix C

Abbreviations Used in the Notes and Bibliography

COLLECTIONS

Annals *The Debates and Proceedings in the Congress of the United States*, ed., Joseph Gales (Washington, D.C.: Gales and Seaton, 1834–56) 42 vols.

Elliot's Debates *The Debates in the Several State Conventions on the Adoption of the Federal Constitution*, ed., Jonathan Elliot (Washington, D.C.: J.B. Lippincott & Co., 1888) 7 vols.

PAH *The Papers of Alexander Hamilton*, ed., Harold Syrett and Jacob E. Cooke (New York: Columbia University Press, 1961–79) 27 vols.

PJM *The Papers of James Madison*, ed., William T. Hutchinson, William M.E. Rachal, *et al.* (Charlottesville, Va.: University Press of Virginia, 1962-) 17 vols.

PTJ *The Papers of Thomas Jefferson*, ed., Julian P. Boyd *et al.* (Princeton, N.J.: Princeton University Press, 1950-) 26 vols.

The Republic of Letters *The Republic of Letters: The Correspondence Between Jefferson and Madison*, ed., James Morton Smith (New York: W.W. Norton, 1995) 3 vols.

WJA *The Works of John Adams*, ed., Charles Francis Adams (Boston: C.C. Little, J. Brown, 1850–56) 10 vols.

WJM *The Writings of James Madison*, ed., Gaillard Hunt (New York: G.P. Putnam's Sons, 1904) 9 vols.

WTJ *The Works of Thomas Jefferson*, ed., Paul Leicester Ford (New York, G.P. Putnam's Sons, 1900–10) 12 vols.

JOURNALS

B.C. L. Rev. *Boston College Law Review*
Conn. L. Rev. *Connecticut Law Review*
Duke J. Const. L. & Pub. Pol'y *Duke Journal of Constitutional Law and Public Policy*
Duke L.J. *Duke Law Journal*
Early Am. Lit. *Early American Literature*

Econ. Hist. Rev. *Economic History Review*
Eng. Hist. Rev. *English Historical Review*
Geo. Wash. L. Rev. *George Washington Law Review*
Har. L. Rev. *Harvard Law Review*
Harv. J.L. & Pub. Pol'y *Harvard Journal of Law and Public Policy*
Hastings Const. L.Q. *Hastings Constitutional Law Quarterly*
Hist. J. *History Journal*
J. Brit. Stud. *Journal of British Studies*
J. Early Repub. *Journal of the Early Republic*
J. Econ. Hist. *Journal of Economic History*
J. Hist. Ideas *Journal of the History of Ideas*
J. Mod. Hist. *Journal of Modern History*
Law & Hist. Rev. *Law and History Review*
Mo. L. Rev. *Missouri Law Review*
N. Ky. L. Rev. *Northern Kentucky Law Review*
N.Z. J. Pub. & Int'l L. *New Zealand Journal of Public and International Law*
Regent U. L. Rev. *Regent University Law Review*
Rev. Pol. *Review of Politics*
S. Tex. L. Rev. *South Texas Law Review*
Stan. L. Rev. *Stanford Law Review*
U. Chi. L. Rev. *University of Chicago Law Review*
U. Pa. L. Rev. *University of Pennsylvania Law Review*
U. Pitt. L. Rev. *University of Pittsburg Law Review*
Wm. & Mary L. Rev. *William and Mary Law Review*
Wm. & Mary Q. *William and Mary Quarterly*
Yale L.J. *Yale Law Journal*

Notes

Preface

1. *Cooper v. Aaron*, 358 U.S. 1, 18 (1958).

Chapter 1

1. *Federalist No. 2*, p. 7 (John Jay) (Bantam Books, ed., 1982).
2. David Hackett Fischer, *Albion's Seed* 6 (1989); Loretto Dennis Szuc and Sandra Hargreaves Luebking, *The Source* 361 (2006); Edward Countryman, *The American Revolution* 18 (1985).
3. For the reign of Elizabeth, see generally, Wallace MacCaffrey, *Elizabeth I* (1993).
4. Succession Act (1604), reprinted in *Constitutional Documents of the Reign of James I*, at 10 (J.R. Tanner, ed., 1960). For a recent biography of James, see generally, Pauline Croft, *King James* (2003). For a brief discussion of James' rise to power and rule, see generally, 2 Winston S. Churchill, *A History of the English Speaking Peoples: The New World* 147–63 (1956) [hereinafter Churchill, *New World*]. The only other claimant to the throne was the daughter of Phillip III of Spain, but securing the throne for a Catholic ruler would have required the conquest of England. Considering that James was already a monarch and could raise forces to fight Spain, the situation was not worth pressing for the Spaniards. See Conrad Russell, *The Crisis of Parliaments* 255–56 (1971).
5. For the intrigues and circumstances forcing Mary to give up the throne, see Alan Stewart, *The Cradle King* 1–37 (2003).
6. John Miller, *The Stuarts* 41 (2004)
7. Succession Act (1604), reprinted in Tanner, supra note 4, at 11.
8. Stewart, supra note 5 at 3.
9. As his own debts mounted, James chose to pay off the debts of several favorites rather than tend to his own fiscal affairs. See Roger Lockyer, *The Early Stuarts* 32 (1999).
10. Once James learned about the Catholic plot to murder him and members of Parliament in 1605 (the "Gunpowder Plot"), he further relied on his friends from Scotland and alienated Englishmen. Stewart, supra note 5, at 222. For the history of the Gunpowder Plot, see generally, Alan Hayes, *The Gunpowder Plot* (1994).
11. James I, *The True Law of Free Monarchies and Basilikon Doron* 167 (Daniel Fischlin and Mark Fortier, eds.) [hereinafter James I, *True Law*].
12. Mark Kishlansky, *A Monarchy Transformed* 34–35 (1996) [hereinafter Kishlansky, *Monarchy Transformed*].
13. See J.P. Summerville, *Politics and Ideology in England, 1603–1640*, at 9 (1986) (discussing divine right of kings).
14. James' theory "was by no means new to England but for some seventy years had been implicit, and often explicit, in the language of supporters of the Tudor monarchy." Harold Berman, *The Origins of Historical Jurisprudence*, 103 Yale L.J. 1651, 1673 (1994); see also Glenn Burgess, *The Divine Right of Kings Reconsidered*, 107 Eng. Hist. Rev. 837, (1992) ("The idea that there was something particularly divine about kingship was one which went back at least to the earliest phases of medieval history.").
15. Sir Thomas Smith, De Republica Anglorum (1583), reprinted in *Sources and Debates in English History: 1485–1714*, at 7 (Newton Key and Robert Bucholz, eds., 2004).
16. Joyce Lee Malcolm, Introduction to 1 *The Struggle for Sovereignty: Seventeenth Century Political Tracts* xxxv–xxxvi (Joyce Lee Malcolm, ed., 1999).
17. James I, TRUE LAW, supra note 11, at 51.
18. *Id.* at 62. Though knowledgeable about

188

the Bible, James ignored God's warning to the children of Israel about how they would be treated by an earthly king: "He will take your sons and make them serve with his chariots and horses, and they will run in front of his chariots. Some he will assign to the commanders of thousands and commanders of fifties, and others to plow his ground and reap his harvest, and still others to make weapons of war and equipment for his chariots. He will take your daughters to be perfumers and bakers. He will take the best of your fields and vineyards and olive groves and will give them to his attendants." 1 Samuel 8:11-15. Undoubtedly, many of James' subjects would find the passage as an accurate description of the reign of the Stuarts. Thomas Paine, during the American Revolution, picked up on this when lambasting the evils of monarchy. See Thomas Paine, Common Sense (1776), reprinted in *Paine and Jefferson on Liberty* 36-37 (Lloyd S. Kramer, ed., 1990).

19. James I, *True Law*, supra note 11, at 62.
20. *Id.* at 66.
21. *Id.*
22. *See id.* at 75.
23. *Id.* at 77.
24. The version I rely on here contains four translated chapters from the original work. Jean Bodin, *On Sovereignty* (Julian H. Franklin. ed., 1992) (1576).
25. See *Black's Law Dictionary* 971 (6th ed. 1991) (describing sovereignty as "[t]he supreme, absolute, and uncontrollable power by which any independent state is governed"). Bodin defined sovereignty as "the highest power of command." Bodin, supra note 24, at 1. Power subject to obligations or conditions was not truly sovereign power. *Id.* at 8.
26. Jeffrey Goldsworthy, *The Sovereignty of Parliament* 17 (1999).
27. Bodin, supra note 24, at 4.
28. *Id.* at 46.
29. *Id.* at 58-59.
30. *Id.* at 51 ("To speak more strictly, law is the command of the sovereign affecting all the subjects in general, or dealing with general interests....").
31. *Id.* at 2.
32. *Id.*
33. *Id.*
34. *Id.* at 104.
35. *Id.* at 3.
36. *Id.* at 89.
37. *Id.* at 13 ("But as for divine and natural laws, every prince on earth is subject to them, and it is not in their power to contravene them unless they wish to be guilty of treason against God."). Natural law is a difficult term to define. Perhaps one of the best descriptions comes from Peter J. Stanlis: "Natural Law was an emanation of God's reason and will, revealed to all mankind. Since fundamental moral laws were self-evident, all normal men were capable through unaided 'right reason' of perceiving the differences between moral right and wrong. The natural law was an eternal, unchangeable, and universal ethical norm or standard, whose validity was independent of man's will: therefore, at all times, in all circumstances and everywhere it bound all individuals, races, nations, and governments." Peter J. Stanlis, *Edmund Burke and the Natural Law* 7 (1986). See also Stanlis, supra, at 251-54.

38. Bodin, supra note 24, at 39.
39. *Id.* at 46.
40. R.R. Palmer and Joel Colton, *A History of the Modern World* 79 (1978).
41. Summerville has gone so far as to describe the church as "the king's ministry of propaganda." Summerville, supra note 13, at 10.
42. The Act of Supremacy (1534), reprinted in A.G. Dickins and Dorothy Carr, *The Reformation in England* 65 (1982).
43. *Id.*
44. An Homily against Disobedience and Wylful Rebellion (1570), reprinted in David Wootton, *Divine Right and Democracy* 94 (2003).
45. *Id.*
46. *Id.*
47. *Id.* at 95; see also Edmund S. Morgan, *Inventing the People* 18 (1988); Burgess, supra note 14, at 841 (noting that divine right theory "rule[d] out the possibility that the people could resist or actively disobey their kings").
48. Homily against Disobedience and Wylful Rebellion (1570), reprinted in Wootton, supra note 44, at 98.
49. William Goodwin, A Sermon Preached Before the Kings Most Excellent Maiestie at Woodstoke (1614), reprinted in 1 Malcolm, supra note 16, at 38 (emphasis omitted). For the scriptural basis of this admonition, see 1 Samuel 26:23, where David, even though Saul was delivered into his hands, refused to "lay a hand on the Lord's anointed."
50. William Goodwin, A Sermon Preached Before the Kings Most Excellent Maiestie at Woodstoke (1614), reprinted in 1 Malcolm, supra note 16, at 40.
51. *Id.* at 41-42 (emphasis omitted).
512. Roger Maynwaring, Religion and Alegiance (1627), reprinted in 1 Malcolm, supra note 16, at 59.
53. *Id.* at 63.
54. Roger Maynwaring, Religion and Alegiance (1627), reprinted in 1 Malcolm, supra note 16, at 64. James I went so far as to call himself a "god." "Kings are justly called gods for that they exercise a manner or resemblance of divine power upon earth, for if you will consider

the attributes to God you shall see how they agree in the person of a king." James I, Speech to Parliament (1610), reprinted in *The Stuart Constitution 1603–1688* at 12 (J.P. Kenyon, ed., 1986).

55. James I and VI, A Speech to the Lords and Commons of the Parliament at White-Hall (1610), reprinted in Wootton, supra note 44, at 108.

56. Mark A. Kishlansky, *The Rise of the New Model Army* 11–12 (1983) [hereinafter Kishlansky, *New Model*].

57. Sir Dudley Carleton, Speech to the House of Commons (1626), reprinted in Kenyon, supra note 54, at 45.

58. The Earl of Salisbury, Speech to Parliament (1610), reprinted in Kenyon, supra note 54, at 11.

59. Donald W. Hanson, *From Kingdom to Commonwealth* 156 (1970).

60. Conrad Russell, *The Crisis of Parliaments* 38 (1971).

61. Kishlansky, *Monarchy Transformed*, supra note 12, at 56.

62. James Whitelocke, Speech on Impositions (1610), reprinted in Kenyon, supra note 54, p. 61.

63. *Id.*

64. Goldsworthy, supra note 26, at 96.

65. *Id.* at 24.

66. William Blackstone, 1 *Commentaries* *143 ("But it is certain that long before the introduction of the Norman language into England, all matters of importance were debated and settled in the great councils of the realm.").

67. 1 Winston S. Churchill, *A History of the English Speaking Peoples: The Birth of Britain* 173–74 and 274 (1956) [hereinafter Churchill, *Birth of Britain*].

68. George O. Sayles, *The King's Parliament of England* 21 (1974).

69. *Id.* at 24.

70. *Id.* at 26. Of course, this does not mean that no conflicts arose. The rebellion against King John and his acceptance of the Great Charter demonstrate that the great tenants-in-chief would fight for their rights or interests if the King exceeded his authority.

71. Churchill, *Birth of Britain*, supra note 67, at 216.

72. See generally, Arthur Hogue, *Origins of the Common Law* 149–65 (1966) (discussing the reforms of Henry II and the development of the various royal courts).

73. Sayles, supra note 68, at 40.

74. *Id.* at 48.

75. Churchill, *Birth of Britain*, supra note 67, at 270–71.

76. Maurice Powicke, *The Thirteenth Century 1216–1307*, at 145–46 (1962).

77. Sayles, supra note 68, at 48.

78. Members of Parliament were representatives of the entire kingdom, not one particular area. See S.B. Chrimes, *English Constitutional Ideals in the Fifteenth Century* 131 (1966).

79. Goldsworthy, supra note 26, at 29. According to Hanson, "from 1327 onwards [the commons] were always summoned to parliament." Hanson, supra note 59, at 168.

80. Hanson, supra note 59, at 168–69. See also Norman F. Cantor, *The English: A History of Politics and Society to 1760*, at 231 (1967).

81. Thomas G. Barnes, Introduction to Coke's "Commentary on Littleton," in *Law, Liberty, and Parliament: Selected Essays on the Writings of Sir Edward Coke* 1, 17 (Alan D. Boyer, ed., 2004).

82. Goldsworthy, supra note 26, at 39. See also William A. Morris, Introduction to *The English Government at Work 1327–1336*, at 27 (James F. Willard and William A. Morris, eds., 1940) ("Parliament was more often an agency to suggest means of obtaining justice than a court to give judgment."). However, we must also remember that when describing themselves in the Act of Succession, the Lords and Commons were "this High Court of Parliament." Succession Act (1604), reprinted in Tanner, supra note 4, at 11.

83. Sayles, supra note 68, at 115.

84. Hanson, supra note 59, at 184.

85. Sayles, supra note 68, at 132–33.

86. *Id.* at 134.

87. Miller, supra note 6, at 48.

88. *Id.* at 116.

89. The Form of Apology and Satisfaction (1604), reprinted in Kenyon, supra note 54, at 30.

90. *Id.* at 31.

91. *Id.*

92. *Id.*

93. *Id.*

94. *Id.* at 32.

95. *Id.*

96. James I, Speech at the Prorogation of Parliament (1604), reprinted in Kenyon, supra note 54, at 37.

97. *Bate's Case* (1606), reprinted in Kenyon, supra note 54, at 55.

98. *Id.*

99. Debate in Committee on the Commons Petition of Right (1610), reprinted in Kenyon, supra note 54, at 38.

100. Commons Petition (1621), reprinted in Kenyon, supra note 54, at 40.

101. *Id.* at 41.

102. King's Letter to the Speaker (1621), reprinted in Tanner, supra note 4, at 279.

103. The Commons Protestation (1621), reprinted in Kenyon, supra note 54, at 42.

104. Small landholders who refused to pay were impressed into military service and sent to fight on the Continent. See Catherine Drinker Bowen, *The Lion and the Throne* 478 (1957). For a history of the forced loan, see Richard Crust, *Charles I, the Privy Council, and the Forced Loan*, 24 J. Brit. Stud. 208, 209–212 (1985).
105. See generally, *Black's Law Dictionary* 491 (6th ed. 1991).
106. *The Five Knights Case* (1627), reprinted in Kenyon supra note 54, at 97.
107. Sir Edward Coke, Speech in Parliament (1628), reprinted in 3 *The Selected Writings of Sir Edward Coke* 1227 (Steve Sheppard, ed. 2003).
108. *Id.* at 1244.
109. *Id.*
110. *Id.* at 1246
111. *Id.* at 1258.
112. *Id.* at 1251.
113. *Id.* at 1263.
114. See Notes of a Bill Brought in by Sir Edward Coke to Secure the Liberties of the Subject (1628), reprinted in *The Constitutional Documents of the Puritan Revolution 1625–1660*, at 65 (Samuel Rawson Gardiner, ed. 1906) [hereinafter Gardiner, *Constitutional Documents*].
115. Petition of Right (1628), reprinted in *From Magna Carta to the Constitution* 19 (David L. Brooks, ed. 1993).
116. *Id.*
117. *Id.* at 19–20.
118. *Id.* at 20.
119. *Id.*
120. *Id.*
121. *Id.*
122. *Id.* at 21.
123. *Id.*
124. *Id.* at 22.
125. *Id.*
126. Christopher Hibbert, *Charles I* 102 (2007).
127. The House of Commons, though not involved in the Duke's death, certainly blamed him for the military situation and many of the King's high-handed uses of prerogative power. See generally, Lockyer, *The Early Stuarts*, supra note 9, at 274–75.
128. See L.J. Reeve, *The Legal Status of the Petition of Right*, 29 Hist. J. 257, 262–63 (1986).
129. Miller, supra note 6, at 28–29.
130. The Remonstrance against Tonnage and Poundage (1628), reprinted in Gardiner, *Constitutional Documents*, supra note 114, at 71.
131. See A.G. Dickens, *The English Reformation* 368 (1993) (describing the Church of England as Calvinist in its theology).
132. See R.C. Sproul, *What Is Reformed Theology?* (1997).

133. R.C. Sproul, *Willing to Believe* 125–43 (1997).
134. Protestation of the House of Commons (1629), reprinted in Gardiner, *Constitutional Documents*, supra note 114, at 81–82.
135. The King's Declaration (1629), reprinted in Gardiner, *Constitutional Documents*, supra note 114, at 95.
136. Lockyer, supra note 9, at 283.
137. For a general discussion of ship money, see Lacy Baldwin Smith, *This Realm of England 1399 to 1688*, at 225 [hereinafter Smith, *This Realm*]; Lockyer, supra note 9, at 284–86.
138. Specimen of the First Writ of Ship-Money (1634), reprinted in Gardiner, *Constitutional Documents*, supra note 114, at 105.
139. Smith, *This Realm*, supra note 137, at 225.
140. For a full discussion of the legal arguments presented, see Richard L. Noble, *Lions or Jackals? The Independence of the Judges in* Rex v. Hampden, 14 Stan. L. Rev. 711 (1962).
141. Bowen, supra note 104, at 479.
142. *Rex v. Hampden* (1638), reprinted in Kenyon, supra note 54, at 101.
143. *Id.* at 102–03.
144. *Id.* at 105.
145. Henry Parker, *The Case of Shipmony Briefly Discoursed* (1640), reprinted in 1 Malcolm, supra note 16, at 109.
146. Laud's apologia (1637), reprinted in Kenyon, supra note 54, at 147.
147. The Scottish National Covenant (1638) reprinted in Gardiner, *Constitutional Documents*, supra note 114, at 127.
148. *Id.* at 129.
149. *Id.* at 133.
150. Rather than seeing the Scots as a danger, many applauded them for standing up to Charles and saw the Scottish army as deliverers. Churchill, *New World*, supra note 4, at 213.
151. Pym's Speech on Grievances (1640), reprinted in Kenyon, supra note 54, at 184.
152. *Id.* at 185.
153. While issues of political liberty certainly animated the people, one should not give short shrift to the religious disputes of the 1630s. See G.P. Gooch, *English Democratic Ideas* 89 (1959) ("It is hardly too much to say that two-thirds of the speeches and pamphlets ... between the meeting of Parliament and the breach with the king in 1642 ... deal with the question of the Church.").
154. Pym's Speech on Grievances (1640), reprinted in Kenyon, supra note 54, at 185–86.
155. *Id.* at 187.
156. *Id.* at 188.
157. *Id.*

Chapter 2

1. The Triennial Act (1641), reprinted in *The Stuart Constitution 1603–1688* at 197 (J.P. Kenyon, ed., 1986).

2. The Act against Dissolving the Long Parliament without Its Own Consent (1641), reprinted in *The Constitutional Documents of the Puritan Revolution, 1625–1660*, at 158 (Samuel Rawson Gardiner, ed. 1906) [hereinafter Gardiner, *Constitutional Documents*].

3. The Grand Remonstrance (1641), reprinted in Kenyon, supra note 1, at 216.

4. Henrietta Maria quoted in Christopher Hibbert, *Charles I*, at 176 (2007).

5. The Nineteen Propositions (1642), reprinted in Kenyon, supra note 1, at 222. According to Gooch, the Nineteen Propositions provided "a scheme of government ... in which the crown was reduced to the place it holds in the Constitution to-day." G.P. Gooch, *English Democratic Ideas* 91 (1959).

6. The orders given to the first commander of parliamentary forces, the Earl of Essex, "directed him to 'rescue' the King and princes, if necessary by force, from the evil counselors into whose power they had fallen." 2 Winston S. Churchill, *A History of the English Speaking Peoples: The New World* 232 (1956) [hereinafter Churchill, *New World*]; see also Edmund S. Morgan, *Inventing the People* 30, 35 (1988).

7. Michael Mendle, *Henry Parker and the English Civil War* 86 (1995).

8. Anonymous, Touching the Fundamental Laws (1643), reprinted in 1 *The Struggle for Sovereignty: Seventeenth Century Political Tracts* 268 (Joyce Lee Malcolm, ed., 1999).

9. *Id.* at 272–73.

10. *Id.* at 274.

11. *Id.* at 275.

12. William Ball, The Rule of a Free-born People (1646), reprinted in 1 Malcolm, supra note 8, at 289.

13. *Id.* at 290.

14. *Id.* at 296.

15. See generally, Diane Purkiss, *The English Civil War* 416–23 (2006) (describing the development of the NMA).

16. The Self-Denying Ordinance (1645), reprinted in Gardiner, *Constitutional Documents*, supra note 2, at 287.

17. In the words of the Earl of Essex: "If we should beat the king ninety-nine times and he beats us once we should all be hanged." Essex quoted in Rebecca Fraser, *The Story of Britain* 344 (2005).

18. Mark A. Kishlansky, *The Rise of the New Model Army* 180 (1979) [hereinafter, Kishlansky, *New Model*].

19. From a Solemn Engagement of the Army (1647), reprinted in *Puritanism and Liberty: Being the Army Debates (1647–9) from the Clarke Manuscripts with Supplementary Documents* 401 (A.S.P. Woodhouse, ed., 1965).

20. *Id.* at 403.

21. From a Representation of the Army (1647), reprinted in Woodhouse, supra note 19, at 404.

22. *Id.* at 406.

23. *Id.* at 407.

24. Antonia Fraser, *Cromwell* 208 (1973) [hereinafter Fraser, *Cromwell*] .

25. Churchill, *New World*, supra note 6, 286–87; Purkiss, supra note 15, at 511-31 (describing Digger experiments).

26. See Gooch, supra note 5, at 119–40; see also G.E. Aylmer, Introduction to *The Levellers in the English Revolution* 9–55 (G.E. Aylmer, ed. 1975).

27. For a biography of Lilburne, see Pauline Gregg, *Free-Born John* (2000).

28. See, e.g., Richard Overton, An Appeal from the Commons to the Free People (1647), reprinted in Woodhouse, supra note 19 at 323.

29. See Gregg, supra note 27, at 162.

30. Richard Overton, An Appeal from the Commons to the Free People (1647), reprinted in Woodhouse, supra note 19, at 334.

31. See Barbara Taft, *The Council of Officers' Agreement of the People*, 28 Hist. J. 169, 170 (1985) (noting that the Levellers "had no more confidence in an unrestricted parliament than in a supreme king").

32. John Lilburne, The Free-man's Freedom Vindicated (1646), reprinted in Woodhouse, supra note 19, at 317.

33. Richard Overton, An Appeal from the Commons to the Free People (1647), reprinted in Woodhouse, supra note 19, at 327.

34. An Agreement of the People, reprinted in Woodhouse, supra note 19, at 444.

35. *Id.* See also Taft, supra note 31, at 180 (observing that the prohibitions of the Agreement were of paramount concern to the Levellers).

36. Commons' Resolutions (1649), reprinted in Kenyon, supra note 1, at 292.

37. *Id.*

38. *Id.*

39. Introduction, *The Trial of Charles I*, at 6 (David Lagomarsino and Charles J. Wood, eds. 1989).

40. The Ordinance for the King's trial... (1649), reprinted in Lagomarsino and Wood, supra note 39, at 17.

41. See Sean Kelsey, *Politics and Procedure in the Trial of Charles I*, 22 Law & Hist. Rev. 1, 3–4 (2004).

42. The Act Erecting a High Court of Justice for the King's Trial (1649), reprinted in Gar-

diner, *Constitutional Documents*, supra note 2, at 357.
43. *Id.*
44. *Id.*
45. Geoffrey Robertson, *The Tyrannicide Brief* 10 (2005).
46. The Charge Against the King (1649), reprinted in Gardiner, *Constitutional Documents*, supra note 2, at 372.
47. *Id.*
48. Trial of the King (1649), reprinted in Lagomarsino and Wood, supra note 39, at 65.
49. Robertson, supra note 45, at 157.
50. Trial of the King (1649), reprinted in Lagomarsino and Wood, supra note 39, at 75.
51. *Id.*
52. Robertson, supra note 45, at 173–74.
53. Act Appointing a Council of State (1649), reprinted in Gardiner, *Constitutional Documents*, supra note 2, at 381.
54. Cromwell quoted in Fraser, *Cromwell*, supra note 24, at 420.
55. Conrad Russell, *The Crisis of Parliaments* 389 (1971).
56. Fraser, *Cromwell*, supra note 24, at 433–34.
57. *Id.* at 448–49.
58. The Instrument of Government (1653), reprinted in Gardiner, *Constitutional Documents*, supra note 2, at 405.
59. *Id.* at 405.
60. *Id.* at 406.
61. *Id.* at 416.
62. Instructions to the major-generals (1655), reprinted in Kenyon, supra note 1, at 322.
63. *Id.* at 323.
64. Fraser, *Cromwell*, supra note 24, at 359.
65. Charles II, The Declaration of Breda (1660), reprinted in Kenyon, supra note 1, at 331.
66. *Id.*
67. Antonia Fraser, *Royal Charles* 184 (1979) [hereinafter Fraser, *Royal Charles*].
68. Over the course of his reign, Charles II had 12 illegitimate children born from seven women. *Id.* at 411.
69. *Id.* at 275–76; Mark Kishlansky, *A Monarchy Transformed* 245–46 (1996) [hereinafter Kishlansky, *Monarchy Transformed*].
70. The Declaration of Indulgence (1672), reprinted in Kenyon, supra note 1, at 382.
71. *Id.*
72. *Id.* at 383.
73. For a study of absolutism in France, see David Parker, *The Making of French Absolutism* (1983).
74. Richard Ollard, *The Image of the King: Charles I and Charles II* 103–04 (1979).
75. The most shameful was the perjury of Titus Oates that led to the witch hunt of the Popish Plot. Fraser, *Royal Charles*, supra note 67, at 355–63.
76. For a brief account of Bloody Mary, see Stephen J. Nichols, *The Reformation* 88–92 (2007). Considering that Catholics made up a very small percentage of the English population, a full-scale return to Rome was unlikely by the 1680s.
77. Joyce Lee Malcolm, Introduction to 2 *The Struggle for Sovereignty: Seventeenth Century Political Tracts* xx (Joyce Lee Malcolm, ed., 1999). See also W.A. Speck, *Reluctant Revolutionaries* 34 (1988).
78. "To their own eventual undoing, the Tories proclaimed, as an essential element of the Anglican Church teaching, the doctrine of divine hereditary right of kings, coupled with the doctrine of non-resistance in its extreme form." G.M. Trevelyan, *The English Revolution 1688–1689*, at 20 (1966).
79. John Brydall, The Absurdity Of that New devised State-Principle, reprinted in 2 Malcolm, supra note 77, at 777.
80. *Id.* at 787.
81. *Id.* (emphasis omitted).
82. Anonymous, The Arraignment of Co-Ordinate Power (1683), reprinted in 2 Malcolm, supra note 77, at 800 (emphasis omitted).
83. Sir Robert Filmer, *Patriarcha* 8–11 (1680).
84. *Id.* at 23.
85. *Id.* at 28–29.
86. *Id.* at 31.
87. *Id.* at 36.
88. *Id.* at 42.
89. *Id.* at 46.
90. *Id.* at 57.
91. Algernon Sydney, *Discourses Concerning Government* 55 (Thomas G. West, ed., 1990).
92. *Id.* at 56.
93. *Id.* at 57.
94. *Id.* at 70.
95. *Id.*
96. *Id.*
97. Gilbert Burnet, An Enquiry Into the Measures of Submission to the Supream Authority (1688), reprinted in 2 Malcolm, supra note 77, at 851.
98. *Id.* at 856.
99. *Id.* at 851.
100. *Id.*
101. *Id.*
102. Frasier, *Royal Charles*, supra note 67, at 407.
103. J.R. Western, *Monarchy and Revolution* 70 (1972); John Miller, *The Glorious Revolution* 3 (1983) [hereinafter Miller, *Glorious Revolution*].
104. Frasier, *Royal Charles*, supra note 67, at 389.

105. Miller, *Glorious Revolution*, supra note 103, at 3.
106. For a good biography of James II, see John Miller, *James II* (1978).
107. Speck, supra note 77, at 43; Robert H. George, *The Financial Relations of Louis XIV and James II*, 3 J. Mod. Hist. 392 (1931) (describing James' request for French financial aid so he could "retain his independence of parliament, and ... prevent it from meddling in foreign affairs").
108. John A. Garraty and Peter Gay, eds., *The Columbia History of the World* 565 (1972).
109. Michael Barone, *Our First Revolution* 93–94 (2007)
110. *Godden v. Hales*, King's Bench, (June 16, 1686), reprinted in Kenyon, supra note 1, at 404.
111. Declaration of Indulgence (1687), reprinted in Kenyon, supra note 1, at 389.
112. Miller, *Glorious Revolution*, supra note 103, at 10; J.R. Jones, *Country and Court* 234–35 (1979).
113. The Invitation to William (1688), reprinted in *The Eighteenth Century Constitution* 8 (E.N. Williams, ed. 1977).
114. *Id.*
115. Western, supra note 103, at 247; Trevelyan, supra note 78, at 54; Richard S. Key, *William III and the Legalist Revolution*, 32 Conn. L. Rev. 1645, 1647–48 (2000).
116. William's Declaration (1688), reprinted in Miller, *Glorious Revolution*, supra note 103, at 106–07. For a discussion of the effect of the Declaration and other uses of propaganda, see Tony Claydon, *William III's Declaration of Reasons and the Glorious Revolution*, 39 Hist. J. 87 (1996).
117. William summons an assembly (1688), reprinted in Williams, supra note 113, at 17.
118. The address of the assembly (1688), reprinted in Williams, supra note 113, at 18.
119. The Bill of Rights (1689), reprinted in Williams, supra note 113, at 27. This broad wording meant different things to Whigs and Tories. "For the Tories, the abdication consisted of James' flight, the vacancy of his physical absence. For the Whigs, the abdication consisted of his violation of fundamental laws, the vacancy of his failure to fulfill the contract between ruler and ruled." Kishlansky, *Monarchy Transformed*, supra note 69, at 285.
120. Barone, supra note 109, at 193.
121. See Gerald Straka, *The Final Phase of Divine Right Theory in England, 1688–1702*, 77 Eng. Hist. Rev. 638, 642 (1962) (arguing that while hereditary right was rejected, the Anglican Church nonetheless believed that William had become king through a providential election).
122. Bernard Bailyn, *The Ideological Origins of the American Revolution* 201 (1967); Trevelyan, supra note 78, at 130; Speck, supra note 77, at 140–41; Jeffrey Goldsworthy, *The Sovereignty of Parliament* 236 (1999); Jeffrey Goldsworthy, *Is Parliament Sovereign? Recent Challenges to the Doctrine of Parliamentary Sovereignty*, 3 N.Z. J. Pub. & Int'l L. 7, 12 (2005). But see Arthur L. Goodhart, *The Rule of Law and Absolute Sovereignty*, 106 U. Pa. L. Rev. 943 (1958); Lord Cooke of Thornton, *The Myth of Sovereignty*, 3 N.Z. J. Pub. & Int'l L. 39 (2005); Stuart Lakin, *Debunking the Idea of Parliamentary Sovereignty: The Controlling Factor of Legality in the British Constitution*, 28 Oxford J. Legal Stud. 709 (2008).
123. William Blackstone, 1 *Commentaries* *149.
124. *Id.* at 150; see also *id.* at 151 ("Like three distinct powers in mechanics, they jointly impel the machine of government in a direction different from what either, acting by themselves, would have done....").
125. *Id.* at 156 (emphasis added).
126. *Id.*
127. *Id.*; see also Edward Countryman, *The American Revolution* 18 (1985).
128. William Blackstone, 1 *Commentaries* *157.
129. A.V. Dicey, *Introduction to the Study of the Law of the Constitution* 9 (Liberty Fund 1982) (1882); see also John V. Jezierski, *James Wilson and Blackstone on the Nature and Location of Sovereignty*, 32 J. Hist. Ideas 95, 103 (1971) ("In short, Parliament was able to do everything that was not naturally impossible, and what it did no authority on earth was able to undo.").
130. John Locke, *Seconnd Treatise of Government* 77–78 (C.B. Macpherson, ed., Hackett Publishing Co. 1980) (1690) (emphasis omitted). Locke wrote after the Glorious Revolution and his *Second Treatise* was an effort to justify the events of 1688–89. For a pithy summary of Locke's thoughts on sovereignty, see James A Gardner, *Consent, Legitimacy and Elections: Implementing Popular Sovereignty under the Lockean Constitution*, 52 U. Pitt. L. Rev. 189, 201–05 (1990).
131. William Blackstone, 1 *Commentaries* *157.
132. *Id.*

Chapter 3

1. William Blackstone, 1 *Commentaries* *105.
2. Martin Howard, Jr., A Letter From a Gentleman at Halifax (1765), reprinted in *Tracts of the American Revolution* 67 (Merrill Jensen, ed., 1967) [hereinafter Jensen, *Tracts*].

3. See Thomas J. DiLorenzo, *How Capitalism Saved America* 43–48 (2004); 1 Clarence B. Carson, *A Basic History of the United States* 112–19 (1992); John C. Miller, *Origins of the American Revolution* 4 (1966) [hereinafter Miller, *Origins*].

4. For overviews of the Navigation Acts, see generally Miller, *Origins*, supra note 3, at 4–7; Edward Countryman, *The American Revolution* 11 (1985); Lawrence Henry Gipson, *The Coming of the Revolution* 22–25 (1954). For a discussion of the economic impact on the colonies, see Roger L. Ransom, *British Policy and Colonial Growth: Some Implications of the Burden from the Navigation Acts*, 28 J. Econ. Hist. 427 (1968) (noting that the effect of the acts was not so great as to warrant colonial secession); Larry Sawers, *The Navigation Acts Revisited*, 45 Econ. Hist. Rev. 262 (1992) (arguing that the acts imposed substantial burdens on America).

5. Gordon S. Wood, *The American Revolution* 14–15 (2002) [hereinafter Wood, *American Revolution*].

6. *Id.* at 13.

7. Edmund S. Morgan, *Inventing the People* 145 (1988).

8. Paul Johnson, *A History of the American People* 94–96 (1997).

9. Wood, *American Revolution*, supra note 5, at 5.

10. Samuel Elliot Morison, *The Oxford History of the American People* 181 (1965) [hereinafter Morison, *Oxford History*]; see also Forrest McDonald, *Novus Ordo Seclorum* 1 (1985) (observing that at the time of the Revolution "probably more Americans had participated directly in government at one level or another than had any other people on earth").

11. Don Cook, *The Long Fuse* 3 (1995).

12. Jack P. Greene, *Peripheries and Center: Constitutional Development in the Extended Polities of the British Empire and the United States 1607–1788*, at 63 (1986).

13. *Id.* at 64.

14. Miller, *Origins*, supra note 3, at 30.

15. Morgan, *Inventing the People*, supra note 7, at 134.

16. Bruce Lancaster and J.H. Plumb, eds., *The American Heritage Book of the Revolution* 50 (1958).

17. Carson, supra note 3, at 141.

18. Johnson, supra note 8, at 104.

19. Carson, supra note 3, at 141.

20. Johnson, supra note 8, at 104; Merrill Jensen, Commentary to Randolph G. Adams, *Political Ideas of the American Revolution* 7 (1958).

21. Countryman, supra note 4, at 43.

22. Wood, *American Revolution*, supra note 5, at 17.

23. *Id.*

24. *Id.* at 18.

25. W.E. Woodward, *A New American History* 126–27 (1938).

26. *Id.* at 126.

27. Johnson, supra note 8, at 132.

28. Miller, *Origins*, supra note 3, at 48.

29. *Id.* at 89. There are 20 shillings in one pound.

30. Cook, supra note 11, at 58.

31. George III, From the Royal Proclamation on North America (1763), reprinted in *Sources and Documents Illustrating the American Revolution* 2 (Samuel Elliot Morrison, ed., 1965) [hereinafter Morrison, *Sources and Documents*].

32. The Sugar Act (1764), reprinted in *Prologue to Revolution: Sources and Documents on the Stamp Act Crisis, 1764–1766*, at 4–8 (Edmund S. Morgan, ed., 1959) [hereinafter Morgan, *Sources*].

33. *Id.* at 4.

34. For a history of the Molasses Act of 1733, see Albert B. Southwick, *The Molasses Act—Source of Precedents*, 8 Wm. & Mary Q. 389 (1951); Richard B. Sheridan, *The Molasses Act and the Market Strategy of the British Sugar Planters*, 17 J. Econ. Hist. 62 (1957).

35. The Act also increased the duties on various luxury items such as linen, silk, and wine. The Sugar Act (1764), reprinted in Morgan, *Sources*, supra note 32, at 5.

36. Wood, *American Revolution*, supra note 5, at 27.

37. The Stamp Act (1765), reprinted in Morgan, *Sources*, supra note 32, at 35–43.

38. Morison, *Oxford History*, supra note 10, at 185.

39. Morgan, *Sources*, supra note 32, at 35–43.

40. For a discussion of the role and evolution of these courts, see Bernard Knollenberg, *Growth of the American Revolution* 276–77 (2003).

41. John Phillip Reid, *Constitutional History of the American Revolution: Abridged* 5–12 (1995).

42. See generally, Larry D. Kramer, *The People Themselves* 9–34 (2004); see also Centinel, Letter VIII, reprinted in *The Anti-Federalists: Selected Writings and Speeches* 91 (Bruce Frohnen, ed. 1999) (explaining that the colonists opposed the Stamp Act and Townshend duties because they were "precedents whereon the superstructure of arbitrary sway was to be reared").

43. The Boston Tea Party — typically treated as a mere tax protest — is a good example of the importance of precedent. Though the Tea Act of 1773 reduced the price of tea, the colonists felt compelled to take action to prevent Parliament from setting a revenue precedent. Under commercial rules, a ship entering a colonial har-

bor was not permitted to leave without offloading its cargo. If the tea was offloaded a duty would be paid; if it was not offloaded within twenty days the cargo would be seized by customs officials who would retain a portion of the merchandise to satisfy the duty. The Tea Party occurred on the nineteenth day that the ships bearing tea had been in the harbor. The colonists destroyed the tea so it could not be seized by the customs officials and the duty technically "paid" to form the basis of a precedent. See Kramer, supra note 42, at 18; John Phillip Reid, *Constitutional History of the American Revolution: The Authority to Tax* 130–32 (1987) [hereinafter Reid, *Authority to Tax*].

44. Pauline Maier, *From Resistance to Revolution* 62 (1991).

45. Hiller B. Zobel, *The Boston Massacre* 27 (1970).

46. Christopher Hibbert, *Redcoats and Rebels* 3 (1990).

47. See Mark Puls, *Samuel Adams* 52 (2006).

48. See, e.g., E. Stanly Godbold, Jr., and Robert H. Woody, *Christopher Gadsden and the American Revolution* 58–59 (1982) (describing riots and mob activity in South Carolina).

49. Henry Mayer, *A Son of Thunder* 78–80 (1991).

50. The French Traveler's Account (1765), reprinted in Morgan, *Sources*, supra note 32, at 46.

51. The Maryland Resolves (1765), reprinted in Morgan, *Sources*, supra note 32, at 53.

52. See James Otis, The Rights of the British Colonies Asserted and Proved (1764), reprinted in Jensen, *Tracts*, supra note 2, at 25 (arguing that the knowledge problem could be solved if only the colonists received representation in Parliament).

53. The Resolutions as Printed in *The Journal of the House of Burgesses* (1765), reprinted in Morgan, *Sources*, supra note 32, at 48.

54. *Id*. See also James Wilson, Considerations on the Nature and Extent of the Legislative Authority of the British Parliament (1774), reprinted in 1 *Collected Works of James Wilson* 8 (Kermit L. Hall and Mark David Hall, eds., 2007) (discussing the doctrine of shared burdens).

55. Reid, *Authority to Tax*, supra note 43, at 239–40.

56. Morgan, *Inventing the People*, supra note 7, at 239–40; Daniel Dulany, Considerations on the Propriety of Imposing Taxes in the British Colonies for the Purpose of Raising a Revenue by Act of Parliament (1765), reprinted in Jensen, *Tracts*, supra note 2, at 95–96.

57. Daniel Dulany, Considerations on the Propriety of Imposing Taxes in the British Colonies for the Purpose of Raising a Revenue by Act of Parliament (1765), reprinted in Jensen, *Tracts*, supra note 2, at 95–96; Reid, *Authority to Tax*, supra note 43, at 87; Morgan, *Inventing the People*, supra note 7, at 239–40; Countryman, supra note 4, at 49.

58. The Connecticut Resolves (1765), reprinted in Morgan, *Sources*, supra note 32, at 55.

59. The Examination of Dr. Benjamin Franklin (1766), reprinted in Morgan, *Sources*, supra note 32, at 144.

60. The Role of William Pitt, reprinted in Morgan, *Sources*, supra note 32, at 136 ("It is my opinion, that this kingdom has no right to lay taxes upon the colonies…. Taxation is no part of the governing or legislative power. The taxes are a voluntary gift and grant of the Commons alone…. When, therefore, in this House we give and grant, we give and grant what is our own. But in an American tax, what would we do?"); Johnson, supra note 8, at 133–34.

61. Wood, *American Revolution*, supra note 5, at 29–30. For a general discussion of mob activity in colonial America, see Countryman, supra note 4, at 74–104 (1985). See also Gordon Wood, *A Note on Mobs*, 23 Wm. & Mary Q. 635 (1966).

62. The Role of William Pitt, reprinted in Morgan, *Sources*, supra note 32, at 141.

63. The Declaratory Act (1766), reprinted in 27 *The Statutes at Large* 19–20 (Danby Pickering, ed., 1767).

64. See Gordon Wood, *Creation of the American Republic, 1776–1787*, at 349 (1998) [hereinafter Wood, *Creation*].

65. Bernard Bailyn, *The Ideological Origins of the American Revolution* 204 (1967).

66. James Otis, The Rights of the British Colonies Asserted and Proved (1764), reprinted in Jensen, *Tracts*, supra note 2, at 19.

67. *Id*. at 21.

68. *Id*. at 21 and 28. See Michael Kammen, *Sovereignty and Liberty* 16 (1988) (observing that Otis was not prepared to embrace popular sovereignty when examining colonial rights).

69. Note, however, that the first volume of the *Commentaries* did not appear until 1765.

70. James Otis, The Rights of the British Colonies Asserted and Proved (1764), reprinted in Jensen, *Tracts*, supra note 2, at 28 and 32–33.

71. See Richard A. Samuelson, *The Constitutional Sanity of James Otis: Resistance Leader and Loyal Subject*, 61 Rev. Pol. 493, 505 (1999) ("In early 1765 Otis realized that British constitutionalism, with or without natural rights, did not necessarily favor the American side of the imperial dispute, and did not necessarily guarantee the rights of Englishmen."); James R. Ferguson, *Reason in Madness: The Political*

Thought of James Otis, 36 Wm. & Mary Q. 194, 198 (1979) ("But he would attempt to move in these new directions while preserving the major assumptions of inherited tradition that justified the absolute power of Parliament.").

72. Bailyn, supra note 65, at 209.

73. See, e.g., Richard Bland, *An Inquiry into the Rights of the British Colonies* (1766), reprinted in Jensen, *Tracts*, supra note 2, at 117.

74. John Dickinson, Letters From a Farmer in Pennsylvania to the Inhabitants of these British Colonies (1768), reprinted in Jensen, *Tracts*, supra note 2, at 133.

75. See *id.*

76. See *id.*

77. Stephen Hopkins, The Rights of the Colonies Examined (1764), reprinted in Jensen, *Tracts*, supra note 2, at 49.

78. *Id.*

79. The Examination of Dr. Benjamin Franklin (1766), reprinted in Morgan, *Sources*, supra note 32, at 146.

80. William Hicks, The Nature and Extent of Parliamentary Power Considered (1768), reprinted in Jensen, *Tracts*, supra note 2, at 183–84.

81. Thomas Jefferson, A Summary View of the Rights of British America (1774), reprinted in Jensen, *Tracts*, supra note 2, at 256. For an excellent discussion of the Summary View, see David N. Mayer, *The Constitutional Thought of Thomas Jefferson* 28–37 (1994).

82. Thomas Jefferson, A Summary View of the Rights of British America (1774), reprinted in Jensen, *Tracts*, supra note 2 at 260; James Wilson made the same point in his writings. See James Wilson, Considerations on the Nature and Extent of the Legislative Authority of the British Parliament (1774), reprinted in 1 Hall, supra note 54, at 29.

83. Thomas Jefferson, A Summary View of the Rights of British America (1774), reprinted in Jensen, *Tracts*, supra note 2, at 263.

84. *Id.* at 268.

85. *Id.* at 276.

86. Joseph Galloway, A Plan of a proposed Union between Great Britain and the Colonies (1774), reprinted in *Colonial Origins of the American Constitution* 392 (Donald S. Lutz, ed., 1998).

87. *Id.* at 393.

88. *Id.* at 392.

89. *Id.*

90. The Declaration of Independence para. 3 (U.S. 1776).

91. *Id.* para. 16.

92. *Id.* para. 33. In his original draft, Jefferson made reference to breaking political connections with Parliament in an effort to accommodate those who thought that Parliament still had some power over the colonies. See Mayer, supra note 81, at 45. The final version simply stated that "all political connection between [the colonists] and the state of Great Britain is, and ought to be, totally dissolved." The Declaration of Independence para. 33 (U.S. 1776).

93. Novanglus, February 6, 1775, www.odur.let.rug.nl/~usa/P/ja2/writings/novan1.htm.

94. James Madison, "Mr. Madison's Report" to the Virginia Assembly, reprinted in 4 *The Debates in the Several State Conventions on the Adoption of the Federal Constitution* 562 (Jonathan Elliot, ed., 1885) [hereinafter, *Elliot's Debates*]; see also Akhil Reed Amar, *Anti-Federalists, The Federalist Papers, and the Big Argument for Union*, 16 Harv. J.L. & Pub. Pol'y 111, 111 (1993) ("The American Revolution, of course, was a revolution that had been fought not simply for freedom, but for localism."); Peter J. Stanlis, *British Views of the American Revolution: A Conflict over Rights of Sovereignty*, 11 Early Am. Lit. 191, 191 (1976) (describing the conflict as one over "the question of sovereignty over America."); Forrest McDonald, *States' Rights and the Union* 4 (2000) [hereinafter McDonald, *States' Rights*] (observing that "what broke apart the empire was an inability to agree on the locus and nature of sovereignty"); Bernard W. Sheehan, Foreword to Bernard Knollenberg, *Growth of the American Revolution* xv (2003) (noting that after the break with Britain the "colonial legislatures in effect functioned in the New World the way the British Parliament did in the old").

95. See Willi Paul Adams, *The First American Constitutions* 13 (1973) ("in 1774 and 1775, during the last phase of public debate before the outbreak of war, the colonial pamphleteers … once again proposed their idea of a number of equal parliaments under one crown as an alternative to the British parliament's claim of exclusive sovereignty.").

96. Scholars deny that the Americans were familiar with the Levellers and their efforts in the 1640s. See Morgan, *Inventing the People*, supra note 7, at 256.

97. Proclamation of the General Court (1776), reprinted in *The Popular Sources of Political Authority* 65 (Oscar and Mary Handlin, eds., 1966).

98. Virginia Declaration of Rights (1776), reprinted in 1 *The Founders' Constitution* 6 (Philip B. Kurland and Ralph Lerner, eds., 1987).

99. Horst Dippel, *The Changing Idea of Popular Sovereignty in Early American Constitutionalism: Breaking away from European Patterns*, 15 J. Early Repub. 21, 36 (1996) ("America's revolutionary elite which was largely responsible for the American constitutions had come to accept

the idea that, in the last resort, political legitimacy could only be derived from the people."); Hannah Arendt, *On Revolution* 156 (1975) (noting that the American revolutionaries eventually understood that "the seat of power ... was the people"); Alexander Hamilton, Remarks on an Act Granting to Congress Certain Imposts and Duties, February 15, 1787, *PAH* 4:75 (it is a "fundamental maxim of republican government that all power mediately or immediately, is derived from the consent of the people, in opposition to those doctrines of despotism which upheld the divine right of kings, or lay the foundations of government in force, conquest, or necessity").

100. See Lance Banning, *The Sacred Fire of Liberty* 443 n.30 (1995). This difference between ultimate sovereignty and legislative sovereignty is clearly expressed in the instruction given by the people of Mecklenburg, North Carolina, to their delegates to the provincial Congress:

1st. Political power is of two kinds, one principal and superior, and the other derived and inferior.

2nd. The principal supreme power is possessed by the people at large, the derived and inferior power by the servants which they employ.

3rd. Whatever persons are delegated, chosen, employed and intrusted by the people are their servants and can posses only derived and inferior power.

4th. Whatever is constituted and ordained by the principal supreme power can not be altered, suspended or abrogated by an other power, but by the same power that ordained may alter, suspend and abrogate its own ordinances.

5th. The rules whereby the inferior power is to be exercised are to be constituted by the principal supreme power, and can be altered, suspended and abrogated by the same and no other.

Instructions to the Delegates From Mecklenburg, North Carolina, to the Provincial Congress at Halifax (1776), reprinted in 1 Kurland and Lerner, supra note 98, at 56.

101. Adams, supra note 95, at 20 ("In Massachusetts the signal step was taken of formally separating the legislative activity and the task of creating a constitution."); Pauline Maier, *Ratification* 139 (2010) (describing the how Massachusetts "transformed popular sovereignty from a theory to a process"). But see Marc W. Kruman, *State Constitution Making in Revolutionary America* 15–33 (1997) (Massachusetts receives too much credit inasmuch as other states understood the constituent power and had elected special conventions to draft constitutions. The difference between Massachusetts and several other states is that the former submitted the constitution for popular ratification while the latter did not).

102. Elisha P. Douglas, *Rebels and Democrats* 188 (1955); R.R. Palmer, *The Age of Democratic Revolution* 222 (1959).

103. See, e.g., Pittsfield Memorial (1775), reprinted in Handlin, supra note 97, at 61–64.

104. Douglas, supra note 102, at 187–88.

105. The Call for a Convention (1779), reprinted in Handlin, supra note 97, at 402.

106. *Id.* at 403.

107. Report of the Committee appointed by the Town (1779), reprinted in Handlin, supra note 97, at 410.

108. *Id.* at 411.

109. Instructions of the Town of Sandisfield (1779), reprinted in Handlin, supra note 97, at 419.

110. See Proceedings of the Convention (1780), reprinted in Handlin, supra note 97, at 432.

111. Douglas, supra note 102, at 208–210.

112. The Constitution of 1780, reprinted in Handlin, supra note 97, at 441.

113. *Id.* at 443.

114. *Id.* at 444.

115. Gordon S. Wood, *Foreword: State Constitution-Making in the American Revolution*, 24 Rutgers L. J. 911, 911 (1993); see also, McDonald, *States' Rights*, supra note 94, at 8; Christina G. Fritz, *Alternative Visions of American Constitutionalism: Popular Sovereignty and the Early American Constitutional Debate*, 24 Hastings Const. L.Q. 287, 290 and 333 (1997).

116. Adams, supra note 95, at 20. But see Kruman, supra note 101, at 33.

117. Thomas Jefferson, *Notes on the State of Virginia* (1781–85), reprinted in *The Complete Jefferson* 652 (Saul K. Padover, ed. 1943).

118. Articles of Confederation, art. II.

119. Report of Proceedings (1787), reprinted in 1 *Elliot's Debates* 118.

120. *Federalist No. 46*, at 237 (James Madison) (Gary Wills, ed., 1982).

121. James Madison, *Notes of the Debates in the Federal Convention of 1787* at 33 (1987) [hereinafter, Madison, *Notes*].

122. *Id.* at 70.

123. *Id.* at 348.

124. *Id.* at 350–51.

125. U.S. Const. art. VII.

126. See Davison M. Douglas, *Foreword: The Legacy of St. George Tucker*, 47 Wm. & Mary L. Rev. 1111, 1111–16 (2006) (providing background on Tucker and discussing his influence).

127. St. George Tucker, On Sovereignty and

Legislature, reprinted in *View of the Constitution with Selected Writings* 20 (Clyde N. Wilson, ed., 1999).
128. *Id.* at 19.
129. James Wilson, Comparison of the Constitution of the United States, with that of Great Britain (1790), reprinted in Hall, supra note 54, at 718–19.
130. *Id.* at 728.

Chapter 4

1. See *The Stuart Constitution 1603–1688* at 75 (J.P. Kenyon, ed., 1986); Harold Berman, *The Origins of Historical Jurisprudence*, 103 Yale L.J. 1651, 1674 (1994).
2. James I, Speech to the judges in Star Chamber (1616), reprinted in Kenyon, supra note 1, at 84.
3. *Id.* at 85.
4. The Declaration of Independence para. 12 (U.S. 1776).
5. Gordon S. Wood, *Empire of Liberty* 400 (2009).
6. Gordon S. Wood, *Creation of the American Republic 1776–1787*, at 157 (1969) [hereinafter Wood, *Creation*].
7. *Id.*
8. *Id.* at 155.
9. *Id.*
10. Jackson Turner Main, *The Sovereign States, 1775–1783*, at 188–89 (1973).
11. *Id.* at 192.
12. *Id.* at 193.
13. Willi Paul Adams, *The First American Constitutions* 267 (1980).
14. M.J.C. Vile, *Constitutionalism and the Separation of Powers* 23 (2d ed. 1998).
15. *Id.* at 151. See also Alexander Hamilton, Remarks on an Act Granting to Congress Certain Imposts and Duties, February 15, 1787, *PAH* 4:75 (part of the executive power is "to execute and interpret the laws"); Anonymous, Four Letters on Interesting Subjects (1776), reprinted in *The Origins of the American Constitution* 6 (Michael Kammen, ed., 1986) (observing that "the judicial power is only a branch of the executive").
16. Thomas Jefferson, *Notes on the State of Virginia* 120 (William Peden, ed., W.W. Norton & Co., 1982) [hereinafter Jefferson, *Notes*]. Even Blackstone in the 1760s recognized the three branches as distinct and counseled for a general separation. See William Blackstone, 1 *Commentaries* *259–60.
17. Massachusetts Constitution (1780), reprinted in 1 *The Founders' Constitution* 13–14 (Philip B. Kurland and Ralph Lerner, eds., 1987).
18. As late as the 1780s, courts "were generally considered an undifferentiated segment of the executive branch." William E. Nelson, Marbury v. Madison: *The Origins and Legacy of Judicial Review* 34 (2000) [hereinafter Nelson, *Origins*].
19. Marc W. Kruman, *State Constitution Making in Revolutionary America* 41 (1997) ("When framers expressed these fears of government, they meant all government, including the legislature.").
20. Adams, supra note 13, at 269–70.
21. Wood, *Creation*, supra note 6, at 161; Akhil Reed Amar, *America's Constitution* 234 (2005) ("Juries were, in a sense, the people themselves, tried-and-true embodiments of late-eighteenth-century republican ideology.") [hereinafter Amar, *America's Constitution*].
22. Forrest McDonald, *Novus Ordo Seclorum* 85 & 289 (1985); Clay S. Conrad, *Jury Nullification* 45–63 (1998).
23. Conrad, supra note 22, at 23.
24. Pauline Gregg, *Free-Born John* 300 (1961)
25. *Id.* at 301–02.
26. William E. Nelson, *Americanization of Common Law* 28–29 (1975) [hereinafter Nelson, *Americanization*]; Wilfred J. Ritz, *Rewriting the History of the Judiciary Act of 1789*, at 30 (Wythe Holt and L.H. LaRue, eds., 1990). Also noteworthy is the jury charge of Chief Justice John Jay in *Georgia v. Brailsford*, 3 U.S. (3 Dall.) 1, 4 (1794) (instructing the jury that it had dominion over "the law as well as the fact in controversy"). See also TJ to Abbé Arnoux, July 19, 1789, *PTJ* 15:282–83 (recognizing that the jurors may "take upon themselves to judge the law as well as the fact").
27. Nelson, *Americanization*, supra note 26, at 28–29.
28. TJ to Edmund Pendleton, August 26, 1776.
29. See Federal Farmer, Letter XV (1788), reprinted in *The Anti-Federalists: Selected Writings and Speeches* 275 (Bruce Frohnen, ed. 1999); A Maryland Farmer, Essay IV (1788), reprinted in Frohnen, supra, at 591 (describing the jury as the democratic branch of the judiciary that is charged with combating "usurpations, which silently undermine the spirit of liberty").
30. Main, supra note 10, at 171–72.
31. *Id.*
32. For a discussion of the case and history of the Two Penny Act, see Henry Mayer, *A Son of Thunder* 58–66 (1991); Bernhard Knollenberg, *Origin of the American Revolution 1759–1766*, at 43–53 (2002).
33. McDonald, supra note 22, at 85; see also Matthew P. Harrington, *Judicial Review Before John Marshall*, 72 Geo. Wash. L. Rev. 51, 53 (2003) ("Indeed, the judiciary was held in rather

low esteem throughout the colonial period, and thus the idea that judges would ultimately determine the constitutionality of legislation would have been unthinkable."); Amar, *America's Constitution*, supra note 21, at 207 (noting that aside from Connecticut and Rhode Island where the colonists named their own judges, "only three of the other fifty men who signed the Declaration of Independence held notable positions on the colonial bench").

34. For a discussion of the councils of revision of Pennsylvania, New York, and Vermont, see Charles Grove Haines, *The American Doctrine of Judicial Supremacy* 73–87 (1932). See also Anonymous, Four Letters on Interesting Subjects (1776), reprinted in Kammen, supra note 15, at 8 (suggesting that a constitution should have a provision for convening a jury every seven or so years to enquire "if any inroads have been made in the Constitution").

35. McDonald, supra note 22, at 153.
36. *Id.*
37. James T. Barry III, *The Council of Revision and the Limits of Judicial Power*, 56 U. Chic. L. Rev. 235, 245 (1989).
38. McDonald, supra note 22, at 153.
39. *Id.*
40. See, e.g., *Federalist No. 22*, at 109 (Alexander Hamilton) (Gary Wills, ed., 1982) (citing "the want of a judiciary" as a significant defect in the Articles of Confederation).
41. William Blackstone, 1 *Commentaries* *259.
42. James Madison, *Notes of the Debates in the Federal Convention of 1787*, at 32 (1966) (1840) [hereinafter Madison, *Notes*].
43. *Id.*
44. *Id.* at 317–18.
45. *Id.* at 318.
46. *Id.*
47. *Id.* at 71.
48. *Id.* at 319.
49. *Id.* at 73.
50. *Id.* at 72.
51. U.S. Const. art III, § 1.
53. See generally, Wythe Holt, "*To Establish Justice*": *Politics, the Judiciary Act of 1789, and the Invention of the Federal Courts*, 6 Duke L. J. 1421 (1989).
53. *Id.* at 32. The proposed council could also review congressional decisions to nullify state law. Under the Virginia Plan, Congress would have had the power to review state legislation.
54. *Id.* at 61.
55. *Id.* at 338.
56. *Id*
57. *Id.* at 340.
58. *Id.* at 61.
59. *Id.* at 79.
60. *Id.* at 338.
61. *Id.* at 81.
62. *Id.* at 341.
63. *Id.* at 336.
64. *Id.* at 337.
65. *Id.*
66. McDonald, supra note 22, at 254.
67. Sylvia Snowiss, *Judicial Review and the Law of the Constitution* 60 (1990).
68. Madison, *Notes*, supra note 42, at 31.
69. *Id.* at 44.
70. *Id.* at 88.
71. *Id.*
72. *Id.*
73. *Id.* at 89.
74. *Id.* at 305.
75. *Id.*
76. *Id.* at 305–06 (internal quotation marks omitted).
77. *Id.* at 390.
78. McDonald, supra note 22, at 255.
79. Madison, supra note 42, at 626.
80. *Federalist No. 78*, at 395 (Alexander Hamilton) (Gary Wills, ed., 1982).
81. *Id.*
82. *Id.*
83. *Id.*
84. *Id.* at 394.
85. *Id.*; see also *Federalist No. 16*, at 79 (Alexander Hamilton) (Gary Wills, ed., 1982) (noting that judges would pronounce unconstitutional acts of Congress void).
86. *Federalist No. 78*, at 395 (Alexander Hamilton) (Gary Wills, ed., 1982).
87. *Id.*
88. *Id.* at 393.
89. *Id.* at 394.
90. *Id.* at 395.
91. *Id.* at 396. See also George W. Carey, *In Defense of the Constitution* 132–38 (1995) (discussing Hamilton's understanding of judicial review).
92. 3 *Elliot's Debates* 553.
93. *Id.* at 325.
94. *Id.*
95. *Id.* at 548.
96. An Old Whig, Essay II (1787), reprinted in Frohnen, supra note 29, at 325; see also Address of the Minority of the Pennsylvania Convention (1787), reprinted in Frohnen, supra note 29, at 545 (complaining that "[t]here is not even a declaration of RIGHTS to which the people may appeal for the vindication of their wrongs in the court of justice").
97. 2 *Elliot's Debates* 196.
98. 4 *Elliot's Debates* 156.
99. *Id.*
100. See U.S. Const. art. I, § 10.
101. *Id.*
102. Remarks of James Wilson in the Pennsylvania Convention to Ratify the Constitution

of the United States (1787), reprinted in 1 *Collected Works of James Wilson* 203 (Kermit L. Hall and Mark David Hall, eds., 2007).

103. *Id*. at 204.

104. For a more thorough discussion of multiple state cases from the Founding era, see William J. Watkins, Jr., *Popular Sovereignty, Judicial Supremacy, and The American Revolution: Why the Judiciary Cannot Be the Final Arbiter of Constitutions*, 1 Duke J. Const. L.& Pub. Pol'y 159, 215–44 (2006).

105. For the ease of the reader, pinpoint citations will be to the Westlaw citation: 1782 WL 5 (Va. Nov. 1782). For a general discussion of judicial review as it developed in Virginia, see Margaret V. Nelson, *A Study of Judicial Review in Virginia 1789–1928*, at 31–39 (1947).

106. *Caton*, 1782 WL at *1.

107. *Id*.

108. *Id*.

109. Edmund Pendleton, Account of "The Case of the Prisoners," in 2 *The Letters and Papers of Edmund Pendleton 1734–1803*, at 426 (David John Mays, ed., 1967) [hereinafter *Pendleton Papers*].

110. *Caton*, 1782 WL at *2.

111. *Id*.

112. *Id*. at *1.

113. Edmund Pendleton, Account of "The Case of the Prisoners," in *Pendleton Papers*, supra note 109, at 417.

114. *Caton*, 1782 WL at *1.

115. Randolph quoted in William Michael Treanor, *The Case of the Prisoners and the Origins of Judicial Review*, 143 U. Pa. L. Rev. 491, 512 (1994).

116. *Caton*, 1782 WL at *2.

117. Tucker quoted in Treanor, supra note 115, at 523.

118. *Id*. at 523.

119. Edmund Pendleton, Account of "The Case of the Prisoners," in *Pendleton Papers*, supra note 109, at 418.

120. *Caton*, 1782 WL at *2.

121. *Id*.

122. *Id*.

123. *Id*. at *3.

124. *Id*. at *4.

125. *Id*. at *7.

126. *Id*.

127. *Id*.

128. *Id*. at *9.

129. *Id*. at * 9.

130. Edmund Pendleton, Account of "The Case of the Prisoners," in *Pendleton Papers*, supra note 109, at 426.

131. *Id*. at *2. This judge was Peter Lyons.

132. 1 *The Law Practice of Alexander Hamilton* 296 (Julius Goebel, Jr., ed. 1964) [hereinafter Goebel, *Law Practice*].

133. *Id*. at 289.

134. *Id*.

135. Statement of Benjamin Waddington (1784), reprinted in Goebel, *Law Practice*, supra note 132, at 317.

136. *Id*.

137. Goebel, *Law Practice*, supra note 132, at 290 and 315.

138. *Id*.

139. *Id*.

140. *Id*. at 292–93.

141. Ron Chernow, *Alexander Hamilton* 196–97 (2004).

142. This is an unreported decision. However, the various briefs and opinions are found in Goebel, *Law Practice*, supra note 132.

143. *Id*. at 299.

144. *Id*. at 357.

145. *Id*. at 382.

146. 8 Co. Rep.107a (1610).

147. *Id*. at 114a.

148. Harold J. Cook, *Against Common Right and Reason:* The College of Physicians v. Dr. Thomas Bonham, in *Law, Liberty, and Parliament* 127, 130 (Allen D. Boyer, ed. 2004).

149. Allen Dillard Boyer, *"Understanding, Authority, and Will": Sir Edward Coke and the Elizabethan Origins of Judicial Review*, 39 B.C. L. Rev. 43, 82 (1997).

150. J.W. Gough, *Fundamental Law in English Constitutional History* 33 (1961).

151. See Elizabeth Read Foster, *The Procedure of the House of Commons Against Patents and Monopolies, 1621–1624*, in Boyer, *Law, Liberty, and Parliament*, supra note 148, at 302, 302–27.

152. Harold J. Cook, *Against Common Right and Reason:* The College of Physicians v. Dr. Thomas Bonham, in Boyer, *Law, Liberty, and Parliament*, supra note 148, at 127, 142.

153. *Dr. Bonham's Case*, 8 Co. Rep. at 114a.

154. See Gough, supra note 150, at 40.

155. William Blackstone, 1 *Commentaries* *91.

156. Sir Edward Coke, Of the High and Most Honourable Court of Parliament, in 2 *The Selected Writings and Speeches of Sir Edward Coke* 1133 (Steve Sheppard, ed., 2003).

157. Opinion of the Mayor's Court (1784), reprinted in Goebel, *Law Practice*, supra note 132, at 393.

158. *Id*.

159. See *id*. at 396.

160. *Id*. at 396–97.

161. *Id*. at 402.

162. *Id*. at 408.

163. *Id*. at 417.

164. *Id*. at 415.

165. *Id*. at 393–419.

166. *Id*.

167. Melancton Smith, *et al.*, Pamphlet on *Ruters v. Waddington* (1784), reprinted in *The Anti-Federalist Writings of the Melancton Smith Circle* 8 (Michael P. Zuckert and Derek A. Webb, eds. 2009).
168. *Id.*
169. *Id.*
170. *Id.*
171. Larry D. Kramer, *The People Themselves* 66 (2004).
172. *Kamper v. Hawkins*, 3 Va. (1 Va. Cas.) 20 (1793). For the ease of the reader, pinpoint citations will be to the Westlaw citation: 1793 WL 248, *1 (Va. Nov. 16, 1793). For a good discussion on the background to *Kamper*, see Charles T. Cullen, St. George Tucker and Law in Virginia 120–26 (Ph.D. Dissertation 1971).
173. *Black's Law Dictionary* 540 (6th ed. 1991).
174. *Kamper*, 1793 WL. at *2.
175. *Id.*
176. *Id.* at *5.
177. *Id.* at *2.
178. *Id.* at *4.
179. *Id.*
180. *Id.*
181. *Id.*
182. *Id.*
183. See *id.*
184. *Id.* at *5.
185. *Id.*
186. *Id.* at *6.
187. *Id.*
188. *Id.*
189. *Id.*
190. *Id.*
191. *Id.*
192. *Id.* at 7
193. *Id.*
194. *Id.*
195. *Id.* at *8.
196. *Id.* at *10.
197. *Id.*
198. *Id.*
199. *Id.* at *11.
200. *Id.* at *12.
201. *Id.* at *11.
202. *Id.* at*14.
203. *Id.* at *15.
204. *Id.*
205. *Id.*
206. *Id.* at *16.
207. *Id.*
208. *Id.*
209. *Id.*
210. *Id.*
211. *Id.*
212. *Id.* at *21.
213. *Id.* at *22.
214. *Id.* at *23.
215. *Id.* at *24.
216. *Id.*
217. *Id.*
218. Advertisement in Report of a case ... 84 (A. M'Kenzie & Co. 1794).
219. *Id.*
220. *Caton*, 1782 WL at *7.

Chapter 5

1. 5 U.S. (1 Cranch) 137 (1803).
2. Cliff Sloan and David McKean, *The Great Decision* xvii (2009).
3. See, e.g., *Cooper v. Aaron* 358 U.S. 1, (1958); *Baker v. Carr*, 369 U.S. 186, 211 (1962) (describing the Court as the "ultimate interpreter of the Constitution"); *United States v. Navarro-Vargas*, 408 F.3d 1184, 1203 n.24 (9th Cir. 2005) (en banc) (noting that *Marbury* "established [the Supreme Court] as the final arbiter of the Constitution") (internal quotation marks omitted); Charles Grove Haines, *The American Doctrine of Judicial Supremacy* 202 (1932) (observing that John Marshall's opinion in *Marbury* "declared that the Supreme Court was the final interpreter and guardian of the federal Constitution."); Warren E. Burger, *It Is So Ordered* 54 (1995) (arguing that *Marbury* established "judicial supremacy").
4. American Bar Association Task Force on Presidential Signing Statements and the Separation of Powers Doctrine, *Report & Recommendation* 23 (2006) ("Definitive constitutional interpretations are entrusted to an independent and impartial Supreme Court, not a partisan and interested President. That is the meaning of *Marbury v. Madison*.").
5. Here we must be careful to distinguish between "judicial review" and "judicial supremacy." Judicial review, as used throughout this chapter is the "[p]ower of courts to review decisions of another department or level of government." *Black's Law Dictionary* 593 (6th ed. 1991). Judicial supremacy holds that courts are the final arbiters of the meaning of the Constitution.
6. See Saikrishna B. Prakash and John Yoo, *The Origins of Judicial Review*, 70 U. Chi. L. Rev. 887, 890 (2003) (distinguishing between judicial review and judicial supremacy and noting that many critics falsely attack the former when they aim for the latter). For an example of a critic conflating judicial review and judicial supremacy, see Mark R. Levin, *Men in Black* 23–33 (2005).
7. What I describe as a "party" in no way resembles the modern version of a political party. As Dumas Malone has observed, "[t]he term 'party' was something of a misnomer at a

time when the affiliations of members of Congress were not a matter of record, and the organization was rudimentary from our point of view. Parties were loose groupings without legal sanction or formal leadership." Dumas Malone, *Jefferson the President: Second Term 1805–1809* xiii (1974).

8. Gordon S. Wood, *Revolutionary Characters* 16–17 (2006).

9. TJ to JM, Dec. 17, 1796, *The Republic of Letters* 2:950; see also TJ to JA, December 28, 1796, reprinted in *The Adams-Jefferson Letters* 262–63 (Lester J. Cappon, ed., 1959) (congratulating Adams on his succession to the presidency). This letter was never received by Adams because James Madison advised Jefferson that the letter would serve no useful purpose.

10. Joseph J. Ellis, *Founding Brothers* 184 (2000).

11. See generally, William J. Watkins, Jr., *Reclaiming the American Revolution: The Kentucky and Virginia Resolutions and Their Legacy* 28–54 (2004).

12. 1 Stat. 596, 596 (1798).

13. 1 Stat. 570, 571 (1798).

14. John Mitchell Mason, The Voice of Warning to Christians on the Ensuing Election of a President (1800), reprinted in *Political Sermons of the American Founding Era 1730–1805*, at 1452 (1991). For a general discussion of the rhetoric aimed at Jefferson, see Dumas Malone, *Jefferson and the Ordeal of Liberty* 479–83 (1962).

15. Bernard A. Weisberger, *America Afire* 229 (2000).

16. AH to John Jay, May 7, 1800, *PAH* 24: 465.

17. Ron Chernow rightly calls this pamphlet "a petulant survey of John Adams's life and presidency" and "an extended tantrum in print." Ron Chernow, *Alexander Hamilton* 622–23 (2004).

18. Stanley Elkins and Eric McKitrick, *The Age of Federalism* 744 (1993).

19. U.S. Const. art II, § 1.

20. TJ to JM, December 19, 1800, *The Republic of Letters* 2:1154.

21. U.S. Const. art. II, § 1.

22. Horatius, The Presidential Knot (1801), reprinted in Bruce Ackerman, *The Failure of the Founding Fathers* 272–73 (2005).

23. Ackerman offers a compelling argument that Marshall was "Horatius." See Ackerman, supra note 22, at 45–54.

24. JM to TJ, January 10, 1801, *The Republic of Letters* 2:1157.

25. *Id.* at 1158.

26. *Id.*

27. JA to John Jay, December 19, 1800, *WJA* 9:91.

28. 1 Stat. 73 (1789). For a history of the Judiciary Act of 1789, see Wilfred J. Ritz, *Rewriting the History of the Judiciary Act of 1789* (1990).

29. For a concise summary of the provisions of the Judiciary Act of 1789, see Henry J. Bourguignon, *The Federal Key to the Judiciary Act of 1789*, 46 S.C. L. Rev. 647, 668–70 (1995).

30. 2 Stat. 90 (1801).

31. JA to John Marshall, February 4, 1801.

32. 2 Stat. 103 (1801).

33. Sloan and McKean, supra note 2, at 53.

34. Fisher Ames, Falkland No. 2, reprinted in *Liberty and Order* 276 (Lance Banning, ed., 2004).

35. Gouverneur Morris to Robert R. Livingston, February 20, 1801, 3 *The Life of Gouverneur Morris* 154 (Jared Sparks, ed. 1832).

36. TJ to John Dickinson, December, 19, 1801.

37. Ackerman, supra note 22, at 132–33. For a good discussion of the various "midnight judges," see Kathryn Turner, *The Midnight Judges*, 109 U. Pa. L. Rev. 494 (1961).

38. TJ to Justice William Johnson, June 12, 1823.

39. Thomas Jefferson, First Annual Message to Congress (1801), reprinted in *The Complete Jefferson* 390 (Saul K. Padover, ed. 1943).

40. *Id.* at 392.

41. A rule to show cause is a "rule commanding a party to appear and show cause why he should not be compelled to do the act required, or why the object of the rule should not be enforced." *Black's Law Dictionary* 926 (6th ed. 1991).

42. Annals of Congress, 7th Congress, 1st sess., p. 25, January 8, 1802.

43. *Id.*

44. *Id.*

45. U.S. Const. art. III, § 1.

46. *Id.*

47. Annals of Congress, 7th Congress, 1st sess., p. 28, January 8, 1802.

48. Annals of Congress, 7th Congress, 1st sess., p. 60, January 13, 1802.

49. Annals of Congress, 7th Congress, 1st sess., p. 58, January 12, 1802.

50. Annals of Congress, 7th Congress, 1st sess., p. 33, January 8, 1802.

51. *Id.* at 38.

52. *Id.* at 36.

53. Annals of Congress, 7th Congress, 1st sess., p. 66, January 12, 1802.

54. 2 Stat. 156 (1802).

55. Richard E. Ellis, *The Jeffersonian Crisis* 60 (1971) [hereinafter Ellis, *Jeffersonian Crisis*]; Jean Edward Smith, *John Marshall* 310 (1996).

56. *Stuart v. Laird*, 5 U.S. (1 Cranch) 299, 309 (1803).
57. 5 U.S. (1 Cranch) 137 (1803).
58. Ackerman, supra note 22, at 136.
59. *Marbury*, 5 U.S. (1 Cranch) at 137–43 (recounting the argument concerning executive privilege).
60. *Id.* at 142–43 (testimony of the clerks).
61. *Id.* at 143–45 (testimony of Lincoln and argument about privilege).
62. *Id.* at 146 (description of Marshall's affidavit).
63. *Id.*
64. *Id.*
65. *Id.* at 159.
66. *Id.* at 162.
67. *Id.*
68. *Id.* at 157.
69. *Id.* at 165–66.
70. *Id.* at 166.
71. *Id.* at 163.
72. *Id.*
73. *Id.* at 168.
74. *Id.* at 173; see also Judiciary Act of 1789, ch. 20, § 13, 1 Stat. 80.
75. U.S. Const. art. III, § 2.
76. *Id.*
77. Akhil Amar, *America's Constitution* 232 (2005).
78. 5 U.S. (1 Cranch) at 176.
79. *Id.*
80. *Id.*
81. *Id.*
82. *Id.* at 177.
83. *Id.*
84. *Id.*
85. *Id.*
86. *Id.*
87. *Id.* at 178.
88. *Id.* at 177.
89. *Id.* at 178. At another point, the Court says that when adjudicating an issue, the Constitution must be "looked into." *Id.* at 179.
90. *Id.* at 178.
91. *Id.*
92. *Id.* at 179.
93. U.S. Const. art. III, § 3.
94. 5 U.S. (1 Cranch) at 179.
95. *Id.*
96. *Id.*
97. See Charles F. Hobson, *The Great Chief Justice* 66 (1996) ("Marshall no doubt drew on *Kamper* and other precedents in writing *Marbury*....") [hereinafter Hobson, *Great Chief Justice*].
98. Ellis, *Jeffersonian Crisis*, supra note 55, at 66.
99. Jack N. Rakove, *The Legacy of Chief Justice John Marshall: Judicial Power in the Constitutional Theory of James Madison*, 43 Wm & Mary L. Rev, 1513, 1513 (2002).
100. TJ to William Johnson, June 12, 1823, *WTJ* 12:259; see also 2 George Lee Haskins and Herbert A. Johnson, *History of the Supreme Court of the United States* 193 (1981) (noting that the first portions of the *Marbury* opinion were more important to the Court than the judicial review section). As Charles F. Hobson, the editor of *The Papers of John Marshall*, has noted: "For nearly a century after the decision, *Marbury* was almost always cited in connection with issues of original jurisdiction and mandamus, not as authority to pronounce laws unconstitutional." Charles F. Hobson, *John Marshall, the Mandamus Case, and the Judiciary Crisis, 1801–1805*, 72 Geo. Wash. L. Rev. 289, 289 (2003). Akhil Amar has also observed that "not until the late twentieth century did the Court begin to describe itself as the 'ultimate interpreter' of the Constitution." Amar, supra note 77, at 215.
101. But see Haskins and Johnson, supra note 100, at 195–96.
102. TJ to William Johnson, June 12, 1823, *WTJ* 12:259.
103. See Hobson, *Great Chief Justice*, supra note 97, at 67 (observing that Marshall's "defense of judicial review fully agreed with the 'departmental' theory of interpretation" espoused by Jefferson and others); David E. Engdahl, *John Marshall's "Jeffersonian" Concept of Judicial Review*, 42 Duke L.J. 279, 280 (1992).
104. TJ to Abigail Adams, September 11, 1804, reprinted in Lester J. Cappon, ed., *The Adams-Jefferson Letters* 279 (1959).
105. *Id.*
106. *Id.*
107. *Id.*
108. *Id.* Jefferson was not the only president to adhere to departmentalism. See Keith E. Whittington, *Presidential Challenges to Judicial Supremacy and the Politics of Constitutional Meaning*, 33 Polity 367, 369 (2001).
109. Thomas Jefferson, Draft of First Annual Message to Congress, December 8, 1801 LC.
110. TJ to Spencer Roane, September 6, 1819, *WTJ* 12:136.
111. Thomas Jefferson, *Notes on the State of Virginia* 221 (William Peden, ed., 1954).
112. TJ to William Johnson, June 12, 1823, *WTJ* 12:259; see also Larry Kramer, *Understanding* Marbury v. Madison, 148 Proc. Am. Phil. Soc. 14, 15 (2004) ("[I]nterpreting and enforcing constitutional law were tasks delegated explicitly and authoritatively to the people themselves. Power finally to say what the constitution meant rested literally with the community at large — understood as a collective body capable of action independent from government.").

Chapter 6

1. See, e.g., Sandra Day O'Connor, *The Threat to Judicial Independence*, October 1, 2006, opinionjournal.com.
2. Raoul Berger, *Government by Judiciary* 324 (1997).
3. Keith L. Dougherty, *Collective Action under the Articles of Confederation* 18 (2001).
4. *Federalist* No. 46, at 237 (James Madison) (Gary Wills, ed., 1982).
5. *Federalist* No. 45, at 236 (James Madison) (Gary Wills, ed., 1982).
6. See generally, *Federalist* No. 17, at 80–81 (Alexander Hamilton) (Gary Wills, ed., 1982).
7. *Federalist* No. 51, at 264 (James Madison) (Gary Wills, ed., 1982).
8. Brutus, Essay I (1787), reprinted in *The Anti-Federalists: Selected Writings and Speeches* 377 (Bruce Frohnen, ed. 1999).
9. See generally, M.E. Bradford, *A Better Guide than Reason* 29–57 (1994).
10. See Jason A. Adkins, *Lincoln's Constitution Revisited*, 36 N. Ky. L. Rev. 211, 213 (2009) (observing that Lincoln believed the Constitution implemented natural rights principles).
11. The best example of this is the Civil Rights Act of 1866. See An Act to Protect All Persons in the United States in Their Civil Rights, and Furnish Means of Their Vindication, reprinted in *American Legal History* (Kermit L. Hall, et al., eds., 1991). The current version of this Act is 42 U.S.C.A. § 1981.
12. Magna Carta, chapter 39 (emphasis added).
13. Hugo LaFayette Black, *A Constitutional Faith* 33 (1968).
14. Sir Edward Coke, 2 Institutes § 46, reprinted in 2 *Selected Writings of Sir Edward Coke* 849 (Steve Sheppard, ed. 2003). But see George W. Carey, *In Defense of the Constitution* 164 (1995) (challenging whether "due process" can be equated with "law of the land").
15. Sir Edward Coke, 2 Institutes § 46, reprinted in Sheppard, supra note 14, at 849.
16. William Blackstone, 1 *Commentaries* *130.
17. AH, Remarks on an Act for Regulating Elections, February 6, 1787, *PAH* 4:35.
18. St. George Tucker, View of the Constitution, reprinted in *View of the Constitution and Selected Writings* 148 (Clyde N. Wilson, ed., 1999).
19. William Rawle, *A View of the Constitution* 114 (Walter D. Kennedy and James R. Kennedy, eds. 1993).
20. Henry Abraham, *Freedom and the Court* 122 (1988).
21. 2 Parker Crim. Rep. 490 (N.Y. Ct. App. 1856).
22. Jacob Howard, Speech on H.R. No. 127 (1866), reprinted in *The Reconstruction Amendments' Debates* 219 (Alfred Avins, ed., 1967).
23. *Id.* at 220.
24. John Bingham, Speech on H.R. No. 63 (1866), reprinted in Avins, supra note 22, at 157. Members of Congress realized that a great shift of power was underway. For example, Robert Hale of New York observed that "the tenor and effect of the Amendment proposed here by this committee is to bring about a more radical change in the system of the Government, to institute a wider departure from the theory upon which our fathers formed it than ever before was proposed in any legislative or constitutional assembly." John Hale, Speech on H.R. No. 63 (1866), reprinted in Avins, supra note 22, at 157. Andrew Rogers of New Jersey was more blunt: "When sifted from top to bottom it will be found to be the embodiment of centralization and the disenfranchisement of the States of those sacred and immutable State rights which were reserved to them by the consent of our fathers in our organic law." Andrew Rogers, Speech on H.R. No. 63, reprinted in Avins, supra note 22, at 150.
25. Quoted in Akhil Reed Amar, *America's Constitution* 387 (2005). For those delving into the incorporation argument further, a good start would be the concurring opinion of Justice Thomas in *McDonald v. Chicago*, 130 S. Ct. 3020 (2010) and the Appendix attached by Justice Black to his dissenting opinion in *Adamson v. California*, 332 U.S. 46 (1947).
26. 83 U.S. 36 (1873).
27. *Id.* at 77.
28. *McDonald*, 130 S. Ct. 3020 at 3061 (Thomas, J., concurring).
29. 198 U.S. 45 (1905). For recent scholarship challenging that idea that the *Lochner* Court was activist in its use of substantive due process, see David N. Mayer, *Liberty of Contract* (2011).
30. 198 U.S. at 57.
31. 261 U.S. 525 (1923).
32. *Id.* at 544.
33. *Id.*
34. *Id.* at 558.
35. *Id.*
36. *Id.* at 559.
37. Franklin Delano Roosevelt, Message to Congress (1937), reprinted in 2 *Documents of American Constitutional & Legal History* 179 (Melvin I. Urofsky, ed., 1989).
38. *Id.*
39. *Id.* at 180.
40. *Id.*
41. 300 U.S. 379 (1937).
42. For arguments that the Court abandoned meaningful review of economic or social policy legislation, see Mayer, supra note 29, at 109.

43. 304 U.S. 144 (1938).
44. *Id.* at 153 n.4. This footnote is subject to varying interpretations. For a summary of those interpretations, see Felix Gilman, *The Famous Footnote Four: History of the* Carolene Products *Footnote*, 46 S. Tex. L. Rev. 163, 173–182 (2004).
45. 410 U.S. 113 (1973).
46. 128 S.Ct. 2641 (2008).
47. U.S. Const. amend. V.
48. *Godfrey v. Georgia*, 446 U.S. 420, 433 (1980) (Marshall, J., concurring); *Callins v. Collins*, 510 U.S. 1141 (1994) (Blackmun, J., dissenting).
49. See, e.g., 3 *Elliot's Debates* 111 and 447–48.
50. *Kennedy*, 128 S.Ct. at 2649.
51. *Id.* at 2650–51.
52. *Coker v. Georgia*, 433 U.S. 584, 598 (1977).
53. *Kennedy*, 128 S.Ct. at 2662.
54. *Id.* at 2664 (emphasis added).
55. See, e.g., Charles F. Hobson, *The Great Chief Justice* 70 (1996) ("With the obsolescence of the departmental theory and the collapse of rigid distinctions between law and politics, the modern Supreme Court is unabashedly understood to be a political institution whose decisions make policy in a way scarcely distinguishable from legislating."); Jesse H. Choper, *Judicial Review and the National Political Process* 55–56 (1980) ("The Supreme Court is involved in the political process in the sense that it participates in making public policy; it is not an organ of the political process in the sense that it is electorally responsible."); Paul D. Carrington and Roger C. Cramton, *Judicial Independence in Excess: Reviving the Judicial Duty of the Supreme Court*, 94 Cornell L. Rev. 587, 590 (2009) (describing the Court as a legislative institution that "sits chiefly to proclaim new law to govern future transactions and relations").
56. 704 F. Supp. 2d 921, 927 (N.D. Cal. 2010).
57. *Id.* at 932.
58. 539 U.S. 558, 571 (2003).
59. *Id.* at 577.
60. *Id.* at 574.
61. *Id.*
62. *Perry*, 704 F. Supp. 2d at 931.
63. *Id.* at 981.
64. *Id.* at 993.
65. *Id.*
66. *Id.* at 994.
67. *Griswold v. Connecticut*, 381 U.S. 479, 527 (1965) (Stewart, J., dissenting).
68. *Id.* at 520–51 (Black, J., dissenting). See also Thomas B. Griffith, *Was Bork Right About Judges?*, 34 Harv. J. L. & Pub. Pol'y, 157, 159 (2011) ("Rather than impose their own value determinations in every case, judges must derive, define, and apply generally applicable neutral principles gleaned from authoritative legal texts.")
69. *Griswold, 381 U.S.* at 521 (Black, J., dissenting).
70. *Id.*
71. The Bill of Rights (1689), reprinted in *From Magna Carta to the Constitution* 39 (David L. Brooks, ed. 1993).
72. Benjamin Wittes, *Conformation Wars* 41 (2006).
73. *Id.* at 38.
74. *Id.* at 39.
75. I do not mean to imply that there was no controversy over judicial nominations before the Warren Court. Eruptions date back to 1795 when the Senate rebuffed Washington's attempt to make John Rutledge chief justice. Other examples of controversy were the successful nomination of Louis Brandeis in 1916 and the unsuccessful nomination of John J. Parker in 1930. See generally, Henry J. Abraham, *Justices, Presidents, and Senators* (1999).
76. A Bill Proposing a Constitutional Amendment to Establish Limited Judicial Terms in Office: Hearings Before the Subcomm. on the Constitution, Federalism, and Property Rights of the Senate Comm. on the Judiciary, 105th Cong., 1st Sess. at 2 (1997) (Opening Statement of the Hon. John Ashcroft).
77. See generally, Mark Tushnet, *Taking the Constitution Away from the Courts* 129 and 177 (1999).
78. 347 U.S. 483 (1954).
79. *Id.* at 137.
80. See, e.g., *Munn v. Illinois*, 94 U.S. 113 (1877) (noting that under some circumstances due process will prohibit state regulation of property).
81. James B. Thayer, *The Origin and Scope of the American Doctrine of Constitutional Law*, 7 Har. L. Rev. 129, 144 (1893).
82. *Id.* at 135.
83. *Id.*
84. *Id.* at 142.
85. Sylvia Snowiss, *Judicial Review and the Law of the Constitution* 189–94 (1990).
86. *Marbury v. Madison*, 5 U.S. (1 Cranch) 137, 179 (1803).
87. *Id.* at 179.
88. *Id.*
89. See Stephen M. Griffin, The Age of *Marbury*: Judicial Review in a Democracy of Rights, in *Arguing* Marbury v. Madison (Mark Tushnet, ed., 2005) ("Yet the voiding power defended by Hamilton and Marshall is analytically distinct from judicial supremacy.").
90. Edmund Pendleton, The Danger Not Over (1801), reprinted in *Liberty and Order* 271 (Lance Banning, ed., 2004).

91. *Id.* at 273.
92. *Id.*
93. William J. Quirk, *Courts and Congress* 101 (2008).
94. *Id.* at 101; see also Tushnet, supra note 77, at 173 ("Judicial review may serve politicians' interests, not their constituents'. Political leaders often find judicial review a convenient way to hand off hard decisions to someone else.").
95. James Madison, *Notes of the Debates in the Federal Convention of 1787* at 79–80 (1987).
96. *Id.* at 338.
97. *Id.* at 337.
98. *Id.* at 340.
99. 3 U.S. (3Dall.) 1, 4 (1794).
100. See American Judicature Society, Judicial Section in the States Appellate and General Jurisdiction Courts (2008).
101. Michael DeBow, et al., *The Case for Partisan Judicial Elections*, 33 U. Tol. L. Rev. 393, 405 (2002) [hereinafter DeBow, *The Case*].
102. Sandra Day O'Connor, *The Essentials and Expendables of the Missouri Plan*, 74 Mo. L. Rev 479, 485 (2009) [hereinafter O'Connor, *The Essentials*].
103. Exec. Order No. 11972, 42 Fed. Reg. 9659 (1977).
104. *Id.*
105. Rachel Paine Caufield, *Reconciling the Judicial Ideal and the Democratic Impulse in Judicial Retention Elections*, 74 Mo. L. Rev. 573, 577 (2009) [hereinafter Caufield, *Reconciling the Judicial Ideal*].
106. DeBow, *The Case*, supra note 101, at 403.
107. O'Connor, *The Essentials*, supra note 102, at 494 (praising the Missouri Plan's contributions to judicial selection).
108. See Mallory Simpson, Iowa voters oust justices who made same-sex marriage legal, November 3, 2010, cnn.com.
109. DeBow, *The Case*, supra note 101, at 397.
110. *Id.* at 394.
111. Larry C. Berkson and Rachel Caufield, Judicial Selection in the United States: A Special Report 1 (2004).
112. *Id.* at 2.
113. O'Connor, *The Essentials*, supra note 102, at 486–87.
114. Theodore Roosevelt, Introduction to William L. Ransom, *Majority Rule and the Judiciary* 4–5 (1912).
115. Caufield, *Reconciling the Judicial Ideal*, supra note 105, at 573.
116. 28 U.S.C. § 371.
117. See Learned Hand, *The Bill of Rights* 73–74 (1958).
118. Willi Paul Adams, *The First American Constitutions* 249–51 (1973).
119. Articles of Confederation art. V.
120. James Madison, supra note 95, at 31.
121. *Id.* at 41.
122. Charles Pickering, *Supreme Chaos* 23 (2005) ("The living Constitution thrust the confirmation process into the culture war by moving the fight over hot-button social issues from the legislative branch to the judicial branch.").
123. U.S. Const. art. III, § 2.
124. *Id.*
125. 3 *Elliot's Debates* 559–60.
126. *Federalist No. 81*, p. 417 (Alexander Hamilton) (Bantam Books, ed., 1982).
127. 74 U.S. 506 (1868).
128. *Id.* at 514.
129. *Id.* at 515.
130. For a good discussion of scholarship aimed at limiting congressional authority over the federal courts, see John Eidsmoe, *The Article III Exceptions Clause: Any Exceptions to the Power of Congress to Make Exceptions?*, 19 Regent U. L. Rev. 95, 129–143 (2006).

Bibliography

Abraham, Henry. *Freedom and the Court* (New York: Oxford University Press, 1988).
_____. *Justices, Presidents, and Senators* (Rowman & Littlefield, 1999).
Ackerman, Bruce. *The Failure of the Founding Fathers* (Cambridge, Mass.: Harvard University Press, 2005).
Adams, Randolph G. *Political Ideas of the American Revolution* (New York: Barnes & Noble, 1958).
Adams, Willi Paul. *The First American Constitutions* (New York: Rowman & Littlefield, 1973).
Adkins, Jason A. *Lincoln's Constitution Revisited*, 36 N. Ky. L. Rev. 211 (2009).
Amar, Akhil Reed. *America's Constitution* (New York: Random House, 2005).
_____. *Anti-Federalists, The Federalist Papers, and the Big Argument for Union*, 16 Harv. J.L. & Pub. Pol'y 111 (1993).
Arendt, Hannah. *On Revolution* (New York: Viking, 1975).
Avins, Alfred, ed. *The Reconstruction Amendments' Debates* (Richmond, Va.: Virginia Commission on Constitutional Government, 1967).
Aylmer, G.E., ed. *The Levellers in the English Revolution* (Ithaca, N.Y.: Cornell University Press, 1975).
Bailyn, Bernard. *The Ideological Origins of the American Revolution* (Cambridge, Mass.: Harvard University Press, 1967).
Banning, Lance. *The Sacred Fire of Liberty* (Ithaca: N.Y.: Cornell University Press, 1995).
Barone, Michael. *Our First Revolution* (New York: Crown, 2007).
Berger, Raoul. *Government by Judiciary* (Indianapolis, Ind.: Liberty Fund, 1997).
Berman, Harold. *The Origins of Historical Jurisprudence*, 103 Yale L.J. 1651 (1994).
Black, Hugo LaFayette. *A Constitutional Faith* (New York: Alfred A. Knopf, 1968).
Blackstone, William. *Commentaries on the Laws of England* (Chicago, Ill.: University of Chicago Press, 1979) [1765], vol. 1.
Bodin, Jean. *On Sovereignty* (Julian H. Franklin, ed.) (New York: Cambridge University Press, 1992) [1576].
Bourguignon, Henry J. *The Federal Key to the Judiciary Act of 1789*, 46 S.C. L. Rev. 647 (1995).
Bowen, Catherine Drinker. *The Lion and the Throne* (Boston, Mass.: Little, Brown, 1957).
Boyer, Alan D., ed. *Law, Liberty, and Parliament: Selected Essays on the Writings of Sir Edward Coke* (Indianapolis, Ind.: Liberty Fund, 2004).

_____. *"Understanding, Authority, and Will": Sir Edward Coke and the Elizabethan Origins of Judicial Review*, 39 B.C. L. Rev. 43 (1997).
Bradford, M.E. *A Better Guide than Reason* (New Brunswick, N.J.: Transaction, 1994).
Burgess, Glenn. *The Divine Right of Kings Reconsidered*, 107 Eng. Hist. Rev. 837 (1992).
Carey, George W. *In Defense of the Constitution* (Indianapolis, Ind.: Liberty Fund, 1995).
Carson, Clarence B. *A Basic History of the United States* (Wadley, Ala.: American Textbook Committee, 1992), vols. 1 & 2.
Caufield, Rachel Paine. *Reconciling the Judicial Ideal and the Democratic Impulse in Judicial Retention Elections*, 74 Mo. L. Rev. 573 (2009).
Chernow, Ron. *Alexander Hamilton* (New York: Penguin, 2004).
Claydon, Tony. *William III's Declaration of Reasons and the Glorious Revolution*, 39 Hist. J. 87 (1996).
Coke, Sir Edward. *The Selected Writings of Sir Edward Coke* (Steve Sheppard, ed.) (Indianapolis, Ind.: Liberty Fund, 2003), 3 vols.
Conrad, Clay S. *Jury Nullification* (Durham, N.C.: Carolina Academic, 1998).
Cook, Don. *The Long Fuse* (New York: The Atlantic Monthly Press, 1995).
Countryman, Edward. *The American Revolution* (New York: Hill & Wang, 1985).
Crust, Richard. *Charles I, the Privy Council, and the Forced Loan*, 24 J. Brit. Stud. 208 (1985).
DeBow, Michael, et al. *The Case for Partisan Judicial Elections*, 33 U. Tol. L. Rev. 393 (2002).
Dicey, A.V. *Introduction to the Study of the Law of the Constitution* (Indianapolis, Ind.: Liberty Fund, 1982) [1882].
Dickens, A.G. *The English Reformation* (University Park, Penn.: The Pennsylvania University State Press, 1993).
Dippel, Horst. *The Changing Idea of Popular Sovereignty in Early American Constitutionalism: Breaking away from European Patterns*, 15 J. Early Repub. 21 (1996).
Dougherty, Keith L. *Collective Action under the Articles of Confederation* (New York: Cambridge University Press, 2001).
Douglas, Elisha P. *Rebels and Democrats* (Chicago, Ill.: Ivan R. Dee, 1955).
Douglas, Davison M. *Foreword: The Legacy of St. George Tucker*, 47 Wm. & Mary L. Rev. 1111 (2006).
Eidsmoe, John. *The Article III Exceptions Clause: Any Exceptions to the Power of Congress to Make Exceptions?*, 19 Regent U. L. Rev. 95 (2006).
Elkins, Stanley, and Eric McKitrick. *The Age of Federalism* (New York: Oxford University Press, 1993).
Elliot, Jonathan, ed. *The Debates in the Several State Conventions on the Adoption of the Federal Constitution* (Washington, D.C.: J.B. Lippincott, 1888), 5 vols.
Ellis, Richard E. *The Jeffersonian Crisis* (New York: W.W. Norton, 1971).
Engdahl, David E. *John Marshall's "Jeffersonian" Concept of Judicial Review*, 42 Duke L.J. 279 (1992).
Ferguson, James R. *Reason in Madness: The Political Thought of James Otis*, 36 Wm. & Mary Q. 194 (1979).
Filmer, Sir Robert. *Patriarcha* (London: Dodo, 2009) [1680].
Fischer, David Hackett *Albion's Seed* (New York: Oxford University Press, 1989).
Fraser, Antonia. *Cromwell* (New York: Grove, 1973).
_____. *Royal Charles* (New York: Dell, 1979).
_____. *The Story of Britain* (New York: W.W. Norton, 2005).
Fritz, Christina G. *Alternative Visions of American Constitutionalism: Popular Sovereignty and the Early American Constitutional Debate*, 24 Hastings Const. L.Q. 287 (1997).

Frohnen, Bruce, ed. *The Anti-Federalists: Selected Writings and Speeches* (Washington, D.C.: Regnery, 1999).
Gardiner, Samuel Rawson. *Constitutional Documents of the Puritan Revolution 1625–1660* (Oxford: Clarendon, 1906).
Gardner, James A. *Consent, Legitimacy and Elections: Implementing Popular Sovereignty under the Lockean Constitution*, 52 U. Pitt. L. Rev. 189 (1990).
George, Robert H. *The Financial Relations of Louis XIV and James II*, 3 J. Mod. Hist. 392 (1931).
Gilman, Felix. *The Famous Footnote Four: History of the* Carolene Products *Footnote*, 46 S. Tex. L. Rev. 163 (2004).
Gipson, Lawrence Henry. *The Coming of the Revolution* (New York: Harper & Row, 1954).
Goldsworthy, Jeffery. *Is Parliament Sovereign? Recent Challenges to the Doctrine of Parliamentary Sovereignty*, 3 N.Z. J. Pub. & Int'l L. 7 (2005).
———. *The Sovereignty of Parliament: History and Philosophy* (Oxford: Clarendon, 1999).
Gooch, J.P. *English Democratic Ideas in the 17th Century* (New York: Harper & Row, 1959).
Goodhart, Arthur L. *The Rule of Law and Absolute Sovereignty*, 106 U. Pa. L. Rev. 943 (1958).
Greene, Jack P. *Peripheries and Center: Constitutional Developments in the Extended Polities of the British Empire and the United States* (New York: W.W. Norton, 1986).
Gregg, Pauline. *Free-Born John: The Biography of John Lilburne* (London: Phoenix, 2000).
Griffith, Thomas B. *Was Bork Right About Judges?*, 34 Harv. J. L. & Pub. Pol'y. 157 (2011).
Hamilton, Alexander. *The Law Practice of Alexander Hamilton* (Julius Goebel, Jr., ed.) (New York: Columbia University Press, 1964), vol. 1.
Handlin, Oscar, and Mary F., eds. *The Popular Sources of Political Authority* (Cambridge, Mass.: Harvard University Press, 1966).
Hanson, Donald W. *From Kingdom to Commonwealth* (Cambridge, Mass.: Harvard University Press, 1970).
Harrington, Matthew P. *Judicial Review Before John Marshall*, 72 Geo. Wash. L. Rev. 51 (2003).
Hibbert, Christopher. *Charles I: A Life of Religion, War, and Treason* (New York: Palgrave Macmillan, 2007).
———. *Redcoats and Rebels* (New York: Avon, 1990).
Hobson, Charles F. *John Marshall, the Mandamus Case, and the Judiciary Crisis, 1801–1805*, 72 Geo. Wash. L. Rev. 289 (2003).
———. *The Great Chief Justice* (Lawrence, Kan.: University Press of Kansas, 1996).
Hogue, Arthur. *Origins of the Common Law* (Indianapolis, Ind.: Liberty Fund, 1966).
Holt, Wythe. *"To Establish Justice": Politics, the Judiciary Act of 1789, and the Invention of the Federal Courts*, 6 Duke L. J. 1421 (1989).
James I. *The True Law of Free Monarchies and Basilikon Doron* (Daniel Fischlin and Mark Fortier, eds.) (Toronto: Center for Reformation and Renaissance Studies, 1996).
Jefferson, Thomas. *Notes on the State of Virginia* (William Peden, ed.) (W.W. Norton, 1982).
Jensen, Merrill, ed. *Tracts of the American Revolution* (New York: Bobbs-Merrill, 1967).
Jezierski, John V. *James Wilson and Blackstone on the Nature and Location of Sovereignty*, 32 J. Hist. Ideas 95 (1971).

Jones, J.R. *Country and Court* (Cambridge, Mass.: Harvard University Press, 1979).
Kammen, Michael. *Sovereignty and Liberty* (Madison, Wis.: University of Wisconsin Press, 1988).
Kelsey, Sean. *Politics and Procedure in the Trial of Charles I*, 22 Law & Hist. Rev. 1 (2004).
Kenyon, J.P. ed., *The Stuart Constitution 1603–1688* (New York: Cambridge University Press, 1986).
Key, Richard S. *William III and the Legalist Revolution*, 32 Conn. L. Rev. 1645 (2000).
Kishlansky, Mark. *A Monarchy Transformed* (London: Penguin, 1996).
———. *The Rise of the New Model Army* (New York: Cambridge University Press, 1983).
Knollenberg, Bernard. *Growth of the American Revolution* (Indianapolis, Ind.: Liberty Fund, 2003).
Kramer, Larry. *The People Themselves: Popular Constitutionalism and Judicial Review* (New York: Oxford University Press, 2004).
Kruman, Marc W. *State Constitution Making in Revolutionary America* (Chapel Hill, N.C.: The University of North Carolina Press, 1997).
Kurland, Phillip B., and Ralph Lerner, eds. *The Founders' Constitution* (Indianapolis, Ind.: Liberty Fund, 1987), 5 vols.
Lagomarsino, David, and Charles J. Wood, eds. *The Trial of Charles I: A Documentary History* (London: University Press of New England, 1989).
Lakin, Stuart. *Debunking the Idea of Parliamentary Sovereignty: The Controlling Factor of Legality in the British Constitution*, 28 Oxford J. Legal Stud. 709 (2008).
Locke, John. *Second Treatise of Government* (C.B. Macpherson, ed.) (Indianapolis, Ind.: Hackett, 1980) [1690].
Lockyer, Roger. *The Early Stuarts* (New York: Longman, 1999).
Madison, James. *Notes of the Debates in the Federal Convention of 1787* (New York: W.W. Norton, 1987).
Maier, Pauline. *From Resistance to Revolution* (New York: W.W. Norton, 1991).
———. *Ratification* (New York: Simon & Schuster, 2010).
Main, Jackson Turner. *The Sovereign States* (New York: New Viewpoints, 1973).
Malcolm, Joyce Lee. *The Struggle for Sovereignty: Seventeenth Century Political Tracts* (Indianapolis, Ind.: Liberty Fund, 1999), 2 vols.
Malone, Dumas. *Jefferson and the Ordeal of Liberty* (Boston, Mass.: Little, Brown, 1962).
Mayer, David N. *The Constitutional Thought of Thomas Jefferson* (Charlottesville, Va.: University of Virginia Press, 1994).
Mayer, Henry. *A Son of Thunder* (New York: Grove, 1991).
McDonald, Forrest. *Novus Ordo Seclorum* (Lawrence, Kan.: University of Kansas Press, 1985).
———. *States' Rights and the Union* (Lawrence, Kan.: University of Kansas Press, 2000).
Mendle, Michael. *Henry Parker and the English Civil War* (New York: Cambridge University Press, 1995).
Miller, John. *The Glorious Revolution* (New York: Longman, 1983).
———. *The Stuarts* (Stanford, Cal.: Stanford University Press, 2004).
Morgan, Edmund S. *Inventing the People* (New York: W.W. Norton, 1988).
———, ed. *Prologue to Revolution: Sources and Documents on the Stamp Act Crisis* (New York: W.W. Norton, 1959).
Morrison, Samuel Elliot. *Sources and Documents Illustrating the American Revolution* (New York: Oxford University Press, 1965).
Nelson, William E. *Americanization of Common Law* (Cambridge, Mass.: Harvard University Press, 1975).

Noble, Richard L. *Lions or Jackals? The Independence of the Judges in Rex v. Hampden*, 14 Stan. L. Rev. 711 (1962).
O'Connor, Sandra Day. *The Essentials and Expendables of the Missouri Plan*, 74 Mo. L. Rev 479 (2009).
Ogg, David. *England in the Reigns of James II and William III* (New York: Oxford University Press, 1984).
Padover, Saul K., ed. *The Complete Jefferson* (New York: Duell, Sloan, & Pearce, 1943).
Parker, David. *The Making of French Absolutism* (London: Edward Arnold, 1983).
Pickering, Charles. *Supreme Chaos* (Macon, Ga.: Stroud & Hall, 2005).
Prakash, Saikrishna, and John Yoo. *The Origins of Judicial Review*, 70 U. Chi. L. Rev. 887 (2003).
Puls, Mark. *Samuel Adams* (New York: Palgrave Macmillan, 2006).
Purkiss, Diane. *The English Civil War* (New York: Basic, 2006).
Quirk, William J. *Courts and Congress* (New Brunswick, N.J.: Transaction, 2008).
Ransom, Roger L. *British Policy and Colonial Growth: Some Implications of the Burden from the Navigation Acts*, 28 J. Econ. Hist. 427 (1968).
Reeve, L.J. *The Legal Status of the Petition of Right*, 29 Hist. J. 257 (1986).
Reid, John Phillip. *Constitutional History of the American Revolution: Abridged* (Madison, Wis.: University of Wisconsin Press, 1995).
Ritz, Wilfred J. *Rewriting the History of the Judiciary Act of 1789* (Norman, Okla.: University of Oklahoma Press, 1990).
Robertson, Geoffrey. *The Tyrannicide Brief* (New York: Pantheon, 2005).
Russell, Conrad. *The Crisis of Parliaments 1509–1660* (New York: Oxford University Press, 1971).
Samuelson, Richard A. *The Constitutional Sanity of James Otis: Resistance Leader and Loyal Subject*, 61 Rev. Pol. 493 (1999).
Sawers, Larry. *The Navigation Acts Revisited*, 45 Econ. Hist. Rev. 262 (1992).
Sayles, George O. *The King's Parliament of England* (New York: W.W. Norton, 1974).
Sheridan, Richard B. *The Molasses Act and the Market Strategy of the British Sugar Planters*, 17 J. Econ. Hist. 62 (1957).
Sloan, Cliff, and David McKean. *The Great Decision* (New York: Public Affairs, 2009).
Smith, Jean Edward. *John Marshall* (New York: Henry Holt, 1996).
Snowiss, Sylvia. *Judicial Review and the Law of Constitution* (New Haven, Conn.: Yale University Press, 1990).
Southwick, Albert B. *The Molasses Act—Source of Precedents*, 8 Wm. & Mary Q. 389 (1951).
Speck, W.A. *Reluctant Revolutionaries* (New York: Oxford University Press, 1988).
Stanlis, Peter J. *British Views of the American Revolution: A Conflict over Rights of Sovereignty*, 11 Early Am. Lit. 191 (1976).
Stewart, Alan. *The Cradle King* (New York: St. Martin's, 1993).
Straka, Gerald. *The Final Phase of Divine Right Theory in England, 1688–1702*, 77 Eng. Hist. Rev. 638 (1962).
Taft, Barbara. *The Council of Officers' Agreement of the People*, 28 Hist. J. 169 (1985).
Tanner, J.R., ed. *Constitutional Documents of the Reign of James I* (London: Cambridge University Press, 1960).
Thayer, James B. *The Origin and Scope of the American Doctrine of Constitutional Law*, 7 Har. L. Rev. 129 (1893).
Treanor, William Michael. *The Case of the Prisoners and the Origins of Judicial Review*, 143 U. Pa. L. Rev. 491 (1994).
Trevelyan, G.M. *The English Revolution 1688–1689* (New York: Oxford University Press, 1966).

Tucker, St. George. *View of the Constitution with Selected Writings* (Clyde N. Wilson, ed., Indianapolis, Ind.: Liberty Fund, 1999).
Turner, Kathryn. *The Midnight Judges*, 109 U. Pa. L. Rev. 494 (1961).
Tushnet, Mark. *Taking the Constitution away from the Courts* (Princeton, N.J.: Princeton University Press, 1999).
Watkins, William J., Jr. *Popular Sovereignty, Judicial Supremacy, and The American Revolution: Why the Judiciary Cannot Be the Final Arbiter of Constitutions*, 1 Duke J. Const. L.& Pub. Pol'y 159 (2006).
Weintraub, Stanley. *Iron Tears* (New York: Free, 2005).
Weisberger, Bernard A. *America Afire* (New York: William Morrow, 2000).
Western, J.R. *Monarchy and Revolution* (Totowa, N.J.: Rowman and Littlefield, 1972).
Whittington, Keith E. *Presidential Challenges to Judicial Supremacy and the Politics of Constitutional Meaning*, 33 Polity 367 (2001).
Williams, E.N., ed. *The Eighteenth Century Constitution* (London: Cambridge University Press, 1977).
Wilson, James. *Collected Works of James Wilson* (Kermit L. Hall and Mark David Hall, eds.) (Indianapolis, Ind.: Liberty Fund, 2007), 2 vols.
Wittes, Benjamin. *Confirmation Wars* (New York: Rowman & Littlefield, 2006).
Wood, Gordon. *Creation of the American Republic* (New York: W.W. Norton, 1969).
_____. *Empire of Liberty* (New York: Oxford University Press, 2009).
_____. *Revolutionary Characters* (New York: Penguin, 2006).
_____. *The American Revolution* (New York: The Modern Library, 2002).
Woodhouse, A.S.P., ed. *Puritanism and Liberty: Being the Army Debates (1647–9). From the Clarke Manuscripts* (Chicago, Ill.: University of Chicago Press, 1965).
Woodward, W.E. *A New American History* (New York: Garden City, 1938).
Wootton, David. *Divine Right and Democracy* (Indianapolis, Ind.: Hackett, 2003).
Zobel, Hiller B. *The Boston Massacre* (New York: W.W. Norton, 1970).
Zuckert, Michael P., and Derek A. Webb, eds. *The Anti-Federalist Writings of the Melancton Smith Circle* (Indianapolis, Ind.: Liberty Fund, 2009).

Index

Adams, Abigail 116
Adams, John 101, 103–104
Adkins v. Children's Hospital 127
Agreement of the People 36–37, 149–51
Alien and Sedition Acts 4, 102
Amar, Akhil 114
Annapolis Convention 71
Apology of the Commons 18
Arminianism 25
Arminius, James 25
Articles of Confederation 9, 71, 79, 120–21
Ashcroft, John 134

Ball, William 34
Bank of Manhattan 102
Barebones Parliament 41–42
Bate's Case 19
Bayard, James 105
Berger, Raoul 119
Blackstone, William 53, 124
Bodin, Jean 12–13
Boston Massacre 65
Bradshawe, John 39
Breckinridge, John 108
Brent, Daniel 111–12
Brown v. Board of Education 134
Burke, Edmund 63
Burnet, Gilbert 47
Burr, Aaron 102–104
Butler, Pierce 80

Calvin, John 11, 25
Charles I: personal rule 25–29; trial 37–40
Chase, Samuel 110
Coke, Sir Edward 22–24, 91, 124
Commentaries on the Laws of England 53–54, 72

Commonwealth v. Caton 2, 86–89, 136
Cooke, John 39–40
Councils of revision, 78, 138–39
Covenanters 28
Cromwell, Oliver 34, 41–43
Cromwell, Richard 42–43

Davie, William R., 85
Declaration of Breda 43
Declaration of Independence 67–68, 75, 123
Declaration of Indulgence 44
Declaration of Rights 52
Declaratory Act of 1766 64–65
Departmentalism 116
Dickinson, John 66
Distraint of knighthood 26
Divine right of kings 4
Dr. Bonham's Case 90–91
Doubtful-case rule 82, 84, 135
Duane, James 91–92
Due process 124–29
Duke of Buckingham 19–21, 24

Edict of Nantes 49
Elizabeth I 10
Ellsworth, Oliver 82, 85, 105
English Civil War 33–35
Ex Parte McCardle 145
Exceptions clause 144–45

Fairfax, Thomas 34
Filmer, Robert 46
Five Knights Case 21–22
Franklin, Benjamin 63, 66, 82
French Revolution 102

Galloway, Joseph 67

Georgia v. Brailsford 139–40
Gerry, Elbridge 80, 81, 138
Ghorum, Nathaniel 138
Glorious Revolution 50–52
Godden v. Hales 49
Goldsworthy, Jeffrey 17
Goodwin, William 14
Grenville, George 58–59
Gunpowder Plot 61

Hamilton, Alexander 3, 83, 90, 101, 124
Happy Convention 137
Harper, William 108
Hat Act of 1732 56
Henry, James 95–96
Henry, Patrick 62, 78
Hicks, William 66
Hooe, Robert 108
Hopkins, Stephen 66
Horatius 104
Howard, Martin, Jr. 55
Hutchinson, Thomas 61

James I 10–12, 15, 17–20, 74
James II 48–52
Jamestown 55–56
Jay, John 9, 104–106, 139
Jefferson, Thomas 4, 7, 67, 101–102, 108, 116
Judicial self-restraint 123–24
Judiciary Act of 1789 106, 114
Judiciary Act of 1801 106
Judiciary Act of 1802 110
Jurisdiction stripping 144–45
Jury nullification 77–78, 139–144

Kamper v. Hawkins 2–3, 93–98, 115–116, 152–85
Kennedy, Anthony 131
Kennedy v. Louisiana 129–30
Key, Philip Barton 107
King, Rufus 81
King-in-parliament 15

Laud, William 27–28
Lawrence v. Texas 131–32
Lee, Charles 108, 111
Levellers 36–37
Lilburne, John 36, 77
Lincoln, Levi 112
Lochner v. New York 126
Locke, John 53
Long Parliament 31
Louis XIV 44, 120
Loyal Nine 60–61

Madison, James 71, 81, 122
Magna Carta 124
Marbury, William 108
Marbury v. Madison 5, 6, 7, 100, 111–116
Marshall, James 112–13
Marshall, John 6, 100–101, 104, 106–107, 135
Martin, Luther 80, 81, 138
Mary Queen of Scots 10
Mason, George 72, 81
Mason, Steven Thomson 109
Massachusetts Constitution of 1780 69–71, 76
Maynwaring, Roger 14–15
McHenry, James 103
Mercantilism 56
Missouri Plan 140–41
Molasses Act of 1733 59
Monck, George 43
Morris, Gouverneur 79, 83, 107, 110

Nelson, William 94–95
New Model Army 34–37
Nicholson, James Hopper 104
Nineteen Propositions 32

O'Connor, Sandra Day 119, 142
Oliver, Andrew 61
Otis, James 65

Pacification of Berwick 28–29
Parker, Henry 33
Parliament: development 16–17; sovereignty 52–54
Parsons' Cause 77–78
Patriarcha 46
Pendleton, Edmund 2, 84, 136
Perry v. Schwarzenegger 131–33
Petition of Right 22–24
Philadelphia Convention 79; judicial review and 80–83
Pickering, Timothy 103
Pinckney, Charles 83
Pinckney, Charles Cotesworth 103
Pitt, William 63–64
Pride's purge 37–38
Proposition 8 131
Provisions of Oxford 17
Pym, John 29–30, 32

Quirk, William J. 137

Ramsay, Dennis 108
Randolph, Edmund 72, 87–88, 143
Rawle, William 125

Reformed theology 25
Restoration 43
Revolution of 1800 117
Rex v. Hampden 26–27
Rights of the British Colonies Asserted and Proved 65
Roane, Spencer 2, 95
Rockingham 63
Roe v. Wade 128–29
Roosevelt, Franklin Delano 127–28
Rule of 80 142
Rump parliament 37–38, 41
Rutgers v. Waddington, 88–93
Rutledge, John 79

Salutary neglect 57
Self-Denying Ordinance 34
Separation of powers 3, 76
Seven Years' War 58
Ship money 26–27
Short Parliament 30
Six Livres de la République 12–13
Slaughter-House Cases, 126
Slavery 123
Smith, Melancton 93
Spanish Match 20
Stamp Act of 1765 59–60
Stuart v. Laird 111
Sugar Act of 1764 59
Summary View of the Rights of British America 66–67
Sydney, Algernon 46–47

Term limits 143–44
Thayer, James B. 135

Thirty Years' War 19
Tonnage and poundage 25
Townshend, Charles 64
Townshend duties 64
Tracy, Uriah 109
Treason Act of 1776 86
Treaty of Dover 44
Treaty of Paris 120
Triennial Act 31–32
True Law of Free Monarchies 12
Tucker, St. George 72, 97–98, 125
Two Penny Act 77
Tyler, John 96–97

United States v. Carolene Products Co. 128

Virginia Declaration of Rights 68
Virginia Plan 72, 79, 82

Wagner, Jacob 111–12
Walker, Vaughn R. 131
Walpole, Sir Robert 57
Warren Court 119
Washington, George 101, 121
West Coast Hotel v. Parrish 128
Whitelocke, James 15
William of Orange 44, 50–52
William the Conqueror 16
Wilson, James 72, 82, 84–85, 125
Wolcott, Oliver 107
Wood, Gordon 56
Wynehamer v. People 125
Wythe, George 88

Yates, Robert 122

www.ingramcontent.com/pod-product-compliance
Ingram Content Group UK Ltd.
Pitfield, Milton Keynes, MK11 3LW, UK
UKHW041957140426
5217IPUK00015B/836